Rembrandt's Ghost in the New Machine

I0471191

Ritchie's Perfect Press—Seattle

Rembrandt's Ghost in the New Machine

By Bill H. Ritchie
Creator of the PressGhost Series

2nd Edition

Ritchie's Perfect Press
A Division of Emeralda Works
Office at: 500 Aloha Street, Unit 105
Seattle WA 98109
(206) 498-9208
ritchie@emeralda.com
www.ritchie-art.com

ISBN 13: 978-1484828144
ISBN 10: 1484828143

Rembrandt's Ghost in the New Machine

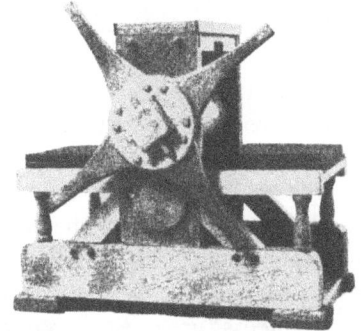

Second Edition

"WeeWoodie Rembrandt Press #1 – 2012"
Handcrafted prototype made by Bill H. Ritchie
and the inspiration for this novel.

By Bill H. Ritchie
Creator of the "PressGhost Series"
Ritchie's Perfect Press—Seattle

About the title and this novel

The 1967 book, "The Ghost in the Machine," by Arthur Koestler, attracted me in the 1980s when I conceived of my trilogy, "Perfect Studios." The full title of my third book was to be, "Ghosts in the New Machine: Between Virtue and Reality." I stopped working on that manuscript around the year 2000, but I always liked the phrase, *ghost in the machine* because, for me, it expresses why, throughout the 50 years I worked with the mechanics of printmaking, video, computers, etc., I sensed the presence of ghostly imprints of the people who either invented or used the technical procedures, machines and instruments to get their works of art done. For Koestler—and the philosopher who coined the phrase, Gilbert Ryle—the phrase may have had deeper meaning; but similar to my idea that the ghosts of artists such as Rembrandt (as well as craftspeople, designers and engineers) are present in my "new" machines—my etching presses.

This book might be called an "info-novel" somewhat like the short TV programs, the "info-mercial." In other words, a production that is too long to be a commercial, but obviously created to persuade the audience, a marketing device. But in defense of my artistic integrity, there is more to it than merely touting the Halfwood Project. Read the *faux-interview* at the back of the book to learn why.   **BR**

Dedicated to Jennifer

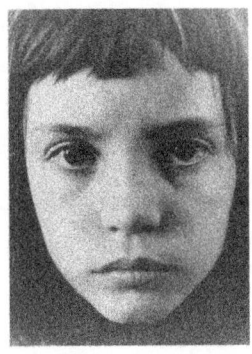

1954-1995

I dedicate this book in memoriam of Jennifer Anne Ritchie Bennett. She was my youngest sister. When I made this photo of her, around 1963, she was about the age of the character, "Mahault," in this story. This name means *powerful battler* in German and French. Jenny was a powerful battler, I think, and she would not mind if I used this picture of her in my book; and she would forgive me for modifying the photo, as seen in later versions of her image, i.e, I added a 17th Century housemaid's bonnet to fit the Mahault in the story.

Rembrandt's Ghost in the New Machine

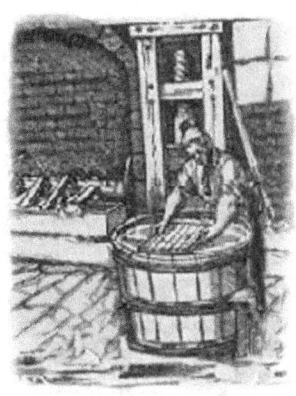

Chapter 1
The Papermaker

1652 – AMSTERDAM: Although it was late in the day, near dinner time, in the Van Gelder and Son paper mill there was a continual constant clattering and banging—the sound of a stamper. Three rocking wood levers the size of fence posts fitted with iron-bound hardwood hammer heads lifted and then fell in quick succession. *Whack, whack, whack!* Their ends caught and slipped off fist-sized teeth on an axle of wood girdled in steel.

Catch and slip, catch and slip, they worked like a clock movement. Driven by a huge cogwheel connected off to the side, the rugged drum turned slowly and another tooth caught the lever's end, raised and let it fall again. *Catch and slip*, whack, *catch and slip*, whack, whack, whack—three in a row, again and again.

The large levers rocked like teeter-totters as the ends were lifted by the blocky protrusions on the rotating axle. Forced up and then let fall again, one after the other in neat precision, the hammer heads

1

slammed down on a dark, water-soaked hardwood plank and rose up. On the plank was piled a clotted mass of wet rags that were being beaten into paper pulp. A worker lifted fork loads of dripping piles of rags that he had scooped up and then plopped the masses onto the plank. His motions that had to be coordinated with each drop of the stampers.

Another man paddled the water with a broad shovel, as if he was rowing a boat, to keep the slurry of paper pulp moving in a circle around the stone-walled tub which contained the stamping engine. Bits of cloth rose and sank again and were scooped up to the plank, mashed, and then let fall back into the turbid water.

The air in this dim, noisy room was damp and the rag pulp reeked of wet dogs. The beating went on interminably, as it had for years, turning rags into pulp to make paper. The linen of old clothing and discarded sheets were piled up against a wall, brought to de Gelder's by rag pickers from all over Amsterdam.

Next to the rag pile squatted several boys, their knees spread wide as they busily pulled pieces from the rag heap, tore them into small bits and tossed them into the tub where they would sink in the swirling slurry.

By those who knew quality paper—the kind needed by the publishing industry—de Gelder was considered to be one of the best paper producers in the Dutch Republic. New book and print publishing enterprises and printing technologies plus the wildly successful Dutch East Indies Company had created a great demand for paper. De Gelder was ambitious, smart, and a hard worker. His paper-making business thrived.

At this moment he stood at a tall, lectern-like

table in a corner far from the stamp mill. With a quill, in the light of an oil lamp, he entered numbers in a ledger. His bewhiskered face was kind. Young he was for an owner of a mill. He was only in his early thirties, but already he had a comfortably round belly. He had a wife and a seven-year old son, Arent. They were in another room with the door closed.

Across the dreary space was the main entryway, and outside, beyond the heavy door, there came a shout. But the voice was drowned out by the clatter of the stamp mill and groaning of the cogwheel as it turned. No one noticed the hollering of the caller as he banged on the door, but it was a customer.

A louder shout of, "De *God-dammit* Gelder!" this time was heard, not by the owner but by the man who wielded the paddle and he leaned his tool against the wall and went over to his boss. To be heard above the noise he leaned in close and said in de Gelder's ear, "Meneer de Gelder, someone is at the door!"

Other workers noticed and turned their heads to see, except one. He was the vat man at another station, leaning over a great boxy tub. He was halfway through his task of dipping the paper mould, a large rectangular screen. He held it with his strong muscled arms, gripping the opposite edges to hold the deckle in place.

He pulled the mould up out of the tub. It held a beautiful field of water and paper pulp fibers in suspension. An expert shake—first this way, then that way—made the watery soup of linen fibers form into an even layer across the screen. By the time all the water had fallen through the wire screen, the fibers were interlocked into an even layer. It would be paper.

Water streamed and fell like rain out the bottom of the mould. He gave the mould one more, well-practiced shake, and one more sheet of Van Gelder Zonen Paper is ready to couch, then press, and finally to hang up and dry.

He went to the post, which is the stack of freshly-made paper sheets just a few steps away. The man with the paper mould removed the deckle. The coucher—as the man at the stack was known in the trade—took the mould, overturned it on the post and lifted the mould off. It left the new sheet of formed paper on the post, glistening wet and with a faint pattern of the wire mould it had laid on. With the mould set aside for the vat man, the coucher expertly threw a heavy wool blanket and he was ready for another sheet of paper from the vat man.

Not far from this two-man operation another man examined a piece of paper from a different post that he moved out of the tall standing press. This press was like a huge torture rack, good for smashing anything down with tons of pressure. A shaft as thick as a man's leg, threaded and fitted into a flat, cast iron platen, would squeeze gallons of water out of a post of freshly-laid paper sheets.

In a drying room nearby there was a web of lines strung tightly across like clotheslines where sheets were hung in rows, as the partly-dried sheets were now strong enough to drape over the line.

At his tall desk, De Gelder had set down his quill and had gone to and unbolted the door. There stood Amsterdam's most famous painter and de Gelder's longtime customer, Rembrandt van Rijn. It was he who rapped at the door and called, trying to be heard.

"Meneer van Rijn. *Goede avond!*[1] *Kom binnen. Welkom,*" said de Gelder. Van Rijn gave the paper maker a big grin and they shook hands. Rembrandt

---

[1] Good evening. Come in. Welcome.

had come on business. He was about to say so when across the room a door opened and the son of the paper maker, Arent de Gelder, entered.

Rembrandt noticed him and called over to the lad, "Arent, boy, you are growing fast. Soon you will take over your old father's work, I think!"

Through the same door Mevrouw de Gelder entered and she registered surprise at seeing van Rijn.

"Meneer van Rijn, *Goede avond*," she said.

The de Gelder's son, Arent, was wide-eyed, awed by the famous painter's presence. While the men returned to the subject of paper for Rembrandt's printing—and as Arent stayed to watch—vrouw de Gelder returned to the family room and closed the door.

***

Weeks later, de Gelder stopped his delivery wagon in front of No. 4 Jodenbreestracht, Rembrandt's fine mansion. It is not many homes in Amsterdam, even in this luxurious district, that have spacious painting and printing studios in them. Van Rijn moved here in the '40s with his wife, Saskia. She had died in this house nine years ago, not long after bearing her fourth child, a boy they named Titus. Their housekeeper, Hendrickje Stoffels, had taken over the house by this time.

In the de Gelder wagon, Arent perched on the seat beside his father. He sat straight and tall, glad to be with his father to make the paper delivery to the famous artist. Above, Mevrouw Stoffels saw them coming, opened out the window and whistled shrilly to de Gelder below.

"Goedmorgen, Meneer de Gelder!" She called down, and without formality she turned and shouted,

"Van Rijn! Meneer Gelder is here!" then withdrew back inside and closed the window.

His father got down from the wagon seat and Arent followed him. From the back of the rig the elder de Gelder gripped the heavy bundle of the paper, lugged it over the walkway and climbed the broad steps to the porch. The door opened and Rembrandt was there. He wore a dirty leather apron. He had been printing, and his hands were black with printing ink. His face had smudges of ink where he had wiped at his forehead. His mass of hair was contained somewhat by a grimy shapeless hat.

"You are just in time, meneer de Gelder. I was on my last sheets. Do you need a hand with that?" van Rijn feigned an offer to help de Gelder with his load.

De Gelder shook his head, huffing and humping the bundle up the stairs. Rembrandt stepped inside as he entered the door and Arent did not hesitate but followed him. He glanced at his hero and entered the foyer.

Rembrandt shut the door. "Watch your step, meneer de Gelder," he said. The elder de Gelder had already headed down the stairs to the studio, as he knew the way. He had delivered paper to Rembrandt before, many times. Arent gawked at the spacious hall and then followed down behind the men.

Inside Rembrandt's printing studio an assistant was busy near a large, wood etching press near the far side of the room. Oil lamp sconces on the wall illuminated the printing studio, and natural light filtered in from many-paned windows high above a work counter.

Agog, Arent surveyed the master's inner sanctum. Unlike his father, he had never been here. Prints were pinned on the wall, and some were clipped to a string stretched across the space between the press and the wall, and they looked like laundry hung to dry. Arent started when, with a sudden loud thud, his father dropped the bundle of paper on a table.

"There it is. One-hundred-fifty sheets, as you ordered, Sir. Do you want to examine them?"

Van Rijn had already recommenced a task at the workbench and he ignored de Gelder's question. Rembrandt was getting ready to print, and he made swiping motions with his hand across his printing plate. The silence was awkward, but no one dared to interrupt van Rijn.

The assistant shot a look at de Gelder and grimaced; de Gelder thought he understood his meaning and he shrugged tolerantly and waited while Rembrandt wiped away at his printing plate.

Finally van Rijn spoke and called over his shoulder, "Young Arent. Come here, boy, and you will see a bit of my magic. You must promise not to tell anyone!"

Arent's jaw dropped and he looked at his father for permission. The elder de Gelder nodded and the boy went to Rembrandt. Arent was shy at first, but curious, so he stood on his tiptoes to see what was on the counter, one hand on the work counter edge. Rembrandt continued to stroke an etched copper plate with his hand, a motion which had a swishing, kissy sound.

Arent surveyed the other paraphernalia cluttering the work area—a gob of glistening black etching ink, ink-smudged glass bottles of amber-colored oils, and inky black rags. Along the ledge above the counter there were hand tools laid about haphazardly, mixed with peculiar carvings, more bottles and some jars stuffed with paint brushes.

Rembrandt went into a teaching mode: "You see how it works? I have worked ink into the lines I etched into the copper. I etched that with acid!" He continued to wipe at the plate. "I wipe off the extra ink, and leave ink in the lines. That's what I want to print. You see?"

Arent nodded. He understood. He had seen etching before, but he had never seen the plates they were printed from. He moved closer toward a kettle-sized, cast iron charcoal brazier above his eye level. Van Rijn pointed to brassier. "Don't touch that, *it is hot.*"

"For my printing ink; softens it. When warm, it prints better—one of my secrets!" and Rembrandt passed his hand over the top of the brazier to underscore his warning not to touch it.

Arent stepped back quickly as Rembrandt abruptly pushed by him and went toward the press. The assistant waited with a small sheet of paper that hung limp, held with a folded tab of paper to keep his fingerprints off. They worked as a team. Rembrandt placed the plate on the press bed and the helper carefully laid down the paper upon it. Next he unrolled a thin, hard gray wool blanket over the paper and plate, covering all.

Rembrandt ordered, "Okay, Arent, grab hold of that press' arm and turn it!" and van Rijn stepped back to watch. Arent went where the master pointed at the great, spreading arms and gripped one with both hands. The wood was thicker than Arent's arm, black and knobby with years of accumulated ink from dirty hands pulling the wooden star wheel around. He pulled the bar with all his might.

"Ugh!" he grunted, but nothing moved. He tried again, and, this time, so hard that he lifted himself clear off the floor! But the press' arm would not budge. Rembrandt laughed.

"What's wrong Arent? Too hard? Har har!" and

he laughed again. "Now, step aside and let the men show how it's done."

Abashed, Arent backed away as Rembrandt and his assistant took the press' arms and, with a groan, the roller slowly moved with the bed and carried the plate, paper and felt blanket through. The press bed stopped. The elder de Gelder moved in closer, gently pressing Arent on the shoulders to see the result close up.

Rembrandt smiled and said, "Don't feel badly, Arent. Bigger boys than you—my students—why they can't turn this press by themselves, either. I tricked you."

The assistant rolled back the felt blankets and the paper revealed a profile of the plate in relief as, under the pressure of the roller, it had made an embossing all around the plate. Rembrandt moved in with a paper gripper and lifted off the sheet by a corner and flipped it over. He leaned in close to scan it; satisfied, he picked it up with the paper tab and held it to show Arent.

"See? Not bad!" and then he handed it over to Arent to take. "*Take it*. Your hands are clean."

Arent made a nest with his hands and Rembrandt laid it in. "There you are, boy. As you tried hard to print it—and your father has brought me paper on short notice—this I present to you. Rembrandt turned away to talk to de Gelder while Arent studied the print. It pictured a man playing cards.

"Meneer Gelder, again I thank you. Please put your charge on my bill." When he heard this, disappointment fell over de Gelder's face. Rembrandt noticed.

"My friend, you see, my hands are filthy, and, besides, I am late to get ready to go out. Hendrickje will be screaming at me any second."

As if on cue, Hendrickje shouted down the stairwell, "Van Rijn. *Time to get ready*. Clean up. The carriage is coming! It's on its way—hurry."

Rembrandt shouted back, "Coming! De Gelder is just leaving. I'm coming," and he winked at de Gelder. Van Rijn said to Arent, "Arent, I have given you a thing of value. When the ink is dry—and I come to pay your father—I want to see the print again. It is no easy thing, etching. Someday, if your father wishes, you may learn the printing trade. Perhaps learn it from me!"

Rembrandt straightened and fixed de Gelder with a beseeching stare. De Gelder knew van Rijn's current financial straits. He set his jaw but said nothing.

As Rembrandt broke away he said, "Excuse me, de Gelder, I have to hurry, you know. My assistant will see you out," and he added a cheerful, "Good day!" as he moved toward the stairs and away.

De Gelder at last objected, "But Meneer van Rijn . . .", and Hendrickje yelled again.

"Rembrandt!"

Rembrandt made haste for the stairs. The elder de Gelder could only relent. The assistant went to the stairs to show courtesy. Saying nothing, he gave de Gelder another look, so as to say, *Rembrandt has no money*.

***

Hendrickje was already dressed for their night out. It was a costume party and she was adorned in a costume reminiscent of bacchanalia. After awhile Rembrandt came into their dressing room. He, too, was costumed in a flamboyant aristocrat's outfit, complete with a gold chain draped around his neck. It

10

was no doubt brass, brought out from his extensive costume supply.

Hendrickje fussed and tucked on his waistcoat as he admired himself in a mirror. He put on a wig with hair that was longer than his own curly mop.

"I will need a hat. Where is that hat?"

"You wear many hats, van Rijn. Which hat?"

"The great, *velvet* one; also, get a plume."

As Hendrickje went to fetch the hat and plume, Rembrandt continued to study his image in the great oval mirror. He wrinkled his brow, winced, twisted his mouth and pulled a couple faces in quick succession.

Hendrickje returned and presented him with a large floppy hat which he put on and adjusted over his wig. She stepped behind to see how he looked in the mirror. With vanity he faced sideway and studied himself.

"*The plume*!" reminded Rembrandt. With a huge ostrich feather, she reached around from behind and swiped it across his nose. He snorted and grabbed it away from her. Hendrickje giggled and backed off as Rembrandt fitted the plume into the brim of his hat. He again admired himself in the mirror as Hendrickje watched over his shoulder, and then van Rijn turned his face to her.

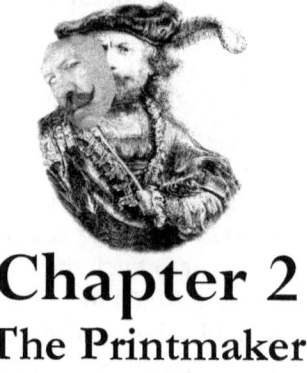

Chapter 2
The Printmaker

SEATTLE, 2010: It was the final, perfect finishing touch to go with the hat—a blue, fake ostrich plume that he got at the costume shop. It was an afterthought, really. Mac put on the great hat with slashed brim and plume over his flowing, rock-musician's wig. Leaving their condo, he and his wife, Faye, went to their car.

While Faye got into the car on the passenger side and was maneuvering her flouncy, white petticoats into a manageable heap, Mac arranged his Flemish gentleman's waistcoat and sank into the driver's seat. His hat and plume barely fit in the headroom of their compact car—a twelve-year old Dodge Neon.

"Are you ready, *ma femme*?" Mac said, as he inserted his key in the ignition and started the motor.

Faye turned to Mac, and her coiled, white bouffant hairdo brushed the headliner. She flashed him a sexy smile, one eyebrow raised flirtatiously.

"*Oui*, chéri *Mac. Mon nom est Marie-Antoinette. Je serai votre compagnon*,"[2] she said softly, deep and breathy.

---

[2] Yes, dear Mac. My name is Marie-Antoinette. I will be your companion.

Mac chuckled, adjusting his hat and revved the car. He looked at her again.

"You look great. I think I might get that camera and take pictures of you, maybe a video, too."

"Save your camera batteries," Faye replied as she adjusted her wig. "But you could use it at the party."

Mac gazed at her, admiringly and thought, *she sure knows how to dress! Like a real Bourbon queen.* Her face was generously made up with white face powder, and she had a beauty mark on her high-boned, powdered cheek.

"I like the beauty mark. Nice touch. How'd you do that? The beauty mark, I mean?" Mac asked.

"Ballpoint," Faye answered.

Mac switched on the car headlights. He pulled the car out of the driveway to the dark street and into the cold, October Halloween night.

At the first intersection they saw a family of three masqueraders. All of them were costumed in pastel, tight-fitting spandex outfits and wearing alien masks. Huge almond-shaped eyes bugged out as they danced through the crosswalk, parading and gesturing at the plumed Netherlandish driver and his queenly passenger.

"Crazy aliens," Faye observed.

After the last of the costumed family crossed, Mac gunned the car and started across the intersection.

Faye said, "Mac, I feel funny not taking anything. Let's take one of those boxes of Rembrandt's Chocolates to the party. We have that one that you put in your new printmaker chest."

"No. That's for the people who come to watch me demonstrate printing etchings with chocolate," Mac replied.

"Oh well, it was just an idea," Faye said. She kept

thinking about a gift for the party. They came to another intersection and another crosswalk and stopped to wait for a teenage couple. The boy was dressed like an able seaman in an old movie, with one arm around the waist of the girl who wore a small white bonnet on her head and wooden clogs—a costume for a Dutch girl. As they watched them pass, Faye brightened and said, "Mac, we have more of those chocolates ordered, I remember!"

Faye loved chocolate. "We could stop by the studio—the workshop—and you could pop in and get those from the chest."

Mac considered it. "Yeah, well, I guess that would be okay," he said, and then added, "Good idea." He turned the car at the next corner and parked in front of his little storefront studio.

"But hurry, Hon," said Faye, "I don't want to be getting there late. It's embarrassing enough wearing these costumes."

Mac got out, dashed around the car, crossed the sidewalk and unlocked the door. As he entered the dark shop, he was met by warm air that smelled of etching ink, solvents and freshly-cut pine lumber— perfumery to any longtime printmaker and, now, wood crafter.

Mac switched on the lights and looked around. His workshop was his favorite place. He also referred to it as his "studio," depending on what he was working on—printmaking or press-making. He had set it up as a printmaker's studio, and then he had outfitted it for woodworking to make presses.

Mac went straight to his latest woodworking project, which was on his workbench. Earlier that day he had finished filling one of these designer furnishings, what he called his "Printmaker Chest." Its contents consisted of (as he claimed in his Web promotions) *"Everything you need to be a printmaker, just add creative juice!"*

Besides being known as a printmaker, Mac was a press maker. He designed little, hand-operated etching presses. He made these table-top machines of half-wood and half-steel, and named them "Halfwoods." He sold them to other printmakers and his advertising slogan was, *"Half wood, half steel, all real."*

To contain the Halfwood Etching Press, and also the supplies for printmaking, Mac started making the printmaker chests. Because Mac loved sailing ships and sea adventures, he designed them to resemble a seaman's chest. He made them using white pine lumber with rope handles and fitted them with fancy brass nameplates and locks. The one on his bench was the fifth chest that he had made.

For a full five seconds Mac gazed admiringly at the newly-finished chest on the bench, already outfitted with a Mini Halfwood press, supplies and the chocolates. Inside also was his new, used digital camera. Quietly, as if he were apologizing to a pet for going away and leaving it home, he said to the chest, "I'd rather be making prints, not going to a Halloween party."

Mac had developed a bad habit of talking to the inanimate things he worked on and this worried him sometimes. Was talking to himself a sign that he was losing his mind? Mac had told Faye about it; and then this worried her, too. She told Mac that he was alone too much and that he should get out more often and see people.

The invitation from their old friend, Dennis, to his Halloween party was timely. Mac and Faye had gone all out to get ready for it, finding their costumes at a Seattle party supply shop.

Mac tried the drop-down door of the chest and then remembered that he had locked it. He found the key in his costume pants pocket and was about to open the chest when he happened to glance over at the far end of the workbench. He recalled that he had left an unfinished task there. It was an old, etched copper plate with a hardened, dull black coating that he needed to clean off and make ready to print.

Mac thought, *That gives me another idea*, and he went over and studied the plate. If he could clean it up, he could take this plate as an accessory to go with his attire for his party role-play as Rembrandt. Since Rembrandt was said to have been something of a boisterous braggart, Mac could show off this copper plate as if it were the etcher's latest creation—an etching plate.

This prospect distracted Mac from his purpose for coming in—to fetch the box of chocolates. Faye beeped the car horn outside, which was their "*Hurry up! We'll be late!*" signal. Hearing this, Mac hesitated, thinking of Faye waiting, and then he made a snap decision to clean the plate and clean it fast!

Getting the chocolates would only take him a second. He hurriedly set the plate on a piece of paper and dribbled some mineral spirits on it from a grimy tin container. With an old cleaning rag in his right hand he started rubbing the solvent into the black coating while he held the plate down with his left hand.

The plate that had come to Mac in a roundabout way: First, there was an email message from a guy in Maine who said he had bought a bucket of copper etching plates at a flea market. He thought they were pretty old. The fellow had asked Mac—who blogged on the Web as a know-it-all printmaking professor, if he could be talked into cleaning the old plates and also to print proofs to see what images were on them.

If the plates proved to have been made by an old master, they would be worth something, the Mainer thought. He wanted to take these to "Antiques Roadshow," but the plates were covered with a black coating and, besides that, he had no proofs.

Mac answered him that he would try. When the plates arrived, some of them were stuck together, and all of them were coated with the hardened, tar-like black substance. They were definitely old—just as the man had described them.

Mac's examination of the plates told him that it was unlikely that there would be any images etched in them that were worth printing. They looked worthless for anything except recycling.

However, Mac knew that if he could get through the black coating on one of them then at least this particular one might be a fairly adequate example of an etching plate like Rembrandt's. It was heavily-coated and thus protected against corrosion. It might be in good shape if he could dissolve the coating and polish it. This plate was about the same size as one of Rembrandt's most famous etchings, "Self Portrait Leaning on a Sill," and small enough to fit in the pants pocket of Mac's costume.

As he rubbed Mac thought, *Probably Rembrandt would show off his latest masterpiece printing plate. That's what I would do, anyway, if I were Rembrandt at a party!*

Once again Mac slipped into his habit of talking to himself and said aloud, "I can kill two birds with one stone," as he dribbled more solvent and rubbed harder. He could clean the plate for the party and then, tomorrow, it would be ready to print on his Mini Halfwood Press that was locked inside the new chest.

The black grime began to soften and come away

from the plate, showing copper color underneath.
Again Faye sounded the car horn. Mac rubbed harder
and faster. The mineral spirits wasn't dissolving the
coating well; it wasn't strong enough. At this rate,
he'd be here all night!

Not to be thwarted, Mac picked up his can of
lacquer thinner, hesitated, and then loosened the lid
and carefully dribbled the noxious fluid onto the
plate. After rubbing some more, he held his breath so
as not to breathe the toxic fumes.

Mac peered closer at the spot he had cleaned and
he thought, *Yes, now it's working!* Copper was
shining through the coating. He added thinner and
rubbed harder. Now he could make out an eye etched
in the copper. Seeing an image appear gradually like
this reminded Mac of the magic of darkroom
photography and how the exposed photo paper going
into the developer tray slowly yielded an image. The
dim red safety light in the photo dark room added to
the mystery and drama of the art—something only the
darkroom photographer could enjoy.

More rubbing and more thinner showed that it
was a man's face in the blackness covering the plate.
Mac leaned closer to get a better look, his nose inches
away from the etched, craggy face. He could see also
the beginnings of a hat. It was a big, floppy affair—a
lot like the hat Mac had rented with his costume! The
vapor of the lacquer thinner filled Mac's nostrils and
irritated his sinuses. He felt dizzy.

"I shouldn't be breathing this," Mac said aloud,
and he heard—for the third time, the car's horn. This
time the horn sound was sustained and persistent; it
grew louder and changed from that of the Dodge
Neon car horn to something else. It was a different
sound. There was a long, drawn-out call, like
someone's voice, a moaning sound like the Doppler

18

Effect, growing louder and then fading, vaguely like words running backwards, echoing back and forth to the sound of the car horn, fading in the distance and now it was getting closer, urgent and harsh!

Mac suddenly felt chilled, and a terrible smell invaded his nose. The smell was different. His head swam and he thought, *Phew, the smell sure isn't lacquer thinner—it's something else. Bad!*

It was an overwhelming stench of manure, so strong it was jumbling Mac's senses and he realized he was in blackness. He felt something hit his leg, like someone kicked him in the leg; Mac realized that he had fallen down. The sound of the car's horn had become a man's voice, as someone yelled in his ear!

His last thought was, *Who is that yelling? And what's he saying?* Mac was dimly aware that a man with a gravelly tone shouted in words Mac didn't understand, *"Mijneer, jij daar! Wakker worden!"*[3]

The voice merged with the fading sound of Faye's leaning on the car horn. In another second the horn was completely drowned out by the man's voice shouting gibberish to Mac, *"Jij Mijneer! Wakker worden!"*[4]

Mac felt an iron grip on his shoulder. Someone was shaking him and shouting in his ear, *"Wakker worden! Wakker worden! Bent U drunken?"*[5]

Mac blinked, trying to clear his eyes. He could hardly see. It was so dark! *Someone turned off my studio lights,* he thought, as he blinked again and then he could make out that a stranger was shaking him and shouting at him in a guttural, foreign language that sounded to Mac's ears like a pig grunting. Paralyzed with fright and unwilling to look, Mac shut

---

[3] Sir, that's here! Wake up!

[4] You sir! Wake up!

[5] Wake up! Wake up! Are you drunk?

his eyes tightly.

A rapid series of images raced into Mac's thoughts. Rational explanations skipped and streamed through his mind, reasons that were—at least maybe—possibilities for what must be happening to him, thoughts such as: *Faye and I went to the party; I must have got drunk and passed out; now I'm lying in the front yard, and that voice must be Dennis' and he's shaking me. It has to be Dennis.* When Mac had opened his eyes for a second, he saw that the man was bearded. Another explanation occurred to him: *Only Dennis—that old hippie—still wears a beard!* He scrunched his eyes shut again.

Mac kept his eyes tightly shut, thinking the illusion would go away, yet the feel of the man's muscular grip on his shoulder was real and unrelenting. Mac's brain was racing, hoping; but *No! This isn't someone's front yard! Here it's hard and wooden, like a deck; and Dennis' yard would never smell like this!*

The smell was like a rotten manure pile, and it stunk to high heaven. The stench was so strong that Mac didn't want to breathe. The air reeked, a thick blend of rotten fish, creosote and saltwater. Heavy, cold dampness swept over and chilled him.

Mac gagged. He was about to vomit.

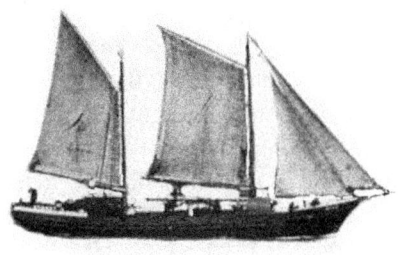

Chapter 3
Dung Boat Arrival

"Bent U ziek?"[6] he bawled in Mac's face.

Mac opened his eyes and choked when he got a good look at the man. He was short. His face was a fright, seamed and ragged, bushy eyebrows, the whites of his eyes set back in dark sockets under the brim of a stubby-billed seaman's cap. At a glance Mac saw that he was dressed in a baggy, rough canvas shirt—like a sailor in the days of tall-masted sailing ships.

Mac swallowed back the acidic taste in his mouth and managed to cry out, "What? Where am I?" as panic tightened his chest. Mac's voice sounded taught and high-pitched with terror, and he felt his nose getting plugged up with snot.

"Where . . .?" he repeated, almost in a scream, but Mac gagged again in his struggle to control his convulsing stomach and his constricting chest. His nose started to run, irritated by the stench of . . . feces! The thought of it was too much to bear; Mac whimpered, *"Is that me I smell?"*

---

[6] Are you sick?

The ugly little man jerked back, surprised and said, "*Bent U een Engelsman?*"[7] Then he switched languages to barely understandable English and he repeated, "*You English?*"

This gruff man had been speaking in a language Mac was unsure of, something like Germanic, Dutch, or Russian, Mac couldn't tell. In the darkness he couldn't make out the man's face. He could only see that he was a scary-looking, bearded man in filthy, smelly clothes.

"Yes," Mac mumbled, and corrected, "*Jah,*" still reeling and unsure what language he should try. "Where am I?" he asked again. He felt the wood deck move underneath him that confirmed that he was on the deck of a ship.

"Am I on a ship?" he cried loudly. "*Ein Schiff?*" he summoned up the words he thought to be German for "*A ship?*"

The man guffawed. "*U bent dronken. Een dronken Engelsman!*"[8] and he laughed again. "*Natuurlijk bent U op een schip, een mest boot, een vuilnis vaarder, en dit is Amsterdam! Houd U mij voor de gek?*"[9] and he turned away, mumbling and shaking his head while making a disparaging, clicking sound with his tongue. "*Een dronken Engelsman!* Har har.*"[10]

"Wait," Mac cried after him. "Wait! Did you say Amsterdam?" as the word *Amsterdam* was the single word that Mac recognized in the man's spiel.

The retreating figure stopped at Mac's cry, turned and looked back at Mac and laughed. The

---

[7] Are you an Englishman?
[8] You're drunk. A drunken Englishman!
[9] Of course you are on a ship, a manure boat, and this is Amsterdam! Do you take me for a fool?
[10] A drunk Englishman!

"Englishman" appeared to him to be so drunk that he was unable to stand and so he lay huddled in the dark. Laughing again, the sailor swung his arm out with a broad sweep into the coming dawn, indicating the horizon that Mac was by now beginning to make out.

"*Ja, Amsterdam*,"[11] and he laughed again.

Another man appeared out of the dark and was coming forward. Mac was terrified, pushing himself away from them and trying to disappear. He heard a growl and saw that the approaching man had a dog with him. It strained toward Mac, growled and licked his chops, but was held back by his master's leash.

"*Wat is hier aan de hand?*"[12] he asked the crewman, who grumbled an answer in reply with something that was, of course, unintelligible to Mac, and gestured toward the *ziek,, dronken Engelsman* who he had stumbled upon in the dark. The sailor acted deferentially toward the second man, so Mac figured the one who was approaching him now would probably be an officer, or the skipper, of the manure boat.

As he ambled forward, pulled along by the dog, Mac pushed himself up against a box. He shook all over and swiped at his nose, trying his best not to start bawling like a baby. Twisting and curling himself into a fetal position, he stifled another urge to throw up.

The skipper, like the sailor, was dressed in the old-time fashion, but his clothes were cleaner and his hat smarter. His chin was stubbly with whiskers. He stooped down, examining the blubbering Mac close to his face. He reached over him and picked up something large, dark and floppy from the deck beside Mac. He looked it over. It was Mac's blue-plumed hat.

---

[11] Yes, Amsterdam.

[12] What is going on here?

The skipper said nothing as he turned the hat around. He took hold of the plume and pulled it out and admired it. He decided to keep the plume and clumsily shoved the hat—minus the feather—on Mac's head. The dog gave one bark in Mac's face. Mac's stomach turned.

Now the skipper squatted on his haunches and he studied the pathetic, sniveling creature on his ship's deck. Mac scooted and forced himself to sit up, conscious that he was being scrutinized. Finally, in English—guttural and Dutch-accented, slowly the man spoke and he seemed to choose his words with care.

"Are you drunk? Or sick?" Then he asked, "Is true? You English?"

His breath was foul. Mac felt queasy.

"Are you English?" the skipper repeated, louder and demanding an answer. Frightened and unsure what to say, Mac's nausea returned and he swiped at his nose.

Louder yet, the man said, "English keel my *broder*, my brother! *I no like English-mann.*"

This was bad news to Mac's way of thinking, and he decided, *I'd better be honest.*

"American," Mac managed to get out. "I'm American," he repeated. The words coming out of Mac's mouth sounded oddly patriotic, but also a little funny, saying them in this strange place, and—as it was blazingly obvious—a different time. He thought, *I sure hope America exists at this time!*

Even in the dim light, Mac saw the whites of his examiner's eyes as they widened and he leaned back on his heels slightly, as if to get a little distance. Mac was glad he had moved back; the man's breath could kill a horse. It was worse than the smell of dung that hung like a cloud over the vessel. The dog barked

24

again.

"*Amerika?*" the skipper muttered, unbelieving. "*Amerika? U bent dronken. Een dronken Engelsman! Amerika! Hah!*"[13] He punctuated this with a laugh, but it was malevolent and humorless.

The skipper twisted his head aside and spat. "*U moet van het schip af! Wij zijn er. Wij zijn in Amsterdam. En neem uw kist mee!*"[14] he said as he stood up and turned to leave. His dog resisted the pull of the leash and looked disappointed that he did not get his master's order to tear Mac apart.

"What? I don't understand," Mac said after him, and he got to his feet but his legs were like rubber. The ship listed and he almost fell. His leg bumped against the box he had been propped against and he grabbed hold of a rope and hung on to it.

Mac swayed there as once again the deck underfoot moved. There was a thud and a shudder. Muffled voices were shouting from the forward deck, and a ship's bell somewhere above rang twice.

He heard Mac call after him, and the skipper stopped and turned back to Mac. He growled, "Um, go off my ship this now. We in Amsterdam here. Bring your . . . *kist*," and he pointed to the box. Mac looked at him blank-faced, not comprehending the meaning of the word, *kist*.

"*Kist?*"

Short-tempered and angry, the man yelled, "*En neem U kist mee. Domme Engelsman!*"[15]

Mac looked to where the man was pointing. The box, the *kist*, it turned out, was his printmaker chest!

---

[13] America? You're drunk. A drunken Englishman! America! Hah!

[14] You need to get off the ship! We are there. We are in Amsterdam. And take your chest!

[15] And take your chest. Stupid Englishman!

He hadn't recognized it, but there it was! The box, what the skipper called his *kist*, was his precious printmaker chest. *How did it get here? How did he get here, to Amsterdam? No, this can't be!* Mac let go of the rope and sat down on the chest. He had to think.

The skipper glared at Mac, his ire was rekindled. He rubbed his chin and was thinking what to do with this miserable, sniveling apparition that had inexplicably turned up on his "*mest boot*." Slowly he came back to Mac, squatted and studied the American's face again. Mac, sitting on his chest, attempted a brave face despite his dread.

"Why you say '*Amerika*'?" the skipper asked.

Mac felt panic again, sensing renewed danger. He thought, *I'd better change to something else.* He forced a smile, trying to act normal. He stood up again and the skipper stood also, alert and looking ready for a fight; but Mac kept his hand on to the rope and straightened to attention and tried to look less like a victim. He put on a brave, American face.

Mac's survival senses were coming to his rescue. By all appearances and references to the English killing his brother, a Dutchman, Mac might be in wartime 17th Century. The United States would not exist yet. He recalled, *but, colonial America? Yes!*

"American," Mac said with pride. "I am from the American colonies." Estimating the time at hand, he refined his statement: "Yes. New Amsterdam," and proudly tapped his chest. He gambled on his scant history education. "New . . . Amsterdam." Mac repeated, as he tried to remember when it was changed to New York.

Mac thought he probably sounded like he was talking to a child, or a visitor from outer space. He felt like an alien, too—like a visitor who landed on a hostile planet. To the man looming over him, in fact,

Mac was like an infant with all his whining and carrying on. Yet Mac dared not declare: "I am from the 21st Century!"

"You sound *English*," the man said, tapping his ear to make his point, and he moved a little closer to Mac. The light was getting better now as the sky was lighter in the east. Mac thought it must be near sunrise. He quickly scanned the eastern horizon and Mac could see the silhouettes of buildings starting to show against the growing light.

One stood out, higher than all the others, with a tower. He flashed back on the *Space Needle* in Seattle. *This sure isn't Seattle and that isn't the Smith Tower, either. More likely it's a church steeple.*

In that instant, Mac also saw on the horizon a singularly unfamiliar shape. It was moving. It was a huge windmill, its sails turning slowly. Here and there were glimmers of dim lights, but definitely not *electric* lights. Overhead a seagull cried. For a fraction of a second Mac was again back in Seattle, listening to familiar sounds of the waterfront, but only in his imagination. *This sure isn't Seattle!*

Still waiting for Mac to answer, the skipper who confronted him grew shifty and acted nervous. The dog added his concerns and grumbled lowly; he was prepared to do Mac harm. His Master shoved a hand under his great coat and it finally occurred to Mac that the skipper probably had a knife on him.

"Scottish," Mac said, without a thought. "I am Scottish, from Scotland. My accent is . . . I speak Scottish-American," he added confidently. Then, without knowing what possessed him to do it, he said, louder, "Ah, Amsterdam. So beautiful!" and he gave the man what he figured was a big, amiable Scottish smile.

His ruse seemed to work. The man nodded,

relaxed, turned and took a step over to the ship's railing.

"Ach," he hacked, and he spit over the side. When he turned and when he came back, he was holding a knife in his hand, pointed at Mac. He almost lost what little control that he still had.

"I the *skipper*! You stowaway on my boat! I cut you," and the man made a couple short, threatening jabs at Mac with his knife. "You have money?"

Mac thought, *This does it! I'm going to faint!* But he managed to nod his head.

"Oh, yes!" Mac said, releasing the rope and reached for his pocket. The skipper tensed. Mac slowed, reached in his pocket and produced some change, quarters, dimes, nickels and pennies, and held them out to him. This felt ridiculous. "It's all I have," he said.

Keeping the knife pointed at Mac, he peered at the coins glinting dully in the half-light. The skipper frowned at the coins and his brow knotted quizzically. Stepping back he said, "Argh! *Wat is dat?* What is that? That is foreign money!"

Someone called out from somewhere on the boat and the skipper called back to them. Duty called, and he was ready to give up on Mac so he returned his knife to its hiding place and, with his dog pulling back, eyeing Mac and probably memorizing his face for future reference.

The skipper moved off as he was needed elsewhere, but over his shoulder the skipper called back, "*Ga van het schip af. Af!*"[16] with an emphatic jab of his thumb. There was no mistaking his meaning: *Get off this ship! Off!*

Mac resumed breathing, returned his hand and let

---

[16] Jump off the ship. Off!

the coins fall back into his pocket. He wondered, *How can I get off?* He couldn't jump overboard. Panicked, looking around for a place to hide for now, he found—at his back, a high wall of rough planking. He reached up and gripped the top and chinned himself up, craning his neck and trying to make out what was in the dark interior of the walled-off area.

The planking was the side of a huge box. From the stench that met Mac's face he did not need light to see that it was a container for manure. That was when he realized, *I'm on a dung boat, a manure scow!* It was true, as the man had said, this was a *mest boot*.

Mac was about to learn about the waste management system in 17th Century Amsterdam, as it was three-hundred-fifty years back in time, a study abroad in space in time; and he started on this manure boat.

All around the deck, activity was picking up. Men shuffled past, shovels over their shoulders, readying to make port. The gaff-rigged scow was being towed; its masts now empty of sails. The dawn light was improving, with the sky turning pearly gray in the east.

Gradually Mac was getting used to the smells and his nausea had subsided; still he worried, wondering how he was going to get off the boat. *He must get off, and soon.*

Somewhere ahead Mac could hear a voice counting off, like a coxswain, calling out the beat for a rowing crew. A few of the workers going by looked Mac up and down, but they said nothing. They were the night crew, and they were almost home, with places to go. A stowaway was no concern of theirs. It was the skipper's problem.

Mac remembered that he was wearing the outfit that he had rented from the costume shop. The label

on the costume had said, "Flemish Duke - 1776."
Eighteenth Century. Maybe the clothes fit in with the
period—whenever "this period" was.

Is Amsterdam Flemish? No, I don't think so, Mac
thought, and he wished he had paid closer attention to
his geography and history lessons. Anyway, an art
professor's sketchy knowledge of history and
geography would not help him to figure out how to
get off a dung boat on Amsterdam's waterfront.

Mac steadied himself with one hand on the rope
and leaned back into the shadows against the plank
wall. He remembered his printmaker chest, and he
hooked his foot around its corner and dragged it
closer while trying not to attract attention.

*His hat! Should he take off his hat? What about
the wig*? Most of the men he saw had long stringy
hair, sort of like his rock musician's wig; so the wig
fit the period, apparently.

Mac felt a shaking beginning in his legs. He
thought it was the ship vibrating, or he was shivering
because he was cold; but the shaking intensified, and
it was fast getting worse. Try as he might, he could
not stop shaking. His teeth chattered; he tightened his
jaw to stop it. His knees literally knocked against
each other and he felt weak, his head floated and he
knew that he was in for a fall.

His knocking knees buckled, he sank and sat
heavily on the printmaker chest, hunched forward and
put his head between his knees. He lost his balance
and fell over sideways on the deck.

The last thing he was conscious of was the sound
of men laughing. Then there was nothing.

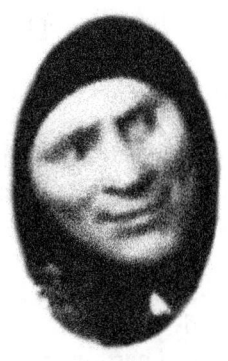

Chapter 4
Guardian Angel from Hell

Mac came to with the sound of a dog barking somewhere nearby. He kept his eyes closed. If he kept his eyes closed, maybe he would find he was only having a dream, and that the barking dog was just a dog that someone was walking, and he had dozed off, and he was on a picnic with Faye, and pretty soon she would awaken him from his sleep.

Any second now. Nothing. *Please, please Faye, wake me up!* But, no Faye.

Instead, there was the dog's constant barking and the horrid smells remained. Full of dread at what he might see, Mac slowly and cautiously opened one eye. The barking was from the dung boat dog, above Mac, at the ship's railing. Mac found himself lying on the quayside.

The wall-like, glistening black side of the scow was about twenty-feet away, tied to the stone quay with thick hawsers, looped around dark wood bollards and holding the dung boat close to the stone pier, cushioned by knotted hemp rope fenders.

Mac realized that he had been left like garbage by

31

the quayside; this was rock bottom, for sure, kicked off a dung boat!

Nonetheless, he was glad to be alive as he remembered his terror in the early dawn. The shaking in his legs was gone. He felt feverish. The sun was high overhead but it was only a silver disc seen through an overcast, early winter sky. Judging from the sun's position, he thought it must be about noontime. There was a chill in the air.

Mac's whole body ached. At his back was something box-like and hard-cornered. With one arm he raised himself up on his elbow and looked around, trying to get oriented. He had been lying on flagstones. The stink of the waterfront seemed to get worse in his nostrils as his head slowly cleared.

A hundred feet farther away, another ship was tied, low in the water. There were two gangplanks from it, and men were rolling barrels down, one man on the uphill side and two below to keep the wood barrels from getting away from them.

Sitting up a little more, Mac could see beyond this to where a ramp was being used to unload shaggy, jug-headed horses from yet another ship.

Here and there were men gathered around the goings-on, busy with their work and mostly ignoring Mac. He got to his feet and brushed off his outfit. A few workers glanced his way and gave him the once-over, perhaps taking note of his costume. Maybe the costume shop didn't get the period quite right but, on a busy dockside in a major seaport, a strangely-dressed foreigner was not enough to draw much attention. No one said anything to Mac.

Stepping back, Mac's foot hit something and caused him to lose his balance and to sit down clumsily. To his surprise, he sat on his printmaker chest—it was the box that he had been leaning against! Some thoughtful soul must have taken pity and got him and his chest off the ship out of their way, and then they left him on the wharf. To them he was just an unfortunate, drunken, sick and lost stowaway; and, by the looks of him, they probably thought this foreigner wouldn't survive for long in Amsterdam.

At the ship's rail above him there was a huddle of several men around the incessantly barking dog and Mac realized that one of them, he recognized as the boat's skipper, was shouting at him, waving a small, dark object.

"Is dit van jouw?" [17] He kept yelling and jabbing his finger at what he held up and pointing at Mac. Mac stood up again and craned his neck to see what it was that the skipper was waving around.

This went on for another few seconds, with a confused Mac gaping open-mouthed at the man, trying to understand what he was saying. Exasperated, the skipper said something that made the others laugh and then he pitched the thing down. It sailed like a Frisbee, and arced down toward the befuddled stowaway Mac who stood below and now who watched the thing as it sailed down toward him.

Just at that moment, a woman approached, oblivious of what was coming down. Mac yelled, "Watch out!" and he leaped forward to shield her. Startled, she ducked and jumped back with a shriek, and almost dropped the wrapped package that she clutched to her bosom. The object missed her and clattered on the stones with a metallic ring.

Angered, she stared at what had been thrown down by the boat's skipper. She glanced at Mac gawping at her and then followed his look as he

---

[17] Is this yours?

33

turned his face again up to the man who had thrown the thing.

She scolded the man above, her voice screeching and shrill as an eagle's. The thrower yelled something back and pointed at Mac. The offended woman shot a black look up at the man, seething and muttering a foreign word that sounded to Mac like an explicative. She stooped to pick up the object and studied it, her expression a mixture of anger and curiosity.

She came to Mac and showed the thing to him.

"*Is dit van jouw?* "[18] she demanded in Dutch. She was still angry and undecided as to who to blame for the near miss. Mac instantly recognized what she proffered as the partly-cleaned, blackened printing plate he had been working on before his nightmare began.

"*Die man zegt dat dit van jouw is,* "[19] she repeated, louder, jerking her head in the direction of the dung boat skipper, who had disappeared. Her voice raised higher: "*Is dat waar?* "[20] Mac realized he must look idiotic with his mouth hanging open in his uncomprehending, dumbfounded state.

What to do? He assumed that she was asking if the thing were his, so he improvised an answer and tried a word that might fit: "*Ja.*" Mac reached for the plate, and he said, "I am sorry. Do you speak English?"

She blinked as he took the plate. She was set back by his words. Her face flushed as she now looked Mac up and down, her eyes narrowed. She appeared to be suspicious and calculating.

Mac thought she might have been in her late fifties. She was heavily clothed in a long black,

---

[18] Is this yours?
[19] The man says this is yours.
[20] Is that true?

layered dress and jacket, and a black scarf bound her head. Around her neck was tied a dark red ribbon, pressing into the flesh under her sharp jaw line and chin.

She studied Mac's floppy hat and stringy wig. Her frown gave way to a bare hint of a smile. Still, her forehead was lined and questioning.

Thinking an introduction might be in order, Mac thought to take off his hat. He swept it from his bewigged head with a theatric flourish in the way he had seen gallantry displayed in plays.

"William Handyside MacRitchie," he crooned, and bowed to her and hoped that he did the gesture correctly. When he straightened again, hat in hand, he added. "At your service!" and pushed aside some of the wig hair that had fallen over his eye.

His fear was subsiding as, on-the-fly, he play-acted a chivalrous self-introduction. The woman shifted her package and cradled it protectively in her elbow as she freed one of her hands. He noticed that her fingers were loaded with rings. He thought, *What's next? Does she expect me to kiss her hand?* But no, she had raised her hand to stroke her chin, and to think what to say to this English-speaking foreigner. Mac was relieved not to have to kiss her hand, but waited and wondered, *Well, is she going to speak English or not?*

She cleared her throat and said quite clearly, "You do not sound . . . *English,"* but her accent was thick and her voice was cold. Waiting, she held her chin pinched between her thumb and forefinger. She knitted her brow and cocked her head, a picture of critical judgment as she continued in her assessment of Mac.

"*Scottish.* I am Scottish," Mac said, and hoped that this would satisfy. It was true; his was a Scottish name stretching back several generations. He tried his best smile and reminded himself, *Faye always said that I had a winning smile.*

The woman was holding him in her gaze. He felt like a mouse before a snake. She was obviously unimpressed with his explanation and she was about to turn away and go when came a hoot from above her that made her stop and glance up. The boat's crew had come back, leaned on the ship's railing and commented in loud, jocular voices; the dog joined in and barked eagerly.

They began laughing and pointing at the two of them, the woman in black and Mac. She shouted back. Mac couldn't understand the insult or threat that she flung at them but, whatever it was, it was effective. The men suddenly stopped laughing and withdrew without another word. The dog followed them, head down, as if he understood her vehement curse.

"Het zijn smerig zwijnen!"[21] she seethed as she turned back to Mac and he thought, *That Dutch word 'zwijnen' sounded a lot like 'swine' to me!*

Then she spoke English and said, "I am sorry. My English not so good. No Scottish. But . . . my name is Mevrouw Macia Schwarzesherz. You look you need help, ja? A place to sleep tonight, maybe?"

Mac smiled. "Oh, ja! I need help." It was the understatement of his lifetime; but as regards to a place to spend the night, Mac said nothing, hoping in his every fiber that he wouldn't be staying all night in this place.

"Hoe kan ik U helpen? How can I help?" she asked. Mac thought her tone and manner were sincere. The thought crossed his mind to say, *Get me*

---

[21] They are filthy swine!

outta' here! But he checked his impulse. A clever response like that wouldn't work. Her question hung in the air. As Mac had made a quantum leap, or he was in a time-warp of some kind, *how in the world could she help?* He speculated: *Maybe it was that lacquer thinner. Maybe I am dreaming. No, you don't smell stink when you dream. Or, maybe I died and this is Hell. Take this woman's offer. Don't lose this chance. Think: first things first. Confirm the time and place. Get . . . a . . . grip!*

What Mac decided was to first ask, "Is this Amsterdam?" gesturing around him. He had to confirm that this really was Amsterdam, as he was told by the men on the boat.

The woman gave him a funny look, like, *Are you kidding? No one is that dumb.* Then she answered, "*Ja, dit is* Amsterdam,"[22] and for the first time she smiled, revealing that she had bad teeth. Mac took her grin to be a good sign despite that it was not a pretty smile.

The smile suggested that this woman was playing along with him, as though she took him for a fool. *That's right*, Mac thought, *Please humor me.*

"Yes, this Amsterdam, Meneer," the woman repeated, and waited for his next words. She smiled coyly. Perhaps she thought that he wanted to play games with her; or could it be that she thought he was flirting with her?

Mac was pondering, *what should I confirm next?* He decided, and blurted, "*When* is it?" He thought, *Yes, that would be good to know. When is this?*

Her smile vanished, and Mac thought, *Uh oh, wrong question.* At that moment, as if on cue, bells began to ring. Mac cheered himself—maybe he had

---

[22] Yes, this is Amsterdam.

said the magic word, "When." The chiming came from several places at once and, in the distance a carillon rang out a hymn.

To the splendid sounds of all the city's bells ringing at once, Mevrouw Schwarzesherz raised her hand to her ear in a demonstrative manner and she said, "You hear? *Het is twaalf uur*,"[23] and she translated. "In English, or Scottish, you say '*twelve o'clock*.'"

Mac shook his head. No, the hour of the day wasn't what he meant by, "*when* is it." She frowned. Seeing her frown Mac thought, *Oh dear! I'm losing at this game.* Again Mac was at a loss of what to say or how to be exact because what he wanted to know was what year, what month, and what day. He started again with, "What day?" he quizzed her for an answer.

"*Het is Zondag,*"[24] she said, and her smile gradually reappeared. "*Zondag*! Sunday," she said as she remembered the English—and probably Scottish—pronunciation of the name for this weekday.

"*Wie bent U, meneer?*"[25] and she asked, appending a question of her own to her answer to Mac's question. "Who are you, Meneer? What is your business here in Amsterdam? You come all the way from Scotland, for why?"

Mac ignored her question and pressed on and he asked her with no effort to conceal his growing eagerness, "What month is it?"

She stepped back a little. His desperation showed and his eagerness made her wary. Mac geared down his interrogation, shrugged innocently, palms out as if

---

[23] It is twelve hours.
[24] It is Sunday.
[25] Who are you, Sir?

to say, *I can't help it, lady!*

"Please . . . The month?" He guessed: "October?"

"Ja, het is Oktober, Meneer,"[26] and again, *"Wie bent U*? Who are you?" It was her turn to ask questions now.

But, again Mac ignored her question and he chanced to ask, "Thirty-first?" He wanted to find a connection with the time on the date when he remembered that he was heading for a Halloween party with Faye, but he felt his panic returning.

"Wat?" she backed off with, *"Ja, een en dertig."*[27]

Mac made a quick calculation and he asked himself: *When was Halloween invented*? Was Halloween always some kind of dark-spirited thing, about witches, death and dark doings? These days, from the look of things around him, this *is* the dark ages. He concluded, *I'd better not ask if it's Halloween.*

The big question came to him next, that which Mac mostly wanted to know and he hesitated before asking, "What year is it?" Not surprisingly, her jaw dropped.

"Je neemt mij voor de gek. Je bent een slechte![28] You make jokes on me. You bad one!" and she giggled. *"Welk jaar is het!"* and she laughed again as she studied his eyes. Then she stopped laughing and composed herself, as if she was thinking, *could it be this Scottish fool really doesn't know what year it is?*

As her mirth subsided she renewed her distrusting look and Mac sensed he was headed for trouble again. He changed his tactic and said, "I mean, how do you say this year, in Dutch?"

She relaxed then and her smile came back. *"Ah!*

---

[26] Yes, it is October, Mister.

[27] Yes, thirty-one.

[28] You fool around with me. You are a bad man!

Zestien zestig. Zestien sestig,"[29] which didn't really help Mac. However, to him, he heard in her answer two of her words that sounded a lot like, "Sixteen-sixty."

He thought: *1660!* And he repeated those two words aloud and tried to mimic her accent. "*Zest-ien ses-tig? Zestien sestig?*" he echoed. Then, in English, "*Sixteen-sixty*?" in a voice an octave higher, his stomach knotted and his throat suddenly went dry. He choked.

"Ja. 'Sixteen-sixty.'"

Mac felt his shoulders drop, and it was only when she said what year it was—1660—that he realized his back, neck and shoulder muscles ached with the tension, his deepest desire right now had been to learn whether this, his nightmare, was a reality. Yes, and there it was, *October 31, 1660!*

Mac was 350 years back in time!

---

[29] Sixteen-sixty.

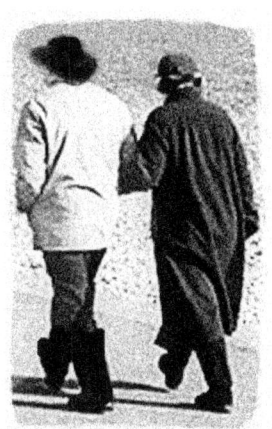

Chapter 5
Sabbatical Study Abroad

Mac tried to stay cool and to act normally, but he felt a wave of dizziness threaten him; and the woman, Mevrouw Macia Schwarzesherz, gave him that suspicious look once again.

"*Alles goed met je?* Will you be all right? Is someone to meet you?" She touched his arm kindly. "You look for a place to sleep tonight? To bed?" She seemed genuinely concerned with Mac's need. He allowed himself the thought that she might well be his guardian angel, sent to protect him.

She asked him the question she had asked before: "Who are you, sir?" She eyed the outfit he wore, her curiosity piqued by (Mac was becoming increasingly aware) his outlander's costume, wig and hat. The Flemish garb was garish compared to what people who were passing by them were wearing. Yet no one, except for this one woman, seemed to be interested in him, or cared what his predicament might be.

Bless her heart, thought Mac.

"*Misschien wel kan ik je helpen,*"[30] she began, then stopped and started over, in English. "Perhaps I can help you, but you must tell me who you are, Meneer Willem . . . Um . . .."

He finished for her, "William MacRitchie," Mac told her for the second time. "William *Handyside* MacRitchie. What I am, Madam, is . . .," and he thought of something fitting and that would be safe, ". . . a scholar. I am here to study," he improvised. This identity might save him, he thought, *I could role-play a scholar, like a professor on sabbatical.* After all, Mac had been a professor of art at a university, and twice took sabbaticals and spent time in Amsterdam. That was in the 1960s and '80s . . . almost three-hundred-fifty years in the future!

"Ah! *Een geleerde!* A scholar!" she said, and gave him a modest, respectful curtsy.

Mac was abashed and, as she noticed, she smiled at his reaction to her show of respect for his high calling. "I am honored to meet you, Sir," she said in a demure and more formal tone. Her English was improving fast, Mac thought, the more that they talked.

"And, what did you come to study, Meneer, if you do not mind my asking you? Will you attend the *Athenaeum Illustre*?" Mac had suddenly gained respectability in this woman's eyes.

He shook his head no. The truth was he had never heard of the *Athenaeum Illustre*, which sounded like an institution where he would not likely be welcomed if his past academic record was to be taken into consideration. Mac had radical ideas in his own time. An institution was no place for him. Probably there

---

[30] Perhaps I can help you.

would be no room for him in such a place in this, the 17th Century, any more than there would be in the 20th Century. It might even be dangerous. As Mac wasn't expecting the question she asked, "*Where do you want to study?*" it took him a few seconds to come up with an answer.

His mind retraced back and forth to his sabbatical days, jetting around the globe, meeting contemporary, name artists of the day. Now, here he was in Amsterdam again, but thrown back to the year 1660, chatting not with a name artist, but with a 17th Century Dutch woman who happened to find him—a dung boat castoff, garbage on the dock—and she had just offered him a bed. He thought, *Maybe she runs a hostel!*

She waited while Mac considered, gazing outward at the forest of tall masts of ships that he could see far out on the bay. *Is that the Zuiderzee?* Mac wondered as he stalled for time and thought how best to answer her question. He shifted his feet and clasped the plate behind his back thoughtfully, *If not to visit the Athenaeum Illustre, then what would a scholar do?* A bright idea came to him.

"No, not the *Athenaeum*," he began, and took a deep breath as he decided on a long shot: "I came to meet Rembrandt van Rijn!" and then he exhaled, relaxed. His decision had a strange effect. Mevrouw Schwarzesherz' eyes widened, as if Mac had said he wanted to meet the head of the Dutch Republic. He crossed his fingers behind his back, hoped for the best, but feared the worst.

"Rembrandt van Rijn? *De fijnschilder?* "[31] she asked. Whether the name was awesome or fearsome to her, he couldn't tell. He looked around; afraid

---

[31] The painter?

everyone had heard him and had stopped in their tracks to stare. But, no, nobody paid him any mind. Only this woman had heard him speak of the celebrated painter, Rembrandt—who was one of Mac's idols of printmaking. Whether her surprise was a good or bad sign, he would soon find out.

Mevrouw Schwarzesherz hesitated no longer; she, too, had made a decision. "We must go! Come. Come. We must go somewhere quiet," and then she said, "Put on your hat and let me take your arm." She shifted her package and clutched it in the crook of her other arm while Mac pocketed his plate.

"*Maak u geen zorgen. Omdat u een bent een bezoeker bent.* [32] Don't worry. By your clothing people will see that you are a foreigner, and that you are with me, and nothing will happen. No one will question." Several people passing by them turned their heads and grinned at her.

Mac suddenly stopped. "Wait! My chest, um, I mean . . . my *kist*!" he said.

She looked where he pointed and saw the chest.

"*Is dat jouw kist*? Is that chest yours?"

"Yes it is! I can't leave it. No."

He couldn't carry the printmaker chest if she was on his arm. Looking around, she tilted toward a boy who lounged a few feet away. The boy had been intently observing them, probably on the lookout for opportunities to make some money.

"*Jongen! Kom hier. Draag de kist van deze geleerde. Blyf dichtby ons. Volg dichtby,*"[33] she commanded the boy, her voice sharp.

Mac figured she said, "Carry that!" because the boy jumped to it and gripped the rope handles and

---

[32] Don't worry, because you are a visitor.
[33] Boy! Come here. Carry the chest of this scholar. Stay close to us. Follow closely.

picked up Mac's printmaker chest. Bashful but expectant, he kept his eyes on Mac.

The woman spoke again, "*Wees voorzichtig. Deze man is een geleerde en u zult voor uw hulp betaald worden.*"[34]

Turning to Mac she said, "You have money?" and nodded toward the boy. "For him?"

"I have foreign money," Mac said, thinking of the loose change he had in his pocket, even though the ship's skipper had denied that it was any good. Plus, he had a dollar and a debit card. The woman considered for a moment as she calculated. Mac felt panic time coming back, but she dismissed the issue for now and indicated that she could pay the boy and she waved them on.

"We can settle money matters later," she said, and nodded in the direction toward the larger buildings at the end of the quay. Now she rested her free hand on Mac's arm, proud to be guiding a foreign scholar to her house; she kept her package tightly in the crook of her other arm.

As they walked off, her bejeweled hand weighing heavily on his arm, Mac was thinking, *Oh! What I'd give for a postcard! I'd write, 'Dear Faye, I am walking with a Dutch lady on a quay in old Amsterdam. Wish you were here. Love, Mac.' I could sure use a postcard now!* Continuing his wild fantasy, he thought, *If I could get that camera out of the chest, I'd take this good woman's picture! On second thought, that's probably a bad idea!*

Mac could hear the boy as he followed behind them. He grunted and scraped along in his wooden clogs, lugging the chest. Mac worried as he let himself think what the locals would do if they saw

---

[34] Boy! Come here. Carry the chest of this scholar. Stay close to us. Follow close.

what was in his box.

Don't drop it, kid. If you do, and it pops open, they'll probably burn me at the stake or something worse. 'Everything you need to be a printmaker! Just add creative juices!' Ha! I sure could use some creativity now. Beam me up, Faye!

Mac's rambling thoughts were interrupted by the woman as she leaned in closer to Mac, as though she did not want anyone—not the boy or someone passing close by—to hear what she was about to tell her escort.

"Do you know what happened to van Rijn?" she asked Mac in a low, confidential manner.

"No. What happened to him?"

The truth was, Mac didn't know for certain whether Rembrandt was even alive in 1660! He wondered, *Is he dead?* Mac wished for an art history cheat-sheet like his students used to have. *If Rembrandt is dead in 1660, then what will I do?*

Quietly the woman went on with her news. "Trouble. *Big trouble.* Poor man. His lovely wife Saskia died nineteen years ago, you know. Then things got worse and he lost his house on the *Jodenbreestraat* and also his art collection and all his treasures. At the end he had to live like a tenant in his own beautiful home. Then his house was auctioned off, sold to a silk merchant and a shoemaker! Poor Rembrandt. *Poor man.* You know? Did you not know?"

"I knew that," Mac lied. "Still, he is a great artist. That's why I . . .," he started to explain, but the woman squeezed his arm when he was in mid-sentence and shushed him. Mac shushed and thought, *She has quite a grip. This was not a woman to mess with.*

Two uniformed men were approaching from the

other direction. Whether they were police or soldiers, Mac didn't know. They nodded and smirked at the lady with a foreigner at her side. They passed by them and said not a word and did not question them, just as she had promised. Mac heard them laughing behind his back as they continued along, but he didn't turn around to see why.

She continued, "Oh, yes, Rembrandt is a great artist still, of that everyone agrees. Almost everyone. He is a great painter." She thought carefully about what she had to say next. "But they say his painting days are over, without a great studio today."

"No studio?" Mac asked her.

"No. All gone. And he has been seen haunting his former house, a ghost of his old self. 'Rembrandt's Ghost,' they call him. Did you know the word for . . . how you say . . . *official*, um, *union* . . . no, *Guild* . . . do you understand '*Guild*'?"

"Yes. 'Guild' I understand. What about it?"

"Because of lawsuits, and the artist's union rules, Rembrandt is not permitted to sell his paintings now. Also, he and his son, Titus, and Rembrandt's second wife—Hendrickje, and their little girl, had to move to the Rozengracht. It is quite a fall from the Breestraat. Quite a scandal. *Een verschrikkelijke schandaal!*"[35]

"Do you understand?" she asked quietly, as some people passing near had turned their heads at her mention of the word "*schandaal*," and, like the soldiers, the passersby smiled over a privately-shared knowledge. Mac could only wonder why they smiled; but the woman went on with her gossiping.

"You must also know that he is not allowed to have any new apprentices. So if you approach him, then you must not appear as a new apprentice. You

---

[35] A terrible scandal.

must appear to be a colleague of the man. He is still a painter of honor, and the Union, the Guild, will not bother you, a foreign professor, and a scholar of the arts." Having concluded her instructions and her chin up, she sniffed importantly; it seemed to Mac that she was proud to be his escort.

Then, suddenly changing the subject, Mevrouw Schwarzesherz said, *"Heb jij honger?* Are you hungry?"

Mac understood the Dutch word for "hungry." The horror and stench of his early morning trials were wearing off, leaving him ravenous. She pointed to a hanging sign, *"De Vier Suikerbroden,"*[36] with an enticing, painted bas relief image of four loaves of cinnamon bread with glistening tops, sprinkled with sugar crystals and spices. Mac salivated.

She said, "A *bakkerij,* a bakery. Come. Come-come!" The bread and rolls displayed in the many-paned window reminded Mac of Seattle's Pike Street Market, only with Amsterdam's stinky air added, with its pervading smells of the waterfront under the aroma of fresh baking bread.

She turned and told the boy to wait, and he gratefully set down the printmaker chest and plopped down on it to rest. Inside now—and with a gentle push, Mevrouw Schwarzesherz steered Mac toward a small table in the back. She spoke to the woman behind the counter who gave Mac a disapproving look.

He sat on a bench behind the table and leaned against the wall. *Sure,* Mac began another inner dialog; *I eat lunch in 17th Century Dutch bakeries whenever I get the chance!* His hunger was making him feel giddy, and he risked a smile.

---

[36] The four sugar loaves.

Could it be that I'm beginning to enjoy this nightmare? He sobered. *No way. Please, Faye, wake me up from this bad dream!*

He watched Mevrouw Schwarzesherz buy a tidbit and go out and give it to the boy. She returned to Mac's table and settled, tucking her package close to her side protectively. In a few minutes, a girl came carrying a tray of bread and cheese, a wood-handled knife and two gray pewter tankards of beer, foam streaming down their sides. A small pot held a clot of butter. Mac wondered about drinking beer on his empty stomach, but he decided it was best not to ask for water, having seen open sewers and filthy alleyways all along their walk.

She lifted her tankard and said, *"Drink!"* and Mac lifted his and drank. He smacked his lips and wiped his mouth. He thought it was the best beer he had ever tasted. Smiling over his pleasure, she ordered another. Mac was feeling better. Inwardly he thanked his lucky stars for having met this woman, convinced as he was now that she was his guardian angel.

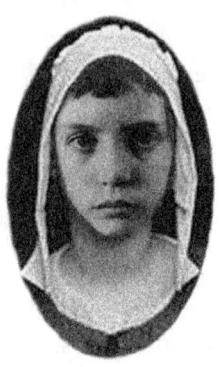

Chapter 6
A Night to Forget

Monday morning, when he opened his eyes after a deep, beery sleep, Mac saw that he was awakening from the worst night of his life. It was embarrassing, humiliating, frightening and stupefying, worse than the time in San Francisco when a woman had invited him to her apartment to see her etchings and he realized she had designs on him.

Mac squeezed his eyes shut and blinked, and hoped that he had only imagined seeing the girl uncurling from his side, moving to the edge of the bed wearing only a loose-fitting shift. His mind flashed, *This can't be! She's not more than fourteen!*

In his panicky mind's eye, Mac instantly saw himself on trial for pedophilia, pleading with a judge, and his attorney trying in vain to defend Mac on grounds of enticement.

Now the girl sat on the edge of the bed and wrapped herself in a rough blanket. She turned and stared at him, her dark eyes wide and imploring.

Mac was reminded of the Vermeer painting, "Girl with the Pearl Earring." Young and comely, she didn't look at all like a child prostitute. Yet, there it was; "Madam" Macia Schwarzesherz got him drunk and here was this girl in bed with him. Slowly, to Mac's fogged mind reality dawned, *figure it out!*

His memory of the seamen's hooting came back, and those smirking police they met—they no doubt got a piece of the action from the Madam after she had relieved Mac, the naïve foreigner, of his money. There it was: Madam Macia Schwarzesherz is a procuress, like the one in yet another Vermeer painting that Mac remembered.

Too late Mac realized this; now, if he survived, it would be a miracle. He knew nothing had actually happened between him and this girl, it couldn't have. The Madam got him too drunk, for one thing; and he wouldn't have, anyway. Nevertheless, if Faye found out, she would never forgive him.

He spoke firmly to the girl, "You must never tell anyone we slept together!"

The girl's mouth dropped open, her lower lip quivered and she made a guttural, baritone sound. Fearful of Mac, she stood up with the blanket tightly wrapped around her and shuffled across the floor barefooted. She stood with her back to the door, trembling with fear.

Mac raised himself up on his elbows and said, more gently, "I'm not going to hurt you," but his words seemed to worsen the situation. She began to make gulping, sobbing noises and slid down the length of the door into a huddle, pulling the blanket closer and winding her forearms around her knees, her hair falling in her eyes. She buried her face and moaned woefully and loud.

"Hey, calm down," Mac said. His head ached, he felt queasy and he needed to go to the bathroom.

"Calm down. I'm not going to do anything," he

51

repeated, but the girl made soft bleating noises and Mac could hear the footsteps of someone coming up the stairs to the room, then loud knocking on the door and, from the other side, Mac heard the Madam's voice yelling something in Dutch. The girl got to her feet, shot a look at Mac and fumbled with the door latch.

The Madam rushed in. She wasn't wearing the scarf now and her gray, thinning hair was a mess. She was wearing a thick quilted robe held together with thongs. Gone was her sweetness. She was fuming. Mac stayed where he was, covering himself and embarrassed no end.

"What is happening?" she demanded in English, moving toward him. "I heard the girl. What did you do?" she demanded to know, and then she began scanning around the room as if she was looking for something.

Mac followed her eyes as they settled on his printmaker chest with the old black printing plate lying on top. She noted his clothes strewn on the floor, his wig and the floppy Flemish hat hung on a peg on the wall. She looked back at him, expecting his answer.

Mac declared, "Nothing! I have done nothing," and he continued to follow her survey of the room, seeing what she saw. Amid the clothing on the floor he caught a glimpse of a scattering of his tiny pocket knife, keys, and his USB flash drive.

She finished her survey and turned back to Mac, and confronted him testily. "What's wrong? Did she not please you? Are you sick?"

Mac did feel sick. By the door, the girl decided it was a good time to leave and she slipped out. Mac did not move. He hid his nakedness under the bed covers.

"You've been going through my things," Mac

said, and gestured to the mess of his things scattered around on the floor. "You should not have done that." He wanted to crawl out of the bed but he was naked; and it was cold, too. "That's no way to treat a guest!" he added.

"Guest? *Guest?* Ha! You are not a guest, Meneer. You are a *customer*. A customer with no money. I can throw you into the street, even naked. You know that?"

She crossed the room and snatched up his pants off the floor. "You have no money, only foreign coins. They are not real silver or gold. Worthless." She dropped his pants on the floor, disgusted.

"I can explain . . .," Mac started, but she cut him off.

"You lie! You say you are a scholar? You are a liar. Show me. Prove to me you are a scholar. Come to see Rembrandt? Ha! Indeed, you are an outcast, I think. Cast away from your own country, no doubt. Yes, you stowed away on a boat and now you think you can fool a poor old woman, ply me with your English gibberish and use my girl!" She punctuated her diatribe with a stamp of her foot.

"Get you dressed or I will throw you out naked. I will have you thrown out the window!" She turned, re-crossed the room, went out the door and slammed it behind her.

Mac began to shudder, whether from cold or from Madam Schwarzesherz' threats, he wasn't sure. He was scared. Mac needed to pee, and he wondered where he could go. He thought, *Chamber pot!* That must be what they do, and he pushed his legs over the side of the bed. His stockings were still on his feet, but the floor felt cold as ice. As he suspected, under the bed was a lidded pot. He was relieved to find it empty. Soon it was not.

He replaced the pot cover and started dressing by putting on his wig and then his clothing. To him the costume looked more ridiculous than ever in his current predicament. He put on the fancy shirt, the pants and jacket and buckled the belt. He got the plate from atop the chest and put it in a pocket of his costume's jacket.

As he was fastening the last buttons, he heard heavy footsteps on the stairs again. This time the door opened and a giant entered. He may have been oversized for his age because something about him made him seem young; but he was barrel-chested and thick-necked. *This would be the bouncer*, thought Mac, quite sure that the outsized boy was not room service.

"Geef me je geldbuidel,"[37] the thug mumbled and gestured, with his hand held out, palm up. Mac couldn't understand the Dutch and could not speak; he stared and his jaw hung open.

"Je geldbuidel!"[38] the big one repeated, louder and moved in on Mac. Mac backed off.

"Give what? I don't understand," and with that the man roughly grabbed Mac's shoulder and jerked him around, frisked him until he felt the plate in one of the pockets; he hesitated, then ignored the plate and next found the bulge of Mac's wallet, which he expertly plucked out of the hip pocket of his pantaloons.

Being up close to the thug Mac held his breath. Everyone he encountered had horrid breath and bad teeth. The young man mumbled and fingered the polished leather of Mac's wallet. He grunted, turned, and went out with it. Mac didn't know whether to go after him or to wait. He thought about the things in

[37] Give me your wallet.
[38] Your moneybag!

his wallet so Mac decided to follow regardless that he would be no match against the guy if it came to a fight over his possessions.

The bouncer was still going down the narrow stairs toward the bottom where Mac could see that there was a hallway and several doors. Mac followed him through one of the doors. There he saw the Madam again.

"Aha. So you dressed," she said, and held her hand out to the bouncer to receive Mac's wallet. The bouncer gave it over and stepped back a little way. She said something to him in Dutch and he left the room and closed the door behind him.

In a second the door opened again and the girl, now dressed in servant's livery and wearing a small white maid's cap, started to come in. She stopped when she saw Mac, blanched, and ducked back out, unnoticed by Madam Schwarzesherz.

She was busy pulling out his cards from his wallet, giving each a cursory glance and frowning at the curious things on them. Was she looking for currency? It crossed Mac's mind that paper currency may not yet be in use in Amsterdam.

"You have strange things here," she said, slowing her search, and suddenly she jerked her hand away with a cry, as if burned, and dropped his wallet on the floor. It landed near his feet and she backed away from him.

"*Wat is dat?*"[39] she shrieked, pointing at cards that now stuck partway out of his wallet. "*What is that*?" madly she repeated, her finger pointed at the cards and wallet where they fell.

Mac grinned. The way she just now reacted to his cards gave him a good idea. He stooped to pick them

---

[39] What is that?

up, mentally rehearsing his next move. He collected his cards, then stood up and methodically checked through them.

It came back to him something he commented to Faye: *Sometimes when you are looking at something that's so familiar you never give it a thought and might not even see it being of interest. You've seen it a million zillion times so it doesn't even register. Then, in the presence of someone who's never seen it, you see it for the first time, and how alien it is if you could see it through their eyes.* The way Madam Schwarzesherz had been startled by the cards that he carried in his wallet was an example.

The cards, his driver's license, debit cards, Costco Membership card, Safeway Club card, and Medicare ID hadn't changed in his time-travel; but now, as Mac had experienced them in the presence of the Madam, through her eyes, these ordinary things looked weird and scary.

Shiny, bright-colored plastic laminates contrasted extremely with the drabness of this 17th Century Dutch house. The bold, red print on the Costco card was a color that was so out of place that it looked garish—almost fluorescent. These simple things might frighten people who were unused to them.

Madam Macia Schwarzesherz, Mac was about to learn, was especially afraid of things she didn't understand—afraid to the point of wild superstitions. She read arcane meanings and fantastic imaginings in strange yet, to Mac, mere ordinary things such as his credit cards.

As Mac saw them through his host's eyes, his wallet was a trove of sinister objects! To this woman, Mac could be a sorcerer, a wizard; so he set his jaw, straightened and took on a cool superiority in his stance. He smiled coldly and spoke to her in a voice soft, low and with measured cadence.

"Ah, my delicate friend, my 'guardian angel' Mevrouw Macia Schwarzesherz, you have realized the truth. I should congratulate you." He saw her eyes widen at his sudden, new manner. He was no longer the silly, helpless foreigner, now that she had glimpsed something that terrified her in the folds of his hiding place. *That's the look I hoped to see. Now I hold the cards,* thought Mac, and he went on.

"You see, Mevrouw Schwarzesherz, it is true, I am a scholar, and it is true that I am a Scot, a MacRitchie. My ancestors are from the Scottish highlands, far away."

Mac was enjoying his dramatic opportunity, like the way he played theatrically with Faye, and Mac loved to make up yarns on the fly. This time, if it worked, his small acting talent might save his neck. Madam Schwarzesherz, still in slight shock, stayed silent as Mac droned on. He was emboldened, but glad that her giant bodyguard was out of the room.

"The MacRitchie clan is part of the powerful MacIntosh known far and wide for their gifts and special powers. What you have found are examples of the powers of the renowned Highlander Sorcerers, he intoned.

She swiped at her brow with the back of her hand, in a sweat despite the cool temperature of the room. Mac noticed and thought, *she really believes this stuff!*

"Do you understand everything I am saying?" He shouted suddenly. She flinched and nodded timorously. "Are you sure? For if you do not understand, I shall have to demonstrate . . .."

"I understand!" she insisted, seriously. "Spare me your sorcery! I am a poor, wretched old soul. Curse me not!"

Mac was now experiencing the dark side of the 17th Century, when magic, spells and curses were part of everyday reality—not simple subjects for video games and movies. People like Madam Schwarzesherz lived as if death lurked around every corner, with wars, plagues of cholera, malaria and pestilence, violent crime, persecution, inquisitions, burning-at-the-stake, hangings, drawing-and-quartering and uncounted instances of rampaging injustices. Although the foundations were being laid for The Enlightenment right in this decade and right here in Amsterdam, it was not yet a time of reason; and a modicum of judicious fairness and times of truth and tolerance were many, many years away.

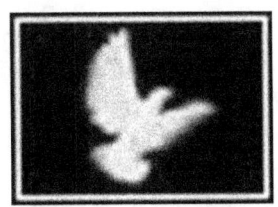

Chapter 7
The Hand that Gives the Bird

Should Mac be ashamed of himself for this trickery? He reasoned that if he took advantage of the old crone with a card trick, it would be no different than the advantages she would take of him, as she had already tried in having used that poor chambermaid to achieve her own ends.

Making a choice, Mac picked out his Visa debit card from those he held. "Look," he said, and he moved closer, presenting the card at her eye level. She jerked her face away, fearing what she had already caught a glimpse of on the card.

"Look!" Mac commanded her. She looked back and focused where Mac pointed, to the little security blue-and-silver hologram—the amazing 20th Century 3D imaging technology—an image of the bird, the white dove

"No!" she screamed, and covered her eyes. "No, take it away!" Mac couldn't help but smile, but quickly he refigured his face to keep up his charade. He could play the sorcerer as well as scholar.

Mac said, "Now you will listen to me, and you will do as I say!"

"Yes, put that away! It is forbidden! 'The hand that gives the bird is forbidden!'" She recited some pre-ordained truth Mac didn't understand. Whatever nonsense it was that she uttered, she obviously believed it, so Mac straightened his back and dropped his tense shoulders. Braver now, he summoned his most demonic mien as a sorcerer, as he was now—to this woman—the "evil one" incarnate.

"You will pay, but not in . . .," and guessed correctly at the current monetary system, ". . . guilders. Instead of guilders, you will help me, you will inform me, and you will take me to Rembrandt," he said, emphasizing each commandment, thrusting a finger skyward. Mac was on a roll. "Understand? You will help!"

"*Ach!* Rembrandt will not see you if I take you to him," she said. "I am known to him, and he has no respect for my art of perfumes and my healing skills. If I bring you, he will not see you. Nor will his son. Nor will his wife! They will scorn you if it is I who brings you to him." She wrung her hands and pleaded, "Pity me, a poor old Jewish woman."

"You must make it possible, for I demand it," yelled Mac, loudly, and it startled even himself. Maybe his theatrics had gotten a little out of hand. However, he thought he could be dead soon if he did not prevail over this woman. He had never yelled at anyone like that before—let alone a woman. Her pitiable whimpering continued.

He repeated: "I don't care. You must make a meeting with Rembrandt possible!" Privately, Mac felt badly for treating the old woman like this, but he stayed firm. He hoped for a way to work around the warning that, if she was Mac's sponsor, it would stigmatize him in Rembrandt's eyes.

She collected herself and appeared to give in. "I will try, if you do not show me to your forbidden images again, I beg you Meneer," and she pressed her face in her palms pitifully.

"Do what you must. Now!" he said, fighting back his empathy. The Madam suddenly raised her face, alight as if with a fresh idea. In his time Mac would have said a light bulb went on, but light bulbs hadn't been invented.

"I can take you instead to his neighbor!" she enthused. "He is an important person in his community. A renowned Sephardic Jew, a Rabbi, a wise man, and kind. He is brave, and he will be willing to talk to me," her composure returned as though she had a new lease on life and there was hope for her. The Rabbi would be her savior. "Yes," as her idea took root and held. She calculated a second: "Yes, he is one who will listen—listen even to me, Ashkenazim that I am. I will take you, yes, and immediately."

"And fetch my *kist*!" Mac reminded her, in case she thought he might have forgotten his printmaker chest, which was still upstairs.

A shadow of disappointment crossed her face as she acknowledged, "Yes, your . . . koffer," and without a pause she shouted toward the door, *"Binnen komen, Pieter!"*[40]

Mac flinched as the door opened immediately and Pieter, as the bouncer was called, strode in. Evidently he had been just outside the door all during the time of their altercation and, Mac assumed, his victory over Madam Schwarzesherz.

She spoke to Pieter rapidly in Dutch. Mac hoped she wasn't telling him, *"Pieter, slit this devil's throat!"* How would Mac know she had not? Mac fingered his cards and raised one to show him as a warning, but Pieter only gave Mac a curious, unafraid

---

[40] Come, Pieter!

61

frown.

He isn't impressed, Mac thought, and returned his cards to his wallet, as his worries seemed to be over for now. There were more orders given to Pieter in Dutch. Soon the printmaker chest and his plume-less hat were brought down. Mac was handed an oversized coat, probably to hide the embarrassment of his costume as much as protection against the cold November air. All the preparations for his departure were made with a relentless barrage of commands from Madam Schwarzesherz.

They were about to leave the house by the front door, when, from the other end of the hallway, the girl appeared and came toward Mac with eyes downcast. She had something in her fist and offered it to him. Mac opened his hand and she spilled his printmaker chest key and some coins into it. He was grateful, but Mac maintained a stern countenance as he looked at her and thought, *She is someone's granddaughter. What are her chances in life? Next to none.*

From his palm he picked out a penny from the change and offered it to her. Surprised, she looked at Madam, who nodded approval. The girl took the penny and turned it over and over, studying the image of Abraham Lincoln on one side and his memorial on the other. Mac wondered, *What must she be thinking?*

As Mac watched, the Madam said something to her in Dutch and the girl dropped the penny as though it had burned her fingers. The madam smirked and said something else, this time in a reassuring tone, bent over and picked up the penny off the floor, pressed it to her forehead with closed eyes, her lips moving silently; then she handed the penny to the girl. Madam Schwarzesherz was a sorcerer or a witch, to Mac's way of thinking, as he watched her show of mumbo-jumbo to exorcize the penny of its poisonous, evil taint.

"Let us go!" Mac said, and Pieter opened the front door. Outside, Mac saw that a horse-drawn wagon waited, summoned earlier by Pieter, supposedly. Pieter put Mac's printmaker chest in the back behind the seat. Madam hoisted herself first onto the seat behind the driver and Mac climbed up after her. She spoke to the driver, and he twisted around in his place to study Mac. The driver was missing an eye and did not wear a patch. His scarred, empty eye-socket was a terror to behold. Inside, Mac was shrieking at the sight but outwardly he sustained his newly-won air of superiority and turned his face away to show that he was too important to pay the driver any mind.

With a *cluck-cluck* the driver coaxed the horse on and, seated by Mac, Madam Schwarzesherz scooted as far from him as she could get. *We are enemies now,* thought Mac, *and there's nothing more to say.*

He settled back to watch the scenery. The street was paved with uneven cobblestones and the wagon's wheels were rimmed with iron, so every hard shock against the stones went right through the wooden seat to Mac's butt-bones and up to his teeth.

His head still ached and he was hungry. His hunger grew now that he had time to think about it and he decided to try out his new power and importance.

"I'm hungry!" he said to Madam Schwarzesherz. The madam turned and looked at him with her mouth open and with unconcealed exasperation. Mac frowned at her to emphasize his point. "I want to eat!" he repeated, and glared at her as if to say he was hungry and he would have his breakfast—or brunch—or she would be food for the Devil!

She relented, sighed and spoke to the driver. Five

minutes later they were getting down from the wagon in front of another bakery.

Inside, Mac went straight to the back to avoid having to order and to pay. His host gave him another black look that said, "Freeloader!" but did not risk his Scottish sorcerer's ire by telling him what she thought of him.

The Madam sat with him, but not as close as she had the afternoon before, when she had got him drunk. He had no stomach for beer this time; he asked for tea. He got a blank look. With some sign language he got across that he wanted, a hot drink.

"Cha?" inquired Mevrouw Schwarzesherz.

"Yes. Hot," Mac said, as the word "cha" sounded enough like tea, so it was safe. *Whatever you do, don't drink the water unless it's boiled,* he remembered Faye's oft-repeated advice when they traveled.

A generous meal came. Bread, cheese and rashers of bacon, thick-cut, greasy and hot, and the customary pot of butter were all set before him. He was starving, and Mac dispensed with his vegetarian scruples and fell hungrily to the bacon and bread.

Madam Schwarzesherz made no move to break bread with him, but she watched him as silent as a stone. Mac was absorbed in the business of eating. The bread was good, with a hard crust and soft but tough brown interior. The bottom of the crust had tiny bits of straw stuck to it.

Mac sliced off a piece of cheese. The taste reminded him of Gouda, only sharper. With the knife he smeared butter on the bread to make it easier to chew, and he stuck on a piece of the cheese. Madam Schwarzesherz watched him, and seemed to take great interest his eating methods; Mac wondered if his table manners were inappropriate; but he didn't care.

He was in charge now. He ignored her and looked around.

People had taken note of him when they first came in, but not anymore. It was quiet compared to the coffee shops in his day, what would be his day if he ever saw his days again. All he noticed were the sounds of people chewing their food, smacking and slurping their beer and issuing an occasional belch. Madam Schwarzesherz made no effort to hide her impatience. Now full and satisfied, Mac pushed the platter away and stood up, anxious to get going. He felt better now.

Again they were trundling along the street, the bad smells diminishing a little as they made their way toward Rembrandt's neighborhood; but they were still in a poor part of town. Filth littered the curb with flies crawling around on garbage. Horse dung lay here and there on the narrow street. He heard the squealing of pigs and saw two huge sows fenced in an alleyway as they passed by, the pigsty smelled of sweet stink. Mac wished he had accidentally wandered onto a movie set and that someone would yell at them, "Get back, quiet on the set!"

This was no movie. The people they passed were not movie stars or extras. Soldiers strode by, and their smart uniforms stood out. Burghers in black and white frocks, too, stood apart from the dingy clothing of the middle-class people and lower-class peasants.

Mac noticed, ahead, that a fancy carriage was coming toward them, one that was more luxurious than the wagon Mac was riding in. Seeing the shiny rig made him feel frumpy and plain. It was painted glossy black and drawn by two gray horses. The windows were covered with leather curtains.

As they passed the carriage, Mac saw a hand move a curtain aside in a window, briefly revealing a man who glanced out at Mac from the dark interior. He was lumpy-faced and had frizzy, curly hair sticking out from under a floppy hat. Then the curtain dropped back as the carriage passed.

That's Rembrandt! Mac recognized him at once from having seen many of Rembrandt's renowned self-portraits. He whispered excitedly to Vrouw Schwarzesherz, "I think I saw Rembrandt! That was him, in that carriage!" Mac suddenly had the feeling of being a groupie and he wanted to jump down and follow, catch up to the carriage and get the great artist's autograph.

He checked his impulse. *That would not be a good idea.* Mevrouw Schwarzesherz turned on Mac and groused, "If that was Rembrandt and he saw me beside you, then I cannot be blamed for what happens now. You are a curse upon me, and the curse will have its way on you, God knows!" She clamped her jaw and her eyes darted around.

Mac twisted around in his seat and watched the back window of the carriage as it went away. He hoped for another glimpse of the artist. Rembrandt was Mac's greatest artistic hero in his own, 20th Century printmaking world.

Their wagon went over a bridge and the neighborhood seemed immediately improved and was almost spotlessly clean. Passing a wide open plaza, Mac saw the first trees that he had seen in Amsterdam. They were elms and they lined a canal.

Beyond the plaza he saw a windmill on an octagonal, solid-looking brick foundation. Above the brickwork were shingled walls and white-framed windows opening out on all the sides. The windmill was an amazing piece of architecture and engineering, with sails that reached higher than MacRitchie's condominium in Seattle.

66

The windmill's great, outstretched arms revolved slowly, their gray canvas-over-wood-frame sails billowed taut and caught the breeze. He could hear the creak and groan of wood struts as they strained against the moving air. From inside the main building Mac could hear the heavy and regular thump-thump sound of a stamp mill.

Seagulls careened and coasted above the square, calling to each other. The sky was overcast and it felt like it might start to rain. Mac's eyes teared-up, thinking of rainy Seattle, and he wished that Faye were with him so that she, too, could view the Amsterdam that he was seeing.

The driver turned the wagon at a corner and then turned again, passed over another canal bridge and continued a little way on with the Madam giving him directions. They came to a stop in front of a narrow, three-story house. Mac looked up at the windows on the second floor in time to see a bearded face appear and then disappear.

Madam Schwarzesherz alighted, went up the steps and rapped with the black, wrought-iron door knocker. She looked back at Mac and motioned for him to stay put.

Mac was about to meet his *real* savior.

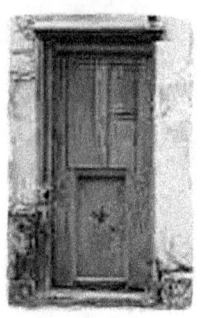

Chapter 8
Door in a Door

As Mevrouw Schwarzesherz rapped the door knocker, Mac waited on the wagon seat. Parked in front of the house which he assumed belonged to the rabbi, he glanced around to see if he could tell which of the homes that stood on either side of the rabbi's might be Rembrandt's house.

The house on the left resembled the limestone-faced one where they were parked; the one on the right was less well-kept.

The house where they parked lacked windows on the street level; the houses on the right and left had many-paned glass windows on all three stories. Mac noted that there was, above the door of the house on the right of the Rabbi's house, a blue and white, delft-glazed image of a crown, with the words, "De Blauwe Kroon," written below it; obviously, it was *The Blue Crown*.

What the Rabbi's house lacked in windows or decoration on the street level, it made up for in colors on the two upper levels. Dark green and bright leaf-green, deep cinnabar and saffron yellow paint had been carefully applied to all the trim around the windows on the upper stories, and even on the mullions separating the many small panes. High above, the third story was faced with scalloped, overlapping shingles, like fish scales, and painted in burgundy. Topping it all off was a pod of beautifully-carved dolphins frolicking up and over the steeply peaked roof of a single dormer from which an octagonal window faced the street. A row of plaques ran along the roofline, all of them carved and painted in uncommonly rich colors that reminded Mac of gay, South American painting.

Mac turned his attention to the front door as once again Madam Schwarzesherz rapped, and from somewhere a voice, like a woman's but raspy and nasal-sounding, called out from somewhere, "*Wie is het?*"[41]

The madam started, stepped back and looked down. There, below waist height, was a small opening with a metal grate—like a ventilator cover.

From inside, through the grate, again the voice demanded, louder this time, "*Wie is het? Wat zijn uw zaken?*"[42]

The woman squatted down to the level of the grating. Mac watched. To his ears the Dutch words coming out of the vent sounded like, "What the heck?" Mac felt suddenly worried and so he called to the woman, "What did they say?"

She stood up, turned to Mac and said, "They said 'Who is it' and, 'What is your business?' Do you want me to say who you are?"

"No! Say you want to speak to the master."

The woman squatted and shouted into the grate: "*Ik vertegenwoordig een bezoeker die wil spreken met de meester van dit huis,*"[43] she said loudly. Mac

---

[41] Who is it?

[42] Who is it? What is your business?

figured that she could see the speaker, but Mac could not see anyone from where he sat.

"*Wie is hij? En wie bent u?*"[44] Whoever was speaking, they sounded annoyed.

Keeping to his seat, Mac called, "What?"

Impatient with her role as go-between and translator for Mac, the woman stood again and straightened, turned and yelled back at him, "They want to know who you are and who I am! Shall I tell them everything you told me?"

Mac nodded and with that she turned and bent down to be heard through the grating, delivering Mac's reason for calling.

"*Een geleerde uit het buitenland,*" she said, "*En Ik ben enkel zijn dienaar.*"[45] He was beginning to think he got a few key words, and Mac interrupted her and asked her to translate what she had just said.

"I told him you are a scholar from abroad, and I am only . . .," she hesitated, glared at Mac, swallowed the bitter pill brought by this person perched on the seat of her wagon, she finished: ". . . only your *servant*!" and she muttered something under her breath which was not intended for Mac's ears.

He suppressed a grin, delighted with his control over her; yet, under the borrowed cloak with his hands hidden, Mac crossed his fingers and hoped with earnest, *this ruse had better work*. The rabbi's house, and whoever it was she was talking to at this moment, was his only hope for a place to stay and get clear of Madam Schwarzesherz.

Finally, the voice said, "*Wachten,*"[46] and there

---

[43] I represent a visitor who wants to speak with the Master of this house.

[44] Who is he? And who are you?

[45] A scholar from abroad, and I'm just his servant.

[46] Wait.

was a clicking, metallic sound.

"What?" called Mac.

"Wait. They said '*wait*'!" the woman snapped back, and she heaved a sigh and looked heavenward, casting hope for redemption.

For awhile all was quiet. The horse stomped a foot and the driver said something to sooth the animal. Mac twisted around on the seat to see if his printmaker chest, his *kist*, was safe.

Of course it was still there, like his loyal pet. His chest was the only contact Mac had with his past and, perhaps, his future—if indeed there was a future for him in old Amsterdam. His printmaker chest might contain he would need if he were to be stranded in the 17th Century for all time.

Or, its contents could get him trouble. Mac didn't ponder that ominous foreboding for long. He realized that the chest's contents—so alien and magical—were things that might make these people want to burn him at the stake for heretic sorcery and witchcraft. In his vivid imagination Mac saw the headlines: *Witch MacRitchie Roasts*!

His grim musing ceased when there was a sound from the front door; but it was not the main door which was opening. Instead it was a smaller door-within-the-door; and through this smaller doorway stepped a fierce-faced, bearded African dwarf. A pointy soft cap with ear flaps covered his overly-large head. He wore an apron dusted with white.

He looked down, at Mac, confirming what her business it was that Madam Schwarzesherz had stated—that she was here to deliver a foreigner who wanted to meet the rabbi.

The African looked up at the woman with doubt; he recognized her, but only said, "*Mijn meester zal spoedig verschijnen,*"[47] in his coarse voice. Then the little dark man (or boy—it was hard for Mac to tell his age) bowed curtly, backed into the opening and pulled the door shut behind him.

Madam Schwarzesherz waited and looked skyward again. She folded her arms; her lips moved, perhaps summoning celestial aid. Mac called to her, "Now what's happening?"

Without looking at Mac she answered, "He said 'the Master of the house will appear shortly.'"

Waiting, Mac amused himself with a silent play on her expression. He thought, *Did she say, 'the Master of the house will appear shortly?' If the Master were to be shorter than the dwarf, then that would be something to see!* It tickled his funny bone. His inner joking was interrupted when there came another metallic sound of a key in a lock and now the main door opened. *This has got to be the master,* thought Mac.

The figure that appeared in the door looked like he stepped out of the dark background of a Rembrandt masterpiece into the light of day. He was tall, which made the dwarf, who stood slightly behind the rabbi, seem even shorter yet. *Back shortly? He's not short at all!* Mac permitted himself a smile.

"*Kan ik u van dienst zijn?*"[48] the rabbi said to Madam Schwarzesherz. The man seemed to Mac to be between fifty and sixty years old. On his head he wore a black Jewish kippeh which held captive a wreath-like mane of abundant curly, gray hair. His beard was fluffy and white. His face was long, accentuated by a straight, narrow nose. Over his tall frame he wore a deep red cloak with a mantle of dark blue velvet fabric edged in green.

His face was stern, but kindly. Upon seeing him,

---

[47] My Master will appear shortly.
[48] Can I help you?

Mac began to feel encouraged about his prospects for survival and he straightened in his seat when the rabbi looked over at him. With keen, dark and perceptive eyes, he regarded Mac, the oddly-dressed stranger on the wagon seat.

Madam Schwarzesherz began to restate her business: "*Ik heb een bezoeker met mij die zegt dat hij uit Engeland of Schotland en die is gekomen . . . .*"[49] The rabbi raised a hand, palm outward, and stopped her from continuing with her explanation. She silenced. Mac had picked out two recognizable words that she had spoken: *Engeland* and *Schotland.*

The rabbi said, "*Terwijl ik weet dat deze plaatsen, laten we allemaal de Engels taal te spreken, als je in staat, vrouw.*"[50] Whatever he said, he said it in a voice and manner that sounded kindly to Mac but Madam Schwarzesherz hesitated, glanced down at Mac and back up again at the man. She seemed to be unsure of something about what he had said and she fell silent.

The rabbi repeated himself, this time in English, "I say, 'it is all right'," and acted as if he spoke English for Mac's benefit.

The rabbi continued: "I speak English and I can understand the Scottish dialect, too, I believe." He looked at Mac with the faintest hint of a smile.

Madam Schwarzesherz began again to explain, more deferentially and entirely in English, "This man I bring to you says he has come to study. He's a scholar and he wants to meet Rembrandt. Therefore, I brought him as he wished, Rabbi Aboab, thinking that you might be able to help him in his quest."

The rabbi continued to assay the visitor, nodding

---

[49] I have a visitor with me who says he is from England or Scotland and who has come . . .

[50] As I know these places, let's all speak the English language, if you are able.

his head with understanding as Madam Schwarzesherz elaborated. Mac sat on the wagon seat and smiled at the rabbi. His fingers were still crossed and hidden from view. He hoped his contrived stratagem would not be evident to this wise-looking man; but the longer the rabbi studied him, the more transparent Mac feared his ruse became.

After a moment the rabbi stepped down the stairs, crossed the narrow sidewalk and stood by the wagon to take a better look at the visitor. Mac began to feel like an exotic specimen. Rabbi Aboab—as the madam had addressed him—was so tall that his eyes were almost on the same level as Mac's, even though he remained sitting on the wagon seat.

Rabbi Aboab said, "Greetings, Sir. My name is Isaac Aboab da Fonseca. I am rabbi in my community. Welcome to Amsterdam," and he offered up his hand to shake Mac's.

Mac uncrossed his fingers, shifted his hands free from within the bulky, borrowed coat and leaned forward to shake the man's hand. He also gave a slight bow, as Mac assumed that this small gesture would be taken as an appropriate show of respect.

Aboab continued speaking as they shook hands and asked, "Is it true, that you are a scholar from the British Isles?" Then he released Mac's hand.

Mac proceeded to answer and thought to choose his words with care, "What I have told the Madam, and what she has told you, I offered to explain the unusual course and circumstances through which I arrived in Amsterdam."

He worried about his wordy explanation and hoped that he wouldn't say the wrong thing or get off on the wrong foot with a story that he would have to recant later on. Mac was trying hard not to lie; and he could see in the man's face that the rabbi sensed

Mac's difficult situation and words that Mac was holding back. It occurred to Mac that the madam, who eavesdropped, might be the reason. Besides, Mac perceived deep wisdom in the man's face and he cautioned himself, *this is one sharp cookie—be careful what you tell him.*

"You are a scholar?" Aboab pressed Mac as he wanted to confirm Mevrouw Schwarzesherz' claim.

"I consider myself to be a scholar, and an artist," replied Mac; and then he added, "Also, I consider myself a gentleman. However, not in the sense of landed gentry as it is meant in the British Isles. My possessions are modest, which pains me at this time, I must confess to you, kind sir."

Aboab studied Mac's face for a time, his own expressing no doubt, no fear, and no threat. The two men's eyes engaged in nonverbal communication, one asking for the truth, the other wishing to tell it yet afraid to try with words that could not be spoken. Not yet. The whole truth could not be told, Mac thought, *Not here, not right now, and not with Madam Schwarzesherz eavesdropping.*

The horse interrupted the silent spell, choosing this pregnant moment to break wind. Both men pretended not to notice, yet they smiled, amused, and the air of tension went away.

"What is your name, sir?" Aboab asked.

"I am William Handyside MacRitchie, at your service, Rabbi Aboab," Mac said, and he dipped his head again in acknowledgement of the man's high station, "and I am honored to make your acquaintance, I am sure. If I may say so, I perceive that you are a scholar, too, in your position as rabbi—a teacher."

Aboab's eyes twinkled. "You're quite perceptive. Yes, you might say as much," he said. "It is a fact that

I spend a great deal of time with my books and my prints when I have opportunities. The Madam, as you refer to the perfumer, Mevrouw Schwarzesherz, said that you want to meet my esteemed neighbor, the *fijnschilder* Rembrandt van Rijn. I take it that this is correct?"

Overhearing this, Mevrouw Schwarzesherz spoke up, as the words of Aboab's question that included her name and her profession had caught her off guard. It bothered her.

"How did you know my name, and the nature of my art—perfume?" she butted in. Aboab turned to her.

"There's little I don't know," he informed her. "Don't worry, *mijn goede dame*,[51] there is no harm intended in this. Early in my life I was a printer, which entailed news-gathering, and it seems I am still something of a clearinghouse of information, and therefore information comes to me from all over the city, including even news in your neighborhood. Also I get information about what occurs concerning ships on the *Ij*," he said. He turned his back on her then and cast a knowing look at Mac.

Mac wondered about what Aboab said, *does that mean he knows about me? That I came by ship? Does he have spies? What else does he know?* The sky had turned dark by now and thunder rolled in the distance. One raindrop plopped on Mac's floppy hat, and soon another. The horse snorted, stomped a hoof, shook his head and rattled the harness. The driver said something to pacify his horse.

---

[51] My good lady.

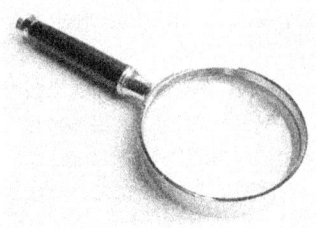

Chapter 9
Jewish Hospitality

"I think I would like to assist Meneer MacRitchie, Mevrouw Schwarzesherz," said the Rabbi to the Madam, and he gave a nod to Mac, who took the cue and climbed down from his wagon seat. Rabbi Aboab turned to meet the woman as she was descending the steps. "I hope you will permit me to offer payment for your trouble in bringing him to me and thus also to Rembrandt's vicinity," he said to her. He nodded his head toward the adjacent house with the blue-and-white glazed tile over the door that read, *De Blaue Kroon*.

Aboab made a gesture to the dwarf, who had listened intently all the while, and who now hopped down the steps and gave some coins to the woman. She glanced at the money he gave her and she looked at the rabbi—pleasantly surprised, it was plain to see.

Mac went to the back of the wagon, dragged his printmaker chest to himself and lifted it by its rope handles. Stepping over the gutter, Mac humped his precious chest around and set it down on the sidewalk at the bottom of the stairs.

Seeing Mac's chest, Aboab said, "And what have we here, may I ask?" and pointed at the chest.

Mac was busy shrugging off the great coat, and

77

he stalled for a little time to consider how he would explain his printmaker chest. He got the coat off and then, as Mac's costume was exposed, Aboab looked him up and down with open surprise as he noted Mac's costume-shop outfit.

The dwarf snorted, punctuating his own amusement at Mac's odd clothes. Mac ignored their reactions, folded the loaned coat and put it on the wagon seat. Aboab resumed his questioning, but now on a different tack.

"Sir, your dress, while it must be fine appointments where you are from, seems strange to my eyes," he said. "I hope you don't think me rude, but, are these your traveling clothes? Surely this is not Scottish fashion—it appears more like the mode they wear in Flanders."

He looked at the printmaker chest on the ground. "And, what of this seaman's chest, I ask you, is this luggage?"

Mac said, "Sir, were it possible to explain in a word, I would do so, but I'm afraid there is too much to tell. I humbly beg for your patience." Mac's mannerisms and choice of words were stilted and sounded odd to his own ears, but the language and style of those gathered here had a decided effect on Mac's own way of speaking. He couldn't help himself, and reasoned, *it's 1660 in Amsterdam, after all! 'When in Rome . . . .'*

Rain was beginning to fall harder now. Aboab said something in Dutch to the dwarf, who bounded back up the steps. Mac was uncertain what to do next.

"May I come in, then?" he asked.

"Yes, we will discuss things. I will dismiss Mevrouw Schwarzesherz. If we cannot come to an agreeable arrangement—that is, you and I—then I can find you a place elsewhere," assured Aboab, and he started up the stairs. He stopped and turned, "Forgive me if I do not offer to carry your chest. Do, please, bring it in."

Mac took his printmaker chest and went up the steps to the door. Mevrouw Schwarzesherz had come down and was already climbing up onto the wagon. She held the overcoat over her head against the gathering rainstorm and she did not bother with a goodbye to Mac. She was grateful to be getting away from him and his wicked "bird-in-the-hand" image; but she regretted that she had not somehow been able to keep possession the Scotsman's *kist*.

She wished that she had done more to him, that she had taken stronger measures and not merely got him drunk. Mac intrigued her, irritated her and scared her all at the same time. She looked at the money Dieners had given her. That was certainly an unexpected development—a good thing, she thought. Very good, indeed it was.

The driver, in his customary way, cluck-clucked to the horse and the wagon rattled off, headed back the way they had come, going back to her neighborhood and her house.

At Aboab's, the instant Mac stepped inside the rabbi's home, he got a breath of fragrant air, a good, familiar smell of baking. It was a welcome respite from the bad smells that seemed to be everywhere outside. He saw the interior was plain and modestly furnished, with wood-paneling on the walls and a black-and-white checkerboard-floored hallway that led straight toward the back. A narrow staircase on the left had fine hemp carpeting fixed in place by brass rods at each stair tread.

Aboab had started up these stairs. Over his shoulder he said to Mac, who waited uncertainly, "Come this way, please."

Mac followed him up the stairs, carefully balancing and picking his way up the narrow treads, walking sideways, crab-like, in order to manage the chest. At the top of the first landing there was another hallway that led to the next staircase. A doorway stood open and Aboab stood there. He motioned Mac to go in.

"We can spend a little time," he said. "Please make yourself comfortable if you can. My wife is away, or she would welcome you. We live a simple life. We seldom have visitors and from so far away as . . . Scotland. You must tell me if there is anything that you find discomforting to you."

Mac looked for a place to set the chest, choosing a corner, and then he came to where Aboab had settled into a chair at an ornate dark wood pedestal table. The table was eye-catching, richly and deeply carved with designs of flowers, fruits and garlands. As Mac took a chair and seated himself, he recognized the wood as being one of the Brazilian hardwoods that he used in his press-making shop!

Aboab noted that Mac was examining the table's carved surface with interest. "Do you like my table?" Aboab asked.

"It's very nice. To be frank, I am surprised by it, because this wood looks familiar to me." Mac stroked the surface, appreciating its well-rubbed finish.

"That wood is called 'dyewood.' It's from Brazil," said Aboab. "The table top was given to me by a community there. I lived in Brazil for many years. The carvings depict the jungle flora." He reached across to Mac's side of the table and pointed to a section of the carving. "Here, for example, are the leaves of the dyewood tree itself, and here, a kind of fig—very delicious."

Mac followed as the rabbi traced around the

carvings with his long-boned index finger, and he stopped on one which, to Mac, looked like an acorn squash.

Aboab continued, "Here, this is one that they regard as sacred, as they make—from the seeds that grow inside—the drink of their gods. It is a strong concoction, apparently. I never tasted it, for I feared that it might be poisonous to a white man, a European such as me. I heard later that the Spanish are experimenting with it."

The pod, Mac realized now, was from the cacao tree, the source of chocolate. That Jews lived in Brazil in the 17th Century surprised Mac. Again he wished that he had paid more attention to his history books; but Mac said nothing of what he was thinking.

Aboab leaned back and said, "But let us talk about you and your purpose in Amsterdam. I hope you do not think me rude, but are you really, as Vrouw Schwarzesherz said, from Scotland?" His eyebrows raised and his forehead crinkled as he questioned Mac.

Mac blushed and felt his own face warm. He cleared his throat. He thought, *The jig's up; time to come clean. What can I lose? My life*? Aboab waited for Mac's answer.

"As I wanted to relate to you outside, my story surprises even me," Mac began carefully, "for I think I am out of my time. You are a scholar and since it is, after all, the 17th Century—plus you have lived in the New World—these things qualify you especially to have tolerance even for the strangest of stories."

And Mac paused here, and then he said, "That, in any case, is what I would assume."

"Please go on," Aboab said, and so Mac began a cautious telling of his story. Every phrase was strategic and crucial to what might happen to him in

81

the ensuing minutes. His plight had become like a game of "Truth or Consequences," with stakes as high as Mac could only imagine.

"My family name, MacRitchie, is Scottish, but I am actually not from Scotland, directly, but from the American colonies, as you may have suspected," and Mac paused again. "I can see in your face, Rabbi Aboab, that you did not think I was really from Scotland."

Aboab said, "You are right, I suspected as much. I know about the colonies in North America. A number of Portuguese Sephardim have gone to New Amsterdam, as you probably know, having been there, perhaps. I considered going myself when we were forced to leave Brazil. But, again, we are not together to talk about my story, but yours. Tell me about your studies, your purpose in coming to Amsterdam. Why is it that you wish to see our painter, Rembrandt van Rijn, in particular?"

"Rembrandt's reputation has spread far," Mac began. "I can't tell you how far, but I learned about him through his prints, by way of his etchings."

"Aha, of course!" Aboab broke in with some enthusiasm. "Perhaps we have found a shared interest. Printing, as you may recall from what I said outside, is one of my trades. Not only am I interested in all forms of printing, but etchings and engravings are my weakness. I should not indulge myself, but I do collect what I can afford. In fact, I have one of Rembrandt's prints. It is an etching of a card player."

Aboab stopped speaking, paused a moment, his hands tent-like in front of his chin, his fingertips tapping lightly together. Then he added, "Perhaps you will come upstairs and I'll show you my etchings if . . . but, now there I go again, I have started talking about my interests. Forgive me. Please continue your

82

story, your needs, and what you bring."

And, as he said this, Aboab shot a meaningful look at the printmaker chest. Mac could tell that its presence bothered the rabbi, but he did not want to open the chest and reveal its contents to anyone. Not yet.

Mac had an inspiration: *The printing plate!* He had put the black-coated copper plate in a pocket in his costume's outer coat. "What brought me here, you might say, is . . . this," he said, and he took the plate out of his pocket and put it forward to Aboab across the table.

"You have a printing plate? Hmm. How interesting," said Aboab as he took it from Mac. Almost holding his breath, Mac waited while Aboab inspected the plate, with its center slightly cleared and the etched lines of a man's face discernible.

"Yes, it is interesting." agreed Mac. "That plate transported me. I thought it might be the work of a Master artist. It made me want to include a visit to Rembrandt in my itinerary."

Aboab studied the plate, turning it over once and then resuming closer study. It was quiet; the only sound was a mantel clock ticking and an occasional clip-clopping of horses passing on the street below, syncopating in and out with the ticking clock. The light where they were sitting was poor, coming as it did from three candles on a ledge that overhung the table.

"A moment, please," Aboab said, scooting back his chair. "I have a magnifying glass," and he stood, crossed the room to a small table and took out a large magnifying glass from a wooden chest on top.

He went to the window where there was better light and studied the plate. Satisfied, he came back. "Would you like to try my glass?"

Mac got up, took the plate and magnifying glass and went to the window to look. Nothing had changed in the copper, despite having been thrown off the ship to the stone wharf; the etched face of the man still had its metallic, dull look in the center where Mac had rubbed it. Under magnification it was harder to see the whole face for details, but the textures were more pronounced.

The magnifying glass itself was crystal-clear and polished clean, rimmed in a band of solid brass, the turned wood handle fitting nicely in the hand. The glass was heavy, but well-balanced. Inscribed on the polished, brass rim he could see a name, "Spinoza," engraved, and a date that he could not make out.

Mac had seen the name, "Spinoza," somewhere before, but he didn't know where or when. *Perhaps Spinoza is the city where it was made*, Mac thought. He re-crossed the room and went back to Aboab, who had taken his seat again, and handed him the magnifying glass and the copper plate.

"The glass helped, indeed. That is a beautiful magnifying glass," Mac said. "I don't think I've ever seen one like it."

Aboab was again studying the plate through the glass under the available light. Hearing Mac's words about the glass itself, Aboab stopped a second and looked at the instrument he was holding as if surprised by what Mac had said about it.

Sidetracked momentarily, Aboab answered, "Hmm? Oh, yes, an acquaintance of mine, from Leiden, made it." Mac thought that something in Aboab's countenance had suddenly changed as he handed the plate back to Mac. "Yes. Well, your plate is interesting, indeed." The rabbi was somewhat abrupt. Then he added, in a tone of finality, "And what else have you to show me, Meneer

84

MacRitchie?" It was a heavy hint that concerned Mac's printmaker chest.

Mac looked around and tried to think of what else he had to show; certainly he could not show what was in his wallet, of that he was sure.

While Mac thought about it, Aboab made up his mind for him: "I think it is time to open your chest," said Aboab.

Into Mac's mind's eye flashed a projected slide image of a historic painting, an image from his student days: Rembrandt's, "Anatomy Lesson of Doctor Tulp." And Mac recalled a pale grey-green cadaver lying on the dissection table, but Mac's memory was not accurate; now the dead body wore his rock-musician's wig and Flemish hat. The cadaver's chest was cut open. Mac's throat tightened.

"My chest?" he squeaked.

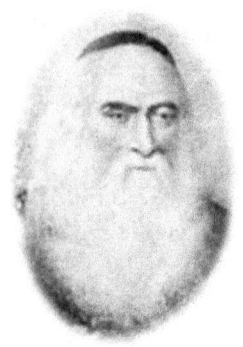

Chapter 10
Going Dutch

It was a heart-stopping moment for Mac, after his host Aboab, suggested—no, one has to say—demanded that Mac open his printmaker chest at that very minute. Here it is difficult to put into words what happened. It was surprising and, for Mac, lucky.

If this were not printed, if it was a scene in a movie instead of a page in a book, then the viewer would see what happened next in slow-motion, focusing on Mac as the unfortunate time-traveler struggles to think of how he can delay the opening of his printmaker chest and reveal the 21st Century wonders inside. Hold that image, almost frozen in time, and, in a suspenseful split second, watch as an aromatic, wispy vapor crosses Mac's nostrils.

Visualize this vaporous illusion, harkening to that which Mac smelled the moment he stepped through the door into Aboab's house—the yeasty smell of bread-making! Now that some minutes have passed, there is the aroma of bread that is baking in an oven downstairs! The fragrance of fresh, Dutch homemade bread is making a wavy pathway—cartoon-like—up from below and it is, to Mac, a delectable smell.

Or, if what has just been described is not a super slow motion view from a movie, and is, instead, a graphic novel, then the graphic artist might have in mind for our eyes to follow those wavy lines across several frames, descend the stairs, working our way down and follow the smell that is titillating Mac, seeking the source of the aroma.

Thus, still holding on the graphic frames, let us take a moment as we have left the nervous Mac and gone, retraced the wavy lines, down, down the narrow staircase and, at the bottom, with a quick turn, go along the checkerboard-tiled hall toward the back, which is, we find, Aboab's kitchen.

At work in the kitchen we discover the dark, fierce-faced, bearded short fellow we first saw as he stepped through the door-in-the-door. His name is Dieners van Santa Catarina and, at this moment, we see him at one of his household duties as baker.

In fact, this gnome-like boy-wonder bakes not only for Rabbi Aboab and his wife, but also for several homes in the Rozengraacht neighborhood—including the van Rijn family next-door. Everyone likes Dieners' crusty sourdough bread very much. Rembrandt likes it better than the bread his wife makes; but he doesn't tell her that.

In our graphic-novel scene, Dieners is opening the oven door and pushing a long, wood-handled paddle, resembling the oar of a rowboat, into the hot interior, and he is slipping it under bread loaves. It is this, the oven door opening and the smell of fresh bread wafting up the stairs to the nose of Mac, who is—at the moment—feeling trapped and wondering what to do about Aboab's order to open up his chest. Our imaginary, graphic passage down to the kitchen took a split second.

Simultaneously—that is, in the same time-frame back upstairs in Aboab's sitting room, another passage is beginning! This is one of Nature's gastrointestinal phenomena, a gas bubble down in Mac's mid-section, meandered noisily along the twisted path of his intestine, a rising crescendo in his grumbling, growling stomach.

Lucky Mac! It was the distraction that he needed because when Aboab heard Mac's stomach complaining, the rabbi's face softened. He forgot, for the moment at least, the pressing issue of opening Mac's chest for inspection.

"Dear me, I am sorry!" the rabbi apologized. "I did not think to offer you something to eat. Were my wife here, she would have done! Perhaps you would like something, a small repast?"

Mac nodded, grateful to escape from having to reveal what his printmaker chest held. He had eaten only an hour ago and should not already be hungry again; but he answered, "Well, actually, I am a little peckish. A little bread, perhaps, would be nice. I cannot help but notice the aroma of baking."

Aboab offered, "Oh, yes, Monday is bread day here. Dieners, the fellow you met at the door, is a baker, and quite a good one, too." With that the rabbi stood up and started toward the door, stopped, and turned back to Mac. "Please come with me, Meneer MacRitchie, I would like to properly introduce the boy, Dieners, to you."

Mac was still sitting where he was, relieved not to comply right now with Aboab's wish to open the chest. As he stood up and followed Aboab down the stairs, Mac thought, *Did he say 'boy'? Why did Aboab referred to the dwarf as 'boy?'* While this "Dieners'" age was hard to guess, Mac's impression of the way he had handled Madam Schwarzesherz was that he acted like a man, not a boy.

They reached the bottom of the stairs and traversed the hall. The kitchen was warm and the air smelled heavenly. Mac saw that the "boy" Dieners was unloading the last, domed-shaped loaf. His creations were dark and warty, with stumpy square nodules standing all over their top crusts. Mac's mouth watered. The baker shut the oven door with a clang and turned toward them as Aboab and Mac came in.

Rabbi Aboab said, *"Dieners, Ik wil je voorstellen aan William MacRitchie. We vonden dat we hebben een gemeenschappelijk belang bij afdrukken."*[52] Dieners swaggered over on his slightly bowed legs, swiped his hand on his flour-dusted apron and extended his hand to Mac, and all this without a change in his gruff expression. A new acquaintance might sense anger in Dieners' face until having gotten to know him.

Mac shook Dieners' hand, which was big in proportion to his body; the dwarf seemed to be made of solid muscle, too. Mac, pumping his hand, felt like he was shaking hands with a brick. *Aha! He's younger than I realized. He's a teenager!* thought Mac.

Without a smile, and still suspicious of this foreigner who had appeared abruptly at the doorstep with the hag, Vrouw Schwarzesherz, Dieners said, *"Het is een genoegen u te ontmoeten,"*[53] and then he hesitated, as if he would say more but he felt inhibited.

Dieners shot a look at Aboab, and in Dutch-accented English he said, "Rabbi, why not I practice

---

[52] Dieners, I want you to meet William MacRitchie. We found that we have a common interest in printing.
[53] It is a pleasure to meet you.

my English?"

"As you suggest, Dieners, let's speak English! A good idea, young man."

Dieners straightened and gave Mac's hand one more hard shake and, by this, added emphasis to his words: "My name is Dieners van Santa Catarina, and I am pleased to make your acquaintance, Meneer," he said, and then he released Mac's hand. "My English is not so good, but I hope I am making myself clear."

Mac nodded and in return introduced himself: "I am William Handyside MacRitchie. You speak English very well; it is a pleasure to meet you, too, Dieners van Santa Catarina."

For the first time since Mac laid eyes on him, the little man smiled, exposing crooked teeth with a couple of gaps. Dieners said proudly, "Rabbi Aboab speaks seven languages. He has taught me English, Portuguese and Spanish! However, we seldom meet with English people. I need the practice. You understand?" Mac nodded. He understood and he was impressed.

Aboab said, "Meneer MacRitchie is not English, Dieners, and although Vrouw Schwarzesherz thought him to be Scottish, he says he is really from the New World. I have not yet learned more. I would like to offer him a little something to eat, for he is hungry." The rabbi nodded to the bread cooling on the table. "It looks as though you have just finished here," Aboab added.

"These are spoken for," said Dieners, glancing at the spread of loaves on his work counter, "but I have other loaf—a kind of sweeter bread, mind you, and already cool. It will go well with our cheese. Would you like some beer, or milk, Meneer?" he offered Mac, and he added, "It is milk that was only just now delivered, cold and fresh."

Mac thought about pathogens, but he decided to take the risk that the milk would not be infected. Dutch cleanliness, to Mac's mind, was legendary. He wasn't ready for beer again, not for awhile.

"If it would be no trouble, I would appreciate some milk," Mac replied, and Dieners bustled off to assemble the food.

Aboab waved Mac toward a table and chairs opposite the oven side of the room. In the back wall was a door set between the eating and the work areas. Next to the door by the table there was a paned window. From where he sat Mac could see a walled back garden. This cozy corner, Mac deduced, served as their dining nook.

In a few minutes Mac was enjoying hard-crusted, chewy bread spread with a thick layer of unsalted butter. A wooden cutting board held a wedge of pale, mild cheese. The milk was cool, and Mac had not tasted any like it since he was a boy on his father's farm. It was sweet and creamy, so rich that Faye would have said that this milk, combined with the heavy, sweet bread, was like a dessert.

Near the work table over in the kitchen area, Aboab carried on a rapid conversation in Dutch with Dieners while Mac worked on a piece of cheese and bread. Then the rabbi came over to join Mac and folded his tall frame onto a bench along the wall. Aboab studied his guest Mac as he ate. After a while, Aboab asked Mac, "Do you like the food?"

Mac answered, "Oh, very much; I appreciate it. You are kind to offer it, and I'm sorry to put you to trouble, dropping in as I have." He added, "I'm sure you must have work to do."

"Yes, I have things to attend to, but it is not a problem. I'll have time later on to catch up. I very much like meeting travelers, after all, and it is uncommon to have a visitor from the American colonies," said Aboab. "You might also say that meeting with foreigners is important to a rabbi's work, therefore my reading and writing can wait."

Aboab was silent as he thought for a moment, and then he launched into the matter of finding a suitable place for Mac—which was the subject uppermost on his mind. He said, "Dieners and I agree that I can invite you to stay here tonight if you wish. I cannot offer you a proper guest room, but there is a bunk bed in the garret which you may use, and a desk. It is apparent that you need a place to rest, and Dieners agrees that you seem like a trustworthy sort. Mevrouw Schwarzesherz may not have perceived your true character in the same way as we do."

Mac was aware that they referred to the woman as "Mevrouw," but, to himself, she would always be "madam," and on this matter the two did not seem inclined to correct him, so he stayed with "madam."

"Madam Schwarzesherz found me cast out on the docks, and she offered me a bed, and food, plus she paid a boy to carry my chest," said Mac. "But she misunderstood my needs." Mac blushed at the memory of the young girl in his bed. Before Mac could tell the whole story, Aboab raised his hand. Mac halted and, quite relieved, did not describe the details of his encounters further.

Aboab said, "She told me—and she was speaking Dutch so you did not understand—that you arrived on a mest boat, a dung boat! And I thought she was joking; but is that true? I can't imagine it! Why—and *how* did you get passage on such a thing? Why *that*? Phew!"

Before Mac could explain, the rabbi thought better of his question and said, "Oh, well, I should not press you on that point. I can judge things for myself.

I perceive that you have an interesting story and your own reasons, so you need not feel obliged to tell me everything," he said apologetically, and then he concluded, "We have more important things to discuss now, I think."

Again Mac was thankful. How could he explain how he got on that stinking boat when he himself didn't know? He was, as is said, having a "distemporal experience," a man out of his time. To say anything he would sound to Aboab and Dieners like a madman, and Mac had a pretty good idea as to what they do with insane people in 17th Century Amsterdam.

He said, "Thank you, Sir, it's true, I can hardly understand it myself. As I said to you earlier—when we met outside—that I perceive you are worldly and that you must have heard many strange stories in your lifetime. My story, when we come to it, may not, therefore, be too implausible for you to believe."

Mac paused, having stated something like a disclaimer, wanting a moment of pregnant silence as he was about to make a promise he desperately hoped that he could keep: "I will not lie to you." He paused again to allow the words and his tone to have an enduring effect.

"As for your invitation to spend the night in the garret, I'm deeply grateful. I will try not to be an inconvenience."

Aboab nodded. "Ah, well yes. You are welcome. But I am not as worldly as you may think, though I have heard many stories that I find hard to countenance; and I've seen many uncommon things. In fact, even in my community, there are strange ideas being discussed. Ah, but . . ." and Aboab stopped and looked upward to the chandelier hanging over the table. All its candles were alight. When he spoke, he intoned in Latin: "'*Tempora mutantur, nos et mutamur in illis*,' The times are changing, and we must change with them."

Mac thought of Bob Dylan's song, *"The Times They are A' Changing,"* as Aboab finished with, "When I rise in the morning, every morning, I brace myself. For every new day, I'm unsure what the hours will bring to my ears and eyes."

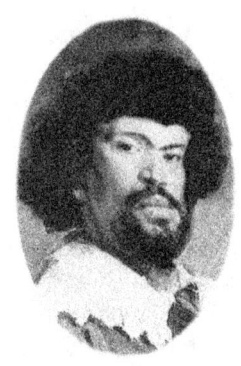

Chapter 11
Dieners' Story

Dieners came again from the working side of the kitchen and this time he carried two fluted green glass roemers of beer with foaming heads. He lifted them up to set them on the table. Then he pulled a chair over—a chair that was higher than Mac's and higher than the bench where Aboab was seated. Dieners climbed up on it and sat down.

He lifted his glass, nodded at Mac and, to Aboab, said, "*L'Chaim*." Aboab took the other glass and replied in the same way. They simultaneously nodded to Mac in acknowledgement and then they drank. Dieners wiped some foam off his bushy mustache, belched, and then he took on a stern countenance and looked straight at Mac. He had something to say, and it was serious, if one were to judge by his face.

"Sir, I will be direct," he began, took another swallow of beer, and went on. "When you came with Mevrouw Schwarzesherz, I had grave misgivings. Yes, grave! I did! She is not one whom people welcome. We call her the 'Black Widow.' She is a witch and an old harlot. I could not imagine any good person to be accompanying her. No good, honest person would fall in with her and have her as a sponsor. That's what I said to myself." He looked to Aboab as if wanting his permission to continue.

With evident caution, the rabbi doffed his flagon in the dwarf's direction. It was a wordless action but was given as if to say, "Carry on." Dieners continued. "I see now, however, that my first impression may have been hasty." He took another drink. "That's all. Now I feel better for having said it!"

Mac started to answer, but Dieners wasn't done. "Another thing; I think also that my being here must seem strange to you, an African living with the renowned Rabbi Aboab da Fonseca."

Mac's face showed what he thought, *You got that right*. Mac nodded and suppressed a smile. He was warming to Dieners' candor.

Now Dieners did smile at Mac, and broadly. "Even though Amsterdam is cosmopolitan—and while the citizens tolerate many different peoples and confessions, regardless of all that, I do not fit in. As you see! Obviously! I think it is only right that you know more about your host, more than what I perceive that you heard from the . . . ah, Black Widow," and he nodded toward Aboab. "You need to know the rabbi is my honored Father."

Mac was taken aback by this revelation and could not conceal his surprise; and the dwarf enjoyed seeing this and he grinned wryly at Mac's shocked reaction.

Now it was Aboab's turn to speak: "What Dieners means is that I adopted him. He was a newborn only hours old when I found him. This happened in Brazil, where the people there dispose of infants who are in any way 'different.' So it was that Dieners was taken into the jungle and left for the predators. Providence sent me on a little exploration along a trail in the

96

jungle. I heard him squalling, and there I found him."

Mac remembered that he had read about the practice of infanticide among some of the world's indigenous people.

"I will add that he had a loud voice!" said Aboab, as he recalled Dieners' screams, a squirming, tiny infant entangled in vegetation on the forest floor. "And feisty—determined to survive, he was!"

"He saved my life," Dieners cut in. "Had it not been for Rabbi Aboab, I would soon have been a little snack for the wild dogs."

Dieners grinned and glanced at Aboab fondly. "The rabbi took me into his community and raised me as his own son. When I was seven, he brought me to the Dutch Republic. This man, I tell you, could have gone to New Amsterdam and started a new life. He could have been a contender for a synagogue in the colonies. However, thinking I would not survive in the new world, and with signs of the English wanting to take over the settlement, we came here instead. It was partly for my sake that he sacrificed an opportunity in the new world."

"There were more reasons than that," Aboab put in quietly. Dieners ignored the rabbi's comment. He was finished with his story so he said no more, satisfied that Mac had learned enough for now.

As for Mac, he was so moved by the story he didn't know what to say. In his eyes, Dieners seemed less the dwarf now and more of a man than many men who stood twice as tall. All this day Mac had wavered between hopelessness and hope, and now his spirit was raised by seeing the love that bonded this unlikely pair—Aboab and his adopted son. In this quiet, reverent moment, Dieners burped and wiped his mustache on his sleeve.

It was getting dark. Outside it was raining and a

few drops tapped on the window glass. Through the window, Mac could see a garden, well past harvest season. Brussels sprouts stalks were still standing, stripped of their buds. Beside a row of cabbages there were beets, some healthy kale and twisted, wilted potato vines.

At the end of the garden was a brick wall with a gate and beyond the wall Mac could see the back of another house. At the moment when he happened to be looking, Mac saw the garden gate open and a woman enter. She was bent under a yoke across her shoulders. Lidded buckets hung from the ends of the yoke, swinging slightly as she clomped in muddy clogs toward Aboab's back door.

Aboab also had seen her coming. He stood up, stepped over to the door, and opened it. As if this were a signal, Dieners got down off his chair. Mac could tell theirs was a practiced routine and that the woman with the yoke was expected.

Dieners went to the opposite corner of the kitchen and picked up a covered pail. He carried it to the door while Aboab held it open. As the dwarf passed Mac with his pail, a faint odor—like that of fermented urine—met Mac's nostrils. He almost gagged when he realized that what Dieners carried was a bucket of pee!

Mac wanted to plug his nose but he refrained and tried to appear indifferent. At the back steps outside the door, words in Dutch were exchanged with the urine collector; and then there was the sound of pouring fluid and the clank of a lid. Mac watched the woman slog away in the rain, buckets swaying to and fro.

Aboab came back in and Dieners followed a minute later, after having rinsed the bucket. Now, to Mac, the spotless Dutch kitchen seemed changed.

Cozy and clean one moment, and in the next moment, he imagined waves of germs lapped at his ankles. He thought, *Seattle recycling was never like this!*

Aboab closed the door and came and stood by the table and folded his arms across his chest. To Mac's thinking, this was a bad sign; folded arms often signaled that a person was about to say something defensively or that they were going to bring up a sensitive subject. Nervous now, Mac thought, *My printmaker chest bugs Aboab.* Mac was sure of it.

"Meneer MacRitchie, I must be direct. As I said before, you are welcome to stay the night. However, there is a condition: I trust you, but I must know what you carry with you in your *kist*," he said. "I do not want to seem meddlesome, but you are something of a mystery, a stranger. There was no advance word of your coming. You arrived in the company of a sponsor of ill repute. My perception seldom fails me, and I am willing to say that I believe you to be trustworthy in spite of her company. Still, your luggage, or whatever it is upstairs, concerns me. Very much."

Mac knew enough about the ill treatment that Jews suffered over the centuries, and therefore it was no wonder the rabbi had to be cautious. He responded, "Of course, I understand and I apologize. I am in need, as you know, and I'm completely and deeply in your debt," and Mac twisted on his chair, preparing to stand and deliver, come what may.

Aboab stopped him, "No, it is settled, then, and I feel the better for it. You will disclose what it is you brought with you, but please remain in your seat. I will retrieve the *kist* and bring it down because Dieners has something to settle with you also, a pecuniary matter that needs to be understood among the three of us."

Dieners was listening to them from the other side of the kitchen where he had returned the bucket to its place and now he stepped forward while Aboab went to the hall and began to go up the stairs.

Dieners said, "You need to know, Meneer MacRitchie, that I am Rabbi Aboab's house manager while his wife is away. Not only do I prepare the food, I also oversee all matters of the house, and this brings us to the subject of money."

Mac's gut tightened.

"We are not wealthy, but we are able to accommodate visitors as we choose. I have known the rabbi all my life, so I can read his actions and I can read between his words. He trusts you. Trust is in his character. As for me, however, I can decide only when I have assurance of liquid compensation."

He paused. Mac was waiting for the bad news.

"Do you understand what I am saying?"

Mac's throat had gone dry. He croaked, "I understand. I can pay."

There was a silent moment. Dieners was waiting for more. Finally he asked, "With what? I can't help but wonder," the dwarf said, finally, "because you, are a foreigner—and from across the ocean—I need to know if you have tender that is of value here in Amsterdam, coinage in silver or gold."

Mac thought of his pocket change—none of which was gold or solid silver. He felt panicky and his heart quickened. Soon he might be on the street, in the onset of night and with no place to stay!

Dieners wasn't finished. "There is another matter, related to the first. It is my understanding that you may be planning to visit our neighbor Rembrandt. What your plans are with him does not concern me. However, if it comes to pass that you will stay longer than just one night as the outcome of your meeting becomes known, then I must know that there is to be forthcoming equivalence."

Mac now felt extremely uncomfortable and he thought, *If there is an original, creative thought in my head, I could sure use it now*. Heavy treads coming down the stairs signaled Aboab's returning and he entered the kitchen, leaning back slightly to counter the weight of Mac's chest that he carried. He didn't look happy; and, at this moment, neither did Dieners.

Mac felt light-headed as the mood in the kitchen seemed to have suddenly changed for the worse. Aboab and Dieners took note as Mac's face paled. He looked stuck. The silence was heavy, and Mac's heart was beating harder now, pounding so impossibly, startlingly loud that he even flinched.

Mac realized, *no, it is not my heart!* The pounding was the door knocker.

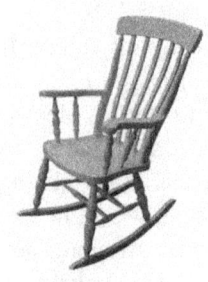

Chapter 12
Stranger Beware

Simultaneously, Aboab and Dieners turned toward the door. They were surprised by the pounding, too. They looked at each other and then Dieners hobbled off to see who it was. Aboab glanced at the clock that sat on a high shelf. Mac followed his glance and noticed the clock for the first time. He thought, *Clock faces have not changed. It is nearly five. November first. Sixteen-sixty. How is it possible?*

From the little distance down the hall he could hear Dieners speak loudly through the grating in the door, and then came a muffled voice in response. Next there was the sound of the door opening, which suggested that the newcomer was welcome, although probably not expected if Mac could judge by the surprised look on Aboab's face.

Not one person, but two men came into the kitchen and Dieners followed behind them.

"*Shalom,*" the two said in unison to Aboab, and then they took a good, hard look at Mac. They did not seem surprised to see him, as it was soon to become obvious that they came because word was out that a mysterious foreign visitor had come to Rabbi Aboab's house.

Aboab said—in English, "Shalom, my friends. I see the news of my visitor has reached you already. Or have you come on another matter?" Mac was surprised that Aboab spoke to the two men directly in English—without a word as to why he chose to do so—and that the visitors registered no surprise.

The taller of the two, who had preceded Dieners and led their way in, spoke first. "You are so perceptive, Rabbi Aboab, and we hope you will forgive us for coming to you uninvited. Yes, we heard that you have a visitor from England, so we thought we would come and introduce ourselves."

Mac had stood up, feeling obsequious and like an object of suspicion or a "person of interest." The men appeared to Mac to be wealthy, dressed in the merchant-class Dutch burgher style—long dark overcoats, broad-brimmed hats and white lacey collars. Self-importance radiated out from them as they stood stiffly and openly evaluated Mac from head to foot.

Said Aboab, "Brothers Pereira, I would like to introduce William Handyside MacRitchie." Mac stepped forward and, with a slight bow, he shook each of their hands in turn as Aboab introduced them to him and began to explain to Mac something of their importance.

"Meneer MacRitchie, these men are members of my community, Abraham Israel Pereira, and his brother, Isaac. They are among our most important leaders in Amsterdam." Then, to the brothers, Aboab said, "Dieners and I were just discussing Meneer MacRitchie's unique situation. So far we have learned that he is actually from New Amsterdam—not from the British Isles as you heard—and he is on a quest with hopes of meeting my esteemed neighbor, Rembrandt van Rijn. Meneer MacRitchie is a scholar."

At this, the one appearing to be the older of the two—the one called "Abraham"—pursed his lips and nodded. Whether he was impressed or doubtful, Mac could not judge.

"A scholar of what?" he asked, his voice a monotone and without warmth. He directed his first question to Aboab. He did not bother to look again at the foreigner. Mac felt as if he had suddenly become invisible. The younger brother silently observed Mac while Abraham spoke; he appeared ready to ask more questions and he was just getting started.

Aboab replied, "A scholar of history, I have gleaned from our conversation thus far, with an interest in printing. We were about to make plans that concern Dieners, myself, and our respectable guest . . .." The rabbi was about to say more but Dieners broke in with unconcealed haste.

"*Mijne Heren* Pereira, I am sorry, but I find I am terribly behind in my preparations for our evening meal for our guest—humble as it is—so I now find myself in an extremely embarrassing situation. I am so regretful that I have to ask you—and I repeat that I am so sorry—may we be excused for now?"

Aboab shot him a look, aghast, but Dieners was effusive; he prattled on and he would not stop. "As we—that is, as I—have so many additional things to arrange with our visitor! Time is of the essence, I fear. I tremble at making my bold request, but hope that you will understand and forgive me." He motioned toward the door showing them the way to the door, with an added, furtive word for Aboab, "Forgive me, Father."

Mac was amazed and, as Dieners' audacity

toward these important-looking men sunk in, he thought, *Dieners is giving them the bum's rush!*

The brothers looked at each other. They, too, were amazed, but they nodded with polite understanding and then actually apologized to Aboab for dropping in unexpectedly. Whatever Dieners' powers were and whatever his motive, Mac had no clue; but it bought him time. It was as though a nonverbal exchange had taken place—but whatever it might have been, Mac had missed it and, before he could think longer about it, Dieners was showing the Pereira brothers to the door.

Mac wanted to sit down again and, as he turned to take his seat, he happened to look toward the window and was surprised to see that it was pitch black outside, which turned the window glass into a mirror. He met his own reflection. Or, rather, he *thought* it was his reflection until he realized, *but no! That face is not mine—not my reflection!*

There was the face of Mevrouw Schwarzesherz' giant, Pieter, looking at him through the glass!

As quickly as Mac saw him, Pieter's face disappeared. Mac wondered if his imagination had played a trick with a reflection from some other source—perhaps it was a reflection from the door down the hall when Dieners closed it, or the candles had fluttered, casting a strange light. He felt sure of what he had seen, however, and thought, *No, it was that bouncer Pieter! Definitely.*

Aboab was speaking in Dutch to Dieners, admonishing him and demanding an explanation for his strange behavior and for showing the important men to the door in the way that he did.

"Dieners, I'm confused. You do some things sometimes that shame me, I must say! I'm surprised at you for your behavior! What manner of

105

arrangement presses you such that you would show
the Pereira brothers the door?"

Dieners' answered, with an attitude of assurance,
that he had a good reason. He explained to Aboab that
he felt danger, and his impetuous ploy solved the
problem before the danger could grow imminent. As
Dieners continued and elaborated, the rabbi nodded,
stroking his beard. He had to agree that Dieners had
done the right thing under the circumstances. Aboab
did not explain it to Mac. It could wait.

Instead, switching back to English, Aboab
explained to Mac that Dieners had to get a payback
arrangement made with him. This matter was a
pressing issue to Dieners because, in the absence of
Aboab's wife, Huisvrouw da Fonseca, the dwarf was
manager of the Fonseca house, and the subject of
money needed to be settled. It was a matter of first
things first.

It was simple: "Money," put in Dieners to Mac in
earnest. "If I am to prepare food for you, and other
accommodations, then I need to know if you have
money, so, please," he said to Mac, "Show me the
money."

Here it was, the time of reckoning. Numbed now
by the series of dramatic events, Mac—almost
automatically—took out his wallet, opened it and
took out a one-dollar bill and handed it to Dieners.

It was an absurd thing to offer and Mac knew it,
but what else could he do? Aboab followed the paper
money with open interest as Mac handed it over.
Dieners scratched his head, hesitated, and then took it
to examine the dollar bill up close.

Aboab leaned down and looked over his shoulder
to see it, too.

"Meneer, what is this?" Dieners said, as his eyes
scanned the words, settled here and there on the

design. He turned it over, surprise on his face that both sides had images printed on them. He held it up and waved it, flapping it like a little paper bird flapping its wings between two fingers. "What?" Dieners repeated.

"It is all I have. It is American currency, paper money," confessed Mac. "I didn't know how to exchange it into your money."

Dieners gave the dollar bill to Aboab, who took his turn and examined the bill on both of its sides. He reached up to a shelf on the near wall for the lighted lamp and brought it down for a better look. Their study stopped as they both looked up, distracted by sounds of retreating footfalls out in the garden and the shutting of the garden back gate.

Aboab looked at Dieners and Dieners looked at Aboab. "*Nacht bodem collector, denk ik,*"[54] suggested Dieners, who thought that it was the sound of the night soil collector. He said it in Dutch, but if Dieners had said it in English, then Mac would have reported that he saw Pieter at the window, and having done what he was sent to do, it was Pieter's steps they heard as he took his leave.

The moment unnerved Mac; everything happened at once; and he didn't know what was going on. He had no inkling of the role the Black Widow's spy would play in the course of Mac's days in Amsterdam.

Aboab came to a decision. He said, "Meneer MacRitchie, what you have offered for payment to stay under our roof, this print—I believe it is an engraving of the finest quality that I have ever seen in my experience. And I have seen much! Speaking for myself, and with Dieners' agreement, you are

---

[54] Night soil collector, I think.

welcome to dine here tonight and sleep in the garret. I will leave the future plans up to Dieners. This print, I—that is, we—accept, at face value."

Dieners nodded agreement, but Mac thought his acceptance was grudging. Mac's printmaker chest was of less interest to Aboab now, compared to his one-dollar bill; and it was Mac's only one.

***

Earlier that afternoon, long before dark and during her ride home, Mevrouw Schwarzesherz felt her bitterness swell as she reviewed the day's events. She had never been so badly treated and embarrassed. She had revealed a weakness to Pieter. Surely he heard her from his place behind the door that afternoon, and he witnessed her deference toward the Scotsman afterward.

No matter. She could fix Pieter if he said anything. The oaf wouldn't dare to tell about it. He was her slave. She thought, *The dolt probably has already forgotten it, anyway, fool that he is.*

By the time she arrived back home, the rainwater had collected on the wagon seat and she felt the dampness penetrating through her clothes and this made her mood worse.

Pieter opened the door before she had time to unlock it. She said nothing to him. She heard sounds in the kitchen, which meant that Mahault had started preparing her evening meal. Vrouw Schwarzesherz was eager to change into dry clothing and went right away up the stairs to change. Then—most importantly—she would hide the coins Rabbi Aboab had given her.

Once in her room she locked the door behind her, took a burning candle from its holder and lit the lamps on each side of her rocking chair. She stood for awhile, gazing at her old rocker. The thought of what lay under it made her smile. Already she felt better as she anticipated the pleasant little task that awaited her. Afterward she would have a little drink to celebrate.

As soon as she had dried herself and changed her house clothes, she poured a glass of wine and set the goblet on the small table beside the chair. Then she pulled the chair toward the center of the room, went to the edge of the carpet nearest the wall and began to roll it toward her. When several of the broad floorboards underneath were exposed, she pressed one end of a board with the heel of her hand. The other end rose up, like a little teeter-totter. She grabbed the other end, raised and lifted the board free and set it aside quietly.

There, in the cavity that had been covered by the board, were several soft, lumpy leather bags. She inhaled the musky smell of the skins like it was perfume. She pulled out one of the sacks and set it down. Its contents jingled as she untied the thongs that held the bag shut. The sound of her bounty of gold coins rubbing against each other was music to her ears.

Reaching into a pocket of her housecoat, she retrieved the coins Dieners had handed her, checked them with a quick bite to reassure herself that they were gold, and added them to the sack. The sound of the coins clinking in the bag to join the others gave her immense pleasure. She tied up the bag, arranged it in the floor cavity, and replaced the board over it.

After she rolled the carpet back over the boards, she pushed her rocking chair back into its customary place, seated herself, reached for her wine and settled in with a long, satisfied sigh.

She thought the day hadn't gone so badly after all. The only thing that went wrong was losing the Scotsman's *kist*. She swirled her glass of wine, took a sip, swished it around in her mouth and then swallowed. After that she laid her head against the pillowed back of the rocking chair and thought, *I must be getting careless. I should have fed him here instead of stopping at the bakery, and prepared him one of my special recipes.*

She smiled at the thought, *I believe another opportunity will come.* Relishing this prospect—this encouraging outlook—she had a new goal in mind and something upon which to meditate. Mevrouw Schwarzesherz took another drink, rocked her chair slowly back and forth and hummed her low, throaty, *Hmm, hmmm.*

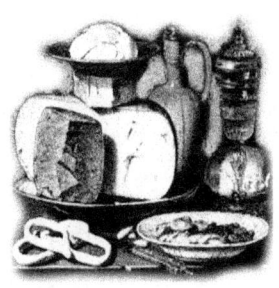

Chapter 13
First Supper

Peahen probably tastes like chicken, Mac thought as he considered the slices of cold white meat that Dieners served on a Delft-glazed plate. Mac's years as a vegetarian had not erased his memory of cold breast of chicken, which Mac thought looked the same as the peahen breast meat prepared by his host for some open-faced sandwiches.

In the kitchen, off to the side in the eating nook, Mac and Aboab were already seated and ready to eat their first supper together. In the center of the table a fat, tall candle cast a warm light on the setting and augmented the candle chandelier overhead. It had been a busy afternoon, but after the unexpected guests had left and the money matter was settled for now, the mood was again quite friendly.

In the quiet of the evening meal, Mac thought of his history lessons. Like many students in their adolescent years, he best remembered historic events that were highlighted with odd and entertaining twists, like the source of the name, "sandwich," that which was given to the serving on the plate in front of him—a peahen, open-faced sandwich. Did Mac dare speak of it as a "sandwich"? No, the sandwich *name* was a hundred years off in the future. The handy, hand-held meal was invented by a gambling Englishman, the Earl of Sandwich, who was so engrossed at playing cards that he ordered his meat between two pieces of bread.

In the minutes after the Pereira brothers left, Dieners had efficiently put together the simple meal for the three of them, Mac's first real supper in Amsterdam. It had been the longest Monday of Mac's life; he was starving and he was drop-dead tired. When Dieners insisted that Mac go ahead—not wait for him to seat himself the table—Mac was happy to begin eating. Peahen *did* taste like chicken. Mac wished for some mayonnaise, but figured mayonnaise was of French origin—and he settled for butter instead.

Mac toyed with the idea of adding a top slice of bread to his open-faced sandwich and, by doing this, he could trump the Brit by a century! *Imagine having a peanut-butter-and-jam "MacRitchie" if the thing were to be named after himself instead of the Earl, now, in 1660!* Mac's musing was interrupted by Dieners as he got up on his high chair to join Mac and Aboab.

"How do you like the food?" Dieners asked Mac.

"It is delicious. It may surprise you, but I have never tasted peahen before. Peahen and peacock are very rare and costly when—I meant—*where* I'm from," Mac said, as he carelessly confused his words. He hesitated, about to take another bite, recovering over the slip in his comment. The two did not seem to notice his mention of "from when" he had come.

"Also here," put in Aboab, "But as it happens, we had a gathering yesterday as a send-off for my wife. She is on a short holiday at Tulpenburg, and this was left-over. I like a simple meal of cold meat. I hope you don't mind."

"Myself, too," said Dieners, as he cut another thick slice of bread from the loaf, swabbed a generous dab of butter on it and offered it to Mac.

Besides the peahen, bread and butter, there were cold red beets—freshly peeled, brilliant globes glistening in the candlelight. Slices of Jerusalem artichoke and unpeeled fruits accompanied them on a large platter in the center of the table.

From somewhere Aboab had produced a bottle of white wine. Mac wondered what kind of wine it might be, as there was no label on the bottle. Perhaps wine labels would be a practice to come later in time, when wine would be more of an art than a necessity. *So much I don't know*, thought Mac, *So much to learn.*

"There is so much we don't know about you, so much to learn, Meneer MacRitchie," said Aboab, "I confess, I grow more curious by the minute."

Aboab poured wine into Mac's goblet, and then some for himself and Dieners. They raised their glasses for a toast. "To your health, Meneer," said Aboab to Mac, and they tried the wine. It was sweeter than what Mac was used to. He guessed it might be a sauterne, or perhaps muscatel.

Aboab said, "I won't press you with my questions until you've finished eating. I expect we will have an interesting conversation after our meal."

Mac set down his wine glass. "Yes," after he swallowed; and he swallowed again at the prospect of the expected questions that he would have to answer. *Gulp! This wine might help.* Perhaps the wine did prepare him for the inevitable because, out of nowhere, the word "faith" flashed into his mind. Mac decided that he had better make his move and trust his intuition. He sensed determination settle upon him, and he thought, *Okay, it's a long shot, but here goes.*

Mac set down his glass and dabbed at the corners of his mouth with a rustic linen napkin. A courageous, inner voice repeated the word "faith" in his ear.

"*Faith!*" Mac stated out loud and added the declarative: "To thine own self be true."

His mouth had taken over his brain! Mac wondered *where did that come from?* He felt himself suddenly subdued and humbled. All was quiet except for the ticking clock on the shelf on the wall.

Aboab was openly surprised. He blinked at Mac's words, so inspired, like a bolt-out-of-the-blue. The words took the rabbi aback also by the profound tone in which Mac gave them. *What other revelations would come?* Aboab wondered. To the rabbi, the phrase was weighty indeed and true, but it was strange that it came from this odd visitor who had impressed Aboab as being naïve for his years. He stared at Mac, waiting to hear what surprises would come out of the visitor's mouth next.

Indeed, Mac had even more to say. "This is what I am thinking, as a preface to what I am going to tell you." He thought for a second, looked down at his hands, which were steady; they did not show the nervous tension that he felt. "You have been tolerant, taking me in as you have, against your better judgment, I should think."

Mac paused, raised his head and looked Aboab steadily and straight in the eye, in a way that he hoped punctuated that he meant what he said. He turned and looked at Dieners and found he watched Mac intently; the dwarf also appeared to be astonished by the weighty axiom Mac had uttered, "To thine own self be true."

Mac was more than an alien from another country: he was a being from another time. He might as well have descended from the sky, carrying in his brain a time machine, a lens through which one could see details of the future. Mac knew that he was taking a chance going further with the dramatic path that he was on. Or, rather it was what Aboab had started by asking from Mac, *nothing but the truth*!

Mac said, "I am from America, it is true, and I am expecting that you want to know more, and, truly, I am glad that I have not waited for you to press me for more details. I want to give you more details in a certain order—in a sequence that would be best for us all."

Mac stalled, but the patient Rabbi Aboab seemed willing to give Mac all the slack that he needed, however long it took. At least, that is what Mac hoped for.

In this, Mac's silent moment, Dieners spoke, tapping the bottle: "More wine, Meneer MacRitchie?" Dieners was not as patient as the rabbi, and maybe he thought that more wine would loosen Mac's tongue.

Mac raised his hand, palm out, in a gesture of "No, thank you," and he repeated, "*To thine own self be true*. As truth is all, it is best to tell you everything about my presence here in order to be true to myself. I am here, yes, and how fortunate it is that it should be here with you that I am . . .." Mac was searching for words, running out of ways to postpone the inevitable.

"I'm from another place and . . .," he took a big breath and let it all out with, " . . . and another time." Mac looked at Aboab and was relieved to see that a smile gradually formed on the rabbi's face. Mac turned and looked at the dwarf again, and was even more relieved to see that a corner of Dieners' usually skeptical, grimacing mouth changed into a mischievous smirk. In this smirk Dieners' face

115

brought to Mac's mind the image of a mischievous little gnome.

Dieners said, "Be careful, Meneer MacRitchie, of what you say henceforth, for my father is a Kabbalist, and will not countenance practical kabbalah—that is, sorcery, magic and such stuff—if you didn't already know, and your words will be taken seriously. Do not jest with the rabbi!" Mac saw that Dieners held out a yellow caution flag. However Dieners was on his side, apparently.

Aboab reached for the long knife lying on the bread board, picked it up, and while he still had a faint smile, his face was unreadable. He was thinking, gazing at the knife which Mac knew to be razor-sharp, then he slowly and methodically began to slice bread. His smile could be interpreted as either one of amusement or of skepticism.

"We come at last to the important thing," Aboab said after the last downward stroke of the knife. The slice of bread fell away. "Your words, '*to thine own self be true*,' inform me that you have made a decision to fortify yourself with the truth. For the past six hours that you have been our guest, you have been evasive, speaking with words of multiple meanings. By your manner I'm reminded of the discussions we have in my circle, when we know, at bottom, that we may never know the truth. But to ourselves, we must persist in knowing. 'Know thyself,' and, as you remind us: 'to thine own self be true'."

In his undergraduate years, Mac and his college roommates had late-night debates (better known as *bull sessions*) that often lasted into the early morning hours; and it was during those discussions that the country boy, Mac, learned what it meant to develop his mind so as to approach and perhaps embrace the ineffable and the unknowable. He learned that one's mind was not to be wasted, and was meant to be enlarged, to be cultivated and watched, like a good farmer and a good steward. Now it suddenly occurred to Mac that those late-night debates about the life of the mind prepared him; it was partly what saved him—in his accidental journey back to the 17th Century—from cracking up.

An animal, like the ones that they put through laboratory experiments, would have probably died when finding itself faced with such extreme changes as Mac was experiencing.

As he mulled over whether he had gone insane and that he imagined all that was happening, he was shaken out of his reflecting by Dieners, who shouted, "I forgot!" and he suddenly got down from his chair. "I haven't delivered their bread to the Rembrandts! I must go do it," and he bustled over to the side where he had put the fresh-baked bread, selected two, and began stuffing the crusty loaves into a linen bag.

Aboab turned to Mac and said, loudly enough for Dieners to hear him, "In most ways, Dieners is like a man twice his age, believe me. But occasionally his attention span belies the teenager that he is." Aboab chuckled; Dieners ignored the rabbi's jibe.

In actuality, Rabbi Aboab wanted to ask Mac questions that he had been saving for an opportunity when Dieners was not present and the boy could not, therefore, listen in. When Dieners was out the door, Aboab chose to ask his visitor the first thing on his mind; but it was not a question Mac expected. He said, "Tell me, Meneer MacRitchie. Where were you born?"

Mac was done with the charade that fate had imposed on him; he had his fill of dancing around the facts of his experience and he was tired of it. *What can Aboab do?* Mac asked himself again, *kill me in his own house? Maybe not. But, I bet he can have me locked up!*

Despite these concerns, Mac answered straightaway: "I said I would never lie to you, Rabbi Aboab. I was born in America, in the town of Yakima."

For a moment Aboab was quiet. A wise man, well-read, and somewhat familiar with the names of the colonies of the new world, he was pondering the settlement name, to himself asking, *Yakima, was that in the Northern New England colonies, or is it in Virginia? Or is Yakima in a newer territory about which I do not yet know?*

Mac took a deep breath to fortify himself and added to what he had just said: "*In 1941.*"

As Aboab did not respond but rather continued his mental exploring of remembered maps of the new world that he had seen. He interrupted his wonderment when it sunk in—the year when Mac had said that he was born.

"Sixteen forty-one, did you say? Impossible! You'd be only nineteen, and—"

Mac did not let the rabbi finish his sentence; he broke in with, "Nineteen," and he repeated, "Nineteen-forty-one. *I was born in nineteen-forty-one*, Rabbi Aboab. Or, I should say, I *am* to be born almost 300 years from now. I am from another time, far from the colonies as they exist in the present day, and far into the future."

Inside, Mac felt something subside in a rush, a release, as if this moment of truth freed him from fear; now he felt victorious and not so suppressed, having heard his own voice at last speak the awful truth. It had a chilling effect on him. Moved with emotion, Mac choked back a sob. *Those words might turn out to be my last,* he thought, *before Aboab calls out for the guard*. Mac pictured in his mind the huge Rembrandt painting, *Night Watch*, which he and Faye saw at the Rijksmuseum. It flashed on an inner screen in Mac's vivid imagination—a crowd of volunteer guardsmen coming out of the dark, crossing the bridge as if on their way to Aboab's, their pikes threatening, muskets loaded, banners waving, marching, coming closer, answering Aboab's urgent summons, to get Mac, tie him up, drag him to the lockup, and try the alien for sorcery and let him rot. What other manner of response would Aboab have, other than to declare Mac to be insane and a danger to society?

At his side of the table, the rabbi was as still as stone with neither a sign of shock nor of surprise. He was deadpan-faced for a few seconds, then his full beard lifted as he raised his chin slightly and he closed his eyes. The room was silent except for the clock. After what might have been thirty seconds (but which seemed like five minutes to Mac) Rabbi Aboab opened his eyes and fixed them, unblinking, on Mac and he said, "I believe you."

This statement was either a major breakthrough, Mac thought, or it was Aboab's way of buying time until he could get away from the lunatic at his table.

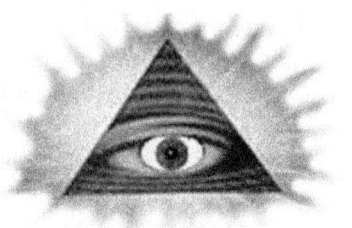

Chapter 14
Futurist

"I believe you, Meneer MacRitchie," Aboab repeated, perhaps to convince himself by saying it twice.

Mac nodded. "Good. Good. I am not lying. I am not insane. I do not pretend to understand how this happened, but I do know that I am from the 21st Century, that I am seventy years old, and that I was born in Yakima, Washington, which is part of what is an, as-yet, uncharted region in the new world—a region that will come to be called the Pacific Northwest of North America."

Aboab said, "We have a lot to talk about, Meneer MacRitchie, indeed. But I must warn you, although I can—and I will—help you, you need to know that if any other person, even my good boy, Dieners, hears you saying such things as you just said to me, the powers ruling Amsterdam will have you imprisoned, even killed, and without mercy." Aboab let that possibility hang in the air and watched Mac's reaction. When Mac nodded his acceptance of what Aboab said, the rabbi went on.

"There is scant tolerance or room for understanding of the kind of things of which you speak, and forbearance for mysticism wears thin in

120

Amsterdam. That you were taken for being English, and yet you survived this long, makes me think you are under the protection of a merciful God. Even I, in my overly-vaunted position, find your good fortune a wonder. You must be possessed of great faith, indeed."

Before Aboab asked his next question—which was obvious that he intended to do, Aboab hesitated long enough for Mac to insert, "Thank you, Rabbi Fonseca. I have been lucky."

"Let me tell you something of my community, Meneer MacRitchie, for I think it important for you to know. Do you know the meaning of *Kabbalah*?"

Mac had heard Dieners mention it in his warning, but Mac had to shake his head "no."

"Kabbalah is a set of Jewish teachings, and studies of the relationship of man to God. We of the Kabbalists seek to understand the meaning of life. Some people, outside of Judaism, think of us as philosophers because we work with the esoteric; but we are not philosophers. To an outsider, a Gentile like yourself, this would be impossible to understand I'm afraid."

Again Mac thought of his student days when discussions of the meaning of life engaged him and stretched his brain and, that having happened, put to ruin his future as a farmer because—once his mind had stretched to reach new dimensions of collegiate intellect—Mac wanted more and more. His mind never returned to its original size. Mac remembered the maxim: *"Mind is like a balloon. If you blow it up—expand it to its fullest, and then even if you let out the air, that balloon is never again the same as it was."*

Aboab stopped, having noticed that Mac didn't appear to be listening and he tilted his head, questioning. Mac noticed and he was embarrassed. "I'm sorry, Aboab," Mac said, "I was remembering my youthful days when I first met with people wiser than myself in such matters as those of which you speak. You reminded me of those times. I remember them and I miss them, although it was decades ago. I look forward to more talks such as we're having now."

"Make no mistake in thinking, Meneer MacRitchie, that you could join this community. You will not be part of it. Not ever. You are probably not aware, for example, that those two who appeared suddenly this afternoon—the brothers Pereira—they did not like you. They came filled with suspicion. I wondered, when Dieners rushed them out, why he did such an audacious, rude thing. Later I realized Dieners sensed that there would be trouble if those two stayed long enough to interrogate you, as they began to do."

Aboab regarded Mac's Flemish jacket and his stringy, rock-musician's wig. "One look at your clothing, which resembles the Flemish style, I must point out, made them ready to pounce. About their power in our city I need only tell you that it goes far. Very far. They are influential men with boundless authority."

Aboab thought about what he was going to add before he said it. Nodding slowly to confirm and shape his thought, he said, "Actually, I think Dieners may have saved your life."

How comforting, thought Mac, and he said, "I like Dieners. Very much."

"He's a good boy; however I am afraid there are those in our city who are rankled at the wonderment that he is being so close to me, that I call him Son, but my station as Rabbi protects Dieners. That fact, and the way that we who stand out, means it is vital that we stick together here in Amsterdam. You do know—," and he suddenly stopped in mid-sentence, as though he'd just thought of something. His eyes widened.

"I believed—believe—you are from the future," Aboab said, and refreshed his newfound understanding. He measured out his next words like a metronome, their weightiness evident. "Then, as you are from the future, you can, that is, you are able, to tell me what will happen."

And at this, just as he had done moments before, Aboab again closed his eyes and lifted his chin in his odd, pensive manner. He was quiet and stayed that way, giving Mac, also, a moment to realize an awful truth. Why hadn't it occurred to Mac before—the obvious thing, the most frightening thing to men with both deep wisdom and common sense?

Mac knew, and he thought, *To know the future is a heavy burden. Aboab knows I know. It is true. I do know the future from now, in 1660, to the second Millennium. I know enough about the plight of Jews. Also I have been to the Netherlands, twice, in the 20th Century; been to the Rembrandtsuis Museum. I saw the house where Anne Frank wrote her diary. My hope now is Aboab will not have me killed in fear of what I know, the messages I could relate, and that I will tell all. These times, the 17th Century, are dark, it is true, and there will be more dark times in the coming years—darker than people can imagine. I cannot unburden myself.*

As though he could read Mac's thoughts, and as though talking in a dream, Aboab said, "You must not tell me," his head was shaking, "no," slowly and his eyes remained closed as he spoke. His words sounded from far away, giving deep and good advice and guided by his intuition.

Aboab did not want to know what was in store. That was final. Then he opened his eyes. "No, you must not tell me anything about the—our—future from this time forward. Somehow we must apply ourselves, resist asking or telling—at any cost."

Aboab made a decision, to be true to his faith, "I will help you if there is a way, although, at this moment, I do not know how to help you."

"I appreciate your words, Rabbi Aboab, and I will tell you nothing about the future of mankind, Jewish or not, henceforth," vowed Mac. "As for your help, if there is one thing I wish for most, it is to return to my home in time. I do not mean that I would leave Amsterdam on a ship to cross the Atlantic because I don't think I would survive. Anyway, I would never meet another man as open-minded as I find you to be."

Aboab was to be Mac's only chance. Mac had often asserted, *When I meet someone new, and I find myself getting to know them, even if our meeting is brief and by a chance passing, I think of these people as gifts placed along my pathway; and I furthermore think that there will come a time when I realize, later—upon reflection, how important they are, or that they were, to me.* Mac wanted to explain this confidence to Aboab, but just then the front door opened and Dieners came back. The little man trotted into the kitchen and made an announcement.

"I have bad news. Our neighbor is drunk!" said Dieners, and he said this with a touch of mirth which, it was immediately obvious, Rabbi Aboab disliked to hear come from the boy's mouth and in the manner in which he spoke.

"Son! That is not a neighborly way to talk about Rembrandt!" Aboab scolded.

Mac was amazed, both by the news of Rembrandt's inebriation and also that, despite a moment ago he had learned Mac's barely credible story, Aboab acted as though he had forgotten. *Was Aboab in a state of shock? Or was his control over himself so great that he could let Mac's revelation simply roll off him? Was this how the Kabbalah prepared a man for the mysteries and surprises of life?*

Mac had expected something to be said concerning his and the rabbi's amazing exchange— perhaps Aboab would break the truth of Mac's origins to Dieners—but, instead, Aboab seemed concerned only with admonishing his son.

"Rembrandt has troubles enough without a show of disrespect by his neighbor's son," Aboab said to Dieners. Once finished, he quieted. Aboab expressed his concern for the van Rijn family as he questioned Dieners, "What is . . . how is Hendrickje? And Titus? And Cornelia? Are they all right? Were they there? Did you see them?"

Without an apology for his transgress, Dieners answered: "They're all right. Hendrickje has seen worse, and I think the little girl has already gone to bed. I did not see Titus. A man his age . . . .." and Dieners trailed off without speculating as to where it was that Rembrandt's nineteen-year old son might be at this hour of night.

In the quiet moment that followed, Mac cleared his throat and said brightly, "Shall we discuss printmaking?" This had the effect on Aboab he had hoped for; and Dieners took this as signal to clear the table and get ready for a display of Mac's things. Mac was proving to be a novelty in Dieners' eyes, and he seemed eager to get the show on the road. The rabbi withdrew the dollar bill from his pocket and put it on the cleared table in the circle of candlelight.

"This print is truly an amazing thing," Aboab said, leaning in closely to get another look at it. "The paper is so thin. It must be Chinese in origin; and it is printed on both sides. Odd symbolism; but some of the signs are familiar to me. The words have colonial meanings, I suppose. I don't understand many of them." His voice had lowered to almost a murmur. "It bears thinking. Tomorrow, in daylight, I will study this more closely with Spinoz . . . with my excellent magnifying glass. The light is too dim for my eyes to make out the fine engraving. I have never seen engraving so regular and precise. If this is an example of what you Americans are capable, then our modern-day Dutch printers are sadly far, far behind."

Here Aboab paused, recalling to his mind Mac's revelation and that this was therefore a 21st Century print. Then, considering for a moment what other out of the ordinary things Mac's chest might hold, Aboab changed the subject.

"I think rather on the morrow that we shall discuss printmaking further. Not now. I feel it is time to show you upstairs, Meneer MacRitchie." With a glance to where Mac's printmaking chest was still sitting on the floor, he continued. "As for opening the chest—that, too, can wait until tomorrow."

Dieners, as he had put the last of the dinner things away, said with surprise, "What? Are we not going to see what more things Meneer MacRitchie has tonight?"

The dwarf was more curious than he had shown himself to be, which surprised Mac, and he hoped that Dieners would not press the issue of opening his chest. For his part, Mac could wait forever to open it; he was worried about the inevitabilities. Would Aboab relent? But Mac didn't have to worry.

"I think not," said Aboab. "I am too tired. It is too dark. Tomorrow we can see everything better in the daylight."

"But I wanted to see it for a long time!" said Dieners, and he stamped his foot.

"No!" said Aboab. "Meneer MacRitchie travels with little, which is a thing remarkable when considering his quest. What little he has we will see in the morning. Now let us take him up—."

"Take him yourself!" said Dieners.

Why the dwarf had turned petulant, and so suddenly, Mac could not understand. A boy who had the face and strength of a man, an African dwarf, prematurely whiskery, he was acting just like the teenager that he was. How otherwise would a teenage, boy/man react to being first praised and then scolded by turns, regardless how wise beyond his years Dieners seemed most of the time?

Plus, Dieners was now faced with housekeeping for a guest who had paid him for it with a piece of thin paper instead of the money that he needed to run the household. Paper money, indeed! Such an idea! Paper could never replace silver and gold, no matter how fine the engraving was. On top of all this, he was put off, bossed by the rabbi, and not allowed to see what was in Mac's mysterious box.

Aboab was lighting some candles as he made excuses for Dieners' churlish outburst. "Meneer MacRitchie, I hope you will excuse Dieners," said Aboab, and he turned toward the hall. "Please bring your chest with you, and I will see you to your room. It's at the top of the stairs. Step carefully, there's not much light to see your way."

With a mixture of relief and embarrassment, Mac got out of his chair and nodded politely to Dieners. "Thank you, Dieners, for the meal. It was excellent.

You are a very capable person, and I look forward to talking with you, and showing you more."

Mac crossed the room and picked up his printmaker chest. He mustered up as much sincerity as he could, turned to Dieners and added, "Much more!" Before he mounted the narrow stairs, he turned again and looked back at the little man, who was standing in the kitchen pouting. Mac called to him, "Good night, Meneer Dieners van Catarina."

"Good night," Dieners replied. Shortly, he added, with a hint of malice that Mac did not catch, "I hope you sleep well." Mac was halfway up the first flight when, Dieners added, yet more quietly, "Very well, indeed." By now Mac was out of earshot.

Starting up the stairs in a side-stepping manner and lugging his cargo, Mac stumbled in the darkness, his toe catching on a stair tread. He wondered about it, *clumsy. Was it the wine?* He drank only one glass, but he felt sleepy, his feet were heavy and he swayed, off-balance with the weight of the printmaker chest which made each step up all the more awkward.

Aboab carried two candles in holders as he led Mac up to the garret at the top of the third staircase. By the time he made the last three steps, Mac had the feeling of a dream as if trying to run through knee-deep water or trying to pull his feet out of mud. At last he was standing on the floor of the garret, and he set down the chest.

Mac felt drowsy. He was entering a macabre dreamland the whole time Aboab showed him around the room—a desk and a ladder leading up to a box-like bunk over it. A down-filled comforter and a hard pillow invited him while Aboab pointed out a pitcher and bowl on the wash stand at the end of the garret, also a chair and a desk under the bunk, plus a chamber pot. Nothing quite registered to Mac's brain;

he was barely cognizant of things in the dimly lit small, cold room. Mac was fading and losing consciousness.

It was like a dream.

But not in a good way.

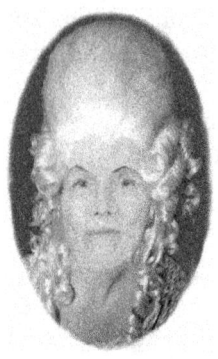

Chapter 15
No Place like Home

"Mac, Mac, wake up!" Faye was near tears.

Mac's head was resting in the crook of Faye's arm. Once again she said to him, her voice breaking. "*Mac!* Wake up! Don't scare me like this!"

Mac rolled his head sideways. Then he snapped his head back, his eyes still closed. She could see the shape of his eyeballs' lenses dancing around under his eyelids, as in rapid eye movement. Suddenly, Mac's eyes popped open!

He said, "Faye?" He could hardly believe it. Mac was back in his shop in his own time!

Faye wiped her teary eyes with her free hand and cried, "Oh, Mac! Don't you ever do that *again*. You hear! You scared me to death. What happened to you?" Her white wig slipped a little on her head, and with her free hand she put it right. Wiping a tear from her eye with the back of her hand, she smeared her ballpoint-pen beauty spot.

Mac's eyes were wide, staring into Faye's face. Such a beautiful, welcome sight! He was afraid to say anything, or do anything, lest he be thrown back in time again to that cold, dark Amsterdam garret in the top of Rabbi Aboab's house.

"Faye! I'm back!"

She blinked and looked perplexed for a moment. "Back? Okay. All right," Faye said again, "I think you must have passed out!"

"Is that what happened? I passed out?" The shock and relief were too much for him and Mac lost control of himself; his face contorted, mouth twisted into a tight smile—more like a grimace—and he began to bawl! He sobbed, his chest heaved with great gasps and tears streamed from his eyes. He was so happy that he couldn't speak.

Faye could only hold Mac's head and wonder. Her eyes glistened. When his crying subsided enough for Mac to form words again, he said one word, then another, and then he began talking so rapidly Faye couldn't understand as his words streamed, tumbling over one another.

"*Youwouldn't believewhathappened, ohmyGod, Iwasbackin-backintime*—," he stammered trying to control himself. He sucked in a deep breath as he struggled to begin an accounting of his fantastic, time-traveler experience.

"Slow down, Honey, it's all right," Faye soothed. "It's okay. It's over. You were lying on the floor. You looked dead! It scared me Mac."

Mac raised himself into a sitting position and looked around his shop. "I don't know what or how it happened, but I was . . . I remember lacquer thinner, maybe. But no! What happened was too real. Faye, listen," and then he stopped as his eyes settled on the printmaker chest. "Thank God, that's back!"

"What's back?" Faye asked, turning her head to follow where he was looking. "What? Your printmaker chest? What are you talking about?"

"Just a minute," Mac said as he got up and went to the bench where the chest sat. He tried the chest door; it was locked. He remembered the key and retrieved it, inserted and twisted the key to unlock the drop-down door. It fell open.

Mac scanned the chest contents. It looked like everything was there and in its place just as it should be: his press, the tools, the camera and his journal. He checked one drawer. It was full; and there was the red box of chocolates, too. Mac heaved a sigh of relief.

"Ah, everything is still here." Brightening, he reached for his journal and pulled it out. "Honey, wait until you see this. You won't believe it. Oh. This is exciting! I think I'm going to have a heart attack," he chortled with anticipation.

"Mac, don't you think we should be going to the party? I hate to be the last ones there." She had a worried frown on her face and still sat on the floor. Recovered from her fright, she straightened her wig and stared up at her husband. Faye watched, puzzled, as Mac—engrossed in his journal—scanned one page and flipped several more.

"Yes!" he said. "It's all here. What I wrote. Oh my . . . oh my!" Faye started to stand to see what he was reading but Mac stopped her. "No, don't get up. Better stay sitting down, because, well . . . just listen to this." Straightening, and in a portentous manner, he began reading his journal to her aloud.

"'Journal entry November 2, 1660. Amsterdam.'" He looked at Faye expectantly.

She looked back at him. The shop was silent in the shop. Mac waited. His eyes twinkled as he looked down at her to watch Faye's amazed response, his eyebrows raised, and with a triumphant, silly smile. Instead of an astonished response, she merely gave a weak smile and a shrug.

Faye broke the silence: "Okay." She checked her wristwatch. "Can we go now?"

"Faye! *Six. Teen. Six-ty!*" Mac burst, unable to contain his excitement. "I wrote those words in 1660! *The 17th Century*! I traveled all the way back to the time of Rembrandt. He was alive and I stayed right next door to him! *I was about to meet Rembrandt in person!*"

As his outburst sunk in, Faye's face went slack, as though she wasn't sure she was acquainted with this raving man. After all her years with Mac, she couldn't recall a performance quite like this.

Mac caught the way she was looking at him. He wanted her to be excited, but she just stared back at him. He tried again. "I know it sounds crazy, but I can tell you all about it. First, I woke up at night on a— you won't believe it—a *dung* boat!"

Faye responded with a nasal whine, "Oh Mac, don't do this now. Come on! Let's just go to the party." She stood, gathered her flowing costume up, dusted off her queenly dress and automatically primped at her coiffure. "Is there a mirror . . . ?"

"No no, listen, yes, we'll go, but let me tell you more," he said. Mac wasn't ready to go—not yet. He was too excited. Dennis' party could wait.

Faye relented. "Okay, tell me more."

"See, they hauled the dung on this boat —*mest*, they call it—out of Amsterdam. It was just coming back with me on it. The skipper had a knife! *And a pit bull*. He said I was a stowaway and was going to toss me overboard! I passed out. I was scared!"

Faye gasped, "A knife? Who had a knife? A pit bull? Mac, this isn't funny! Really. Stop it. Now!"

"I know, I know. I passed out. It stunk there. You wouldn't believe how it stunk!" Then Mac hesitated, raised one sleeve and sniffed the fabric.

"Do I stink?"

"No. You don't stink." She grinned. "Finish your story so we can go, okay?"

"Okay. Let's see." Mac paused, remembering more and enthused at his recall of the details. He didn't notice that Faye only humored him. "When I woke up it was day. They'd put me off the boat, onto the wharf. A woman came along. I didn't know it, but she was a procuress, and . . .."

"A what?" Faye interrupted him.

"A *procuress*, a madam, like a pimp, you know," Mac answered. He saw Faye frown. "Anyway, she took me in. She treated me for lunch. But I realized later she was getting me ready for, well," and he hesitated as the memory of the young girl in his bed came back to him.

"Listen, Faye, I swear, nothing happened. They gave me beer and I passed out and when I woke up I was in bed with this little girl!"

"Mac, that's sick! This really isn't funny. You're taking this too far," Faye said. She was angry now, and she started toward the door. "I've heard quite enough. Come on. Let's go!"

"Wait, really, that was nothing, I didn't touch the kid, believe me! See, the madam thought I wanted a prostitute but of course she was wrong! Wait until you hear the best part. Please?"

Faye dropped her shoulders and sighed, biting her lip. Mac took that to mean *okay*.

"I fooled the old madam with a debit card! No kidding! When she saw the hologram of the bird on the back of the card, she freaked! People back then were so superstitious, they're afraid of anything, so I played that up and that way I got her under my control and told her to take me to Rembrandt . . .."

Faye stopped him. "Mac, I must say, that's a

pretty good story. You ought to write it down when you get a chance, but we've got to get to the party."

Faye was at the door and concerned about her husband; this live-action role play seemed more serious than Mac's usual bantering.

Mac stopped her with, "I'll skip forward . . .."

"If you can make it fast," Faye said.

Mac noticed that she glanced at her wristwatch and his face fell. "You think I'm making this all up, don't you?" He looked again at the journal he still held as a voice inside said, *read more—read it all to her!*

"Faye, what I'm telling you really happened. I have it here, in my hand . . .," he held it up with a dramatic flourish, ". . . *total proof*! These are notes I wrote when I was alone in my garret . . .."

"Your *garret*?"

"Yes, the man I was staying with, a rabbi . . .."

"You stayed with a rabbi? I thought you said you were in a whorehouse!"

Mac took Faye's response as a good sign. He knew he could supply answers to any question she had. Let her cross-examine me—that would be a good thing! He had the truth, right down to the details. Faye, the most important person in his life, the one who always had stood behind him no matter how crazy things got, was listening. His hopes rose.

"No, that was only the first night. Then I was at the house of a Jewish rabbi named Isaac Aboab da Fonseca, and he just happened to live right next door to Rembrandt. Rabbi Aboab took me in. He had an African teenage dwarf living with him . . .." At this he noticed Faye smiled as though something tickled her funny bone.

She said, "*A dwarf*? Were there any more dwarfs, Mac? Like, *Mac and the Seven Dwarfs*? That's a cute

135

twist!" She looked him up and down. "But somehow that Flemish outfit doesn't go with the story," she added, and smirked at her wit.

The two were silent for a moment, staring at each other. He took a deep breath, held for a count of five and exhaled. For a minute Mac had thought she was coming around to believe his story. Faye was only being nice.

"Look," he said, a little more firmly than he meant to, then, softening, he started over. "Look, I have probably a thousand-word account here. I wrote it for you. I didn't know if I would ever get back, alive, to the 21st Century. I thought somehow you would read what's here. I wanted you to know that whatever happened to me, I loved you, Faye."

His last words were full of sentiment. These got her attention. He looked at the journal in his hands and back at Faye. Mac could see, thanks to this book, and, now that he was home with Faye, she would know he had thought of her. That's the most important thing.

"Okay," she said. "Read it." Faye's eyes glistened—either by tears forming or she was just happy to hear him say it, her emotions were stirred. She was touched by his declaration of love, and she loved him, too.

Mac began again.

"November 2, 1660, Tuesday. Amsterdam. Faye, if you ever get this it will be another miracle. I don't know where to begin, and writing this here, it's too much to comprehend. I actually wish I'd wake up and find that I was temporarily insane!

"Because insanity would be better than this. I will therefore pretend that you will get this somehow and read it and, even better, that we will be together reading it and laughing about it. Right now that

seems impossible.

"I will describe it: I'm in a tiny room. There's a bunk bed, and under it, a desk. To say it is rustic would be an understatement. It's cold. I'm freezing. There is no heat source, just a candle. It's damp.

"I wish I knew history better. I'm staying at the house of a Jewish rabbi, Isaac Aboab da Fonseca. He's well traveled, lived in Brazil, and the amazing thing is he helps me.

"I can hear voices downstairs, sounds like an argument. I hope they haven't called the guards. This is really scary, but Aboab said he's going to introduce me to Rembrandt. I get the impression Rembrandt is in some kind of trouble. I told them I am a scholar from the American colonies here to study art, my safest strategy."

Mac paused and looked up from reading the journal. Faye was giving him that look again, as though he was a stranger to her, with her lips pursed in a little pucker as though she were wondering if psychiatric analysis would be covered by Medicare.

"Is there more?" she asked.

Good, thought Mac, *she believes me!*

"Yes," he said, and turned to another page. He read silently to himself a few words ahead. "Well," he said, "On second thought, I feel a little funny reading this part, Faye. It gets kind of emotional."

"It's okay. You needed to write it down, and I'm listening. Go ahead. Read." Mac didn't notice when she looked at the clock Mac kept on a shelf.

Mac cleared his throat and continued.

"This is almost like it was when you and I were here the first time, in 1969, when we traveled—remember? If I get back in time to you, I promise to work harder, and I know you'll be there, a loyal wife and friend. Then this whole nightmare will have been

worthwhile somehow. "

Mac had to stop reading a second and cleared his throat again because his emotions rose up and his voice cracked. With a faint smile he gave up and closed the book softly. "Now I rest my case. I meant every word, you know, from my heart." Faye was silent. She dug into a pocket in her fancy dress and took out a hanky and dabbed at her nose. She was touched, Mac thought.

"Mac, I think it's wonderful what you wrote." She looked at her watch—and this was the third time she did. "Can we go now? It's almost eight. The party started at six, you know."

Confusion swept over Mac. He scrunched his eyelids tightly shut, as if to clear his vision, but it was his mind that was in turmoil. Strange it was, now, as Faye seemed so indifferent to what had happened to him. Faye seemed distant from him and the distance was growing, as if she was sliding away. He kept his eyes shut a second more.

He opened his eyes and began to say something, but he found it difficult to form words. It was hard to speak, and getting harder. He managed to ask her, "Faye," How long—?" His words felt thick in his throat, as though he had a mouth full of something. Then he tried again, slower, "How long was I out?" His words sounded like a phonograph record slowing down. Faye's answer, however, was normal.

"Well, I waited about five minutes in the car. I beeped for you to hurry up. Then I couldn't see you so I came in and you were on the floor. Then you woke up. Three or four minutes . . ..

Mac was confused. He looked at his journal he still held and then he set it on the bench beside his printmaking chest. He looked at Faye. He looked around the shop. Everything was just the same as it had been that afternoon when he'd shut his shop door at the end of the day; but now he wasn't sure and things were starting to get foggy.

He grinned. "Then I dreamed the whole thing?"

"No," Faye said, a touch of mirth in her voice, as she repeated an old joke they had shared so often, "No, Mac. *This* is the dream."

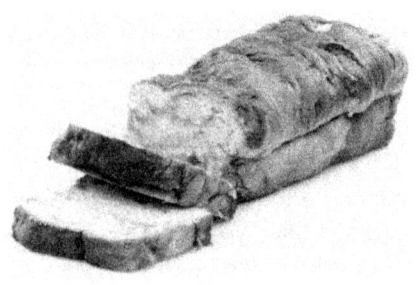

Chapter 16
Sugar and Spice

Mac's eyes shut tight and he kept them shut, but his brain was wide awake and the dream vanished without a trace, not a wisp of the vision of Faye and his being back in the shop. Instead of any trace of a memory or recall of the familiar pine lumber and ink smells of his workshop, there were the odors of the garret—mildew and oil smoke from a lamp burning somewhere.

There was a new smell, the welcome aroma of baking bread, blending with cinnamon and ginger. It must have been this burnt-sugary smell, so delicious smelling, that woke Mac up. Yet, he did not want to open his eyes. He dreaded what he would see. He wanted to get back to something that he had dreamed, but he couldn't remember what it was. *Not at all!*

All he could think of was that something delicious was baking, like it had been when, yesterday, Dieners baked bread; but, this morning, burnt-brown sugar-sweet, with spices and a hint of butter were added.

As he imagined sticky rolls baking, Mac wanted to lose himself in the prospect of having one of those rolls for breakfast. Then a notion popped into his head that he would write in his journal the very first thing today—before breakfast. His new blank journal should be in his printmaker chest. A strong instinct urged him to write. He might forget things if he didn't start writing now, start a log of all that was happening to him. If he got back to the future—or if he didn't—there would be a record.

Lying there, adjusting to the cold, damp air, he planned his moves: *He would open his chest, he would get his pen and his journal and he would write.* Mac often did write notes to himself, but he didn't usually feel as strongly compelled as he did now. He thought he'd start by writing, *November 2, 1660. Amsterdam.*

In a brief, silent self-admonishment he thought, *you must wake up and face the day!* Then Aboab's words came back to him: *"There is hardly a day that I awaken that I don't find some amazing thing that the hours bring."*

Into the dimness of the dawn, Mac said aloud, "Well, Rabbi Isaac Aboab da Fonseca, today is going to be one of those days, I betcha!"

With a brave push, he kicked back the comforter.

The spices and burnt sugar aroma of baking reminded Mac of Faye's apple pie. The memory was helping motivate him to make the greater effort to get out of the box-like bunk bed in which he'd spent his first, dream-filled night at Aboab's.

He had kicked back the comforter and inured himself to the cold. Yet he delayed. He had dreamed something but he couldn't remember what. He lay where he was, closed his eyes again, feigning sleep and trying to get the dream to come back, pushing, urging his memory to yield it up by begging, *please, just give me a hint.* It didn't work. His subconscious had locked it away for good and would not deliver up its secret.

Mac began to mull over the past two days, accounting for what happened, getting ready to write it down.

Is this Tuesday? he asked himself. *Yes. Tuesday it is.* He rolled over; leaving the only warm place there was and the chilling, damp air of the housetop garret enveloped him. He got instant goose bumps. Mac calculated the fastest way to get down the three rungs of the ladder and to get into his clothes. Shivering and shaking, he hurried into his outfit. The costume had taken on a musty smell and was, like everything else in Amsterdam, cold and damp.

Putting on and buttoning the Flemish costume took him back to two nights ago on the evening when he was getting ready to go to the Halloween Party with Faye. He made himself stop thinking about what had happened to him. Obsessing over this was probably an invitation to madness. He had to deal with the here-and-now.

His compulsion to write in his journal still held him. If nothing had changed inside his printmaker chest, then his journal would be right where he had put it. Everything would still be in place.

Words he had declared upon his waking echoed in his mind: *This would be the kind of day Aboab said he was accustomed to expect, a day of amazing things*.

Mac wondered *what if Dieners were to discover the secret that I came from the 21st Century?* Only Rabbi Aboab knew. If Dieners were also to know, then Mac would have to allow whatever followed to unfold as it may. He could not stop it. Again, he dismissed this line of thinking, as the main thing for Mac to do now was to open the printmaker chest and to get started on his writing. Mac needed to be busy with a project or he would dwell too much on his situation. He would lose his mind, if he had not, in fact, already gone off the deep end.

Mac's eyes were adjusting to the dimness of the garret. In the few minutes since his waking up, it had lightened noticeably. What little natural light there was came through an octagonal window in the triangle-topped wall that faced out on the street.

Even with the scant warm air from the kitchen down three floors below that found its way up to the garret, aromatic with spicy, burnt-sugar, it did not help his chills. Mac's stomach rumbled and he wondered what Dieners was baking at this time that smelled so good. He thought of Faye and how she loved cinnamon rolls and, again: *I wish she were here.*

The night before, he had staggered up the last flight of stairs almost overcome by waves of dizziness, but with strong determination, he had managed to reach the top. Mac's printmaker chest was on the floor where he had left it.

Aboab had made no move to help; the rabbi had probably been absorbed in his own thoughts. He had probably wondered how he would deal with this incredible development, giving food and shelter to a man, a gentile from the American colonies, who claimed to be from the future and yet who seemed normal otherwise.

As the morning light got better, Mac saw the layout of the room more clearly. The bed was a high bunk under which was a simple desk with a long, bare top. Mac picked up his chest and set it on the desktop. At the moment that he was looking around wishing for a candle and something with which to light it, Mac saw a flickering movement—a light that animated the ceiling—and there were footfalls on the stairs.

143

Someone was coming up to the garret and it looked as though light was on its way! The light-bearer was Aboab, who called up to Mac in a mixture of Dutch and English: "Goedemorgen, Meneer MacRitchie. You are awake?"

Mac was quick to respond: "Yes, I am awake and dressed, rabbi."

Aboab reached the top and paused. He was carrying a fat, lighted candle in a holder. His lined and bearded face, lit from below, reminded Mac of special, dreadful effects in a Gothic movie; but this was not a creepy face. Rabbi Aboab was smiling and friendly.

"Good morning," Aboab said again, in English, and he nodded politely to his guest as he turned to the near wall and lifted the candle to the sconce to light it. When the flame had taken hold, he brought the candle to the desk and set it there. He surveyed the room and he noticed that Mac had moved the chest to the desktop.

Mac followed the rabbi's look and, eager to put off the chest's opening longer, said, "Good morning, sir," said Mac. "I'm glad to see you. Thank you for last night's meal, for your understanding, and for the bed. I appreciate it." Mac was shivering. He was not yet warmed up.

Aboab said, "You are welcome. I hope you slept well. Not too cold?"

"A little," Mac allowed.

"As you must be hungry, you may come down whenever you please. There will be a housemaid coming later. Her name is Mahault. She's mute, but not deaf. She understands a little English but, of course, cannot speak it."

Aboab surveyed the room a final time and, as he sensed that all was in order, he turned away to go back downstairs. "You would probably like to have some time alone, so I will go. Come down when it pleases you, Meneer MacRitchie."

"Thank you," said Mac, "I plan to do some writing in my journal. Rabbi Aboab, may I ask what it is baking that I can smell? It smells so good."

"That's Dieners' *suikerbrood*. Today he prepares sugar loaves for his customers. They say his are the best in Amsterdam. I don't partake of it. However, he may offer you some, it's his business. I leave it to him."

Aboab was now at the top of the steps and about to go down when he stopped and added, "He is, by the way, in a less confrontational mood this morning. I alluded to your, ah, predicament, but I did not go into details. He is mollified. The boy is highly intelligent and, given time, he can reach his own conclusions. Rest assured, he knows the grave danger of wagging tongues. Yet, be careful what you tell him." With a parting glance at the chest, Aboab went down the dark staircase. Mac heard him say over his shoulder, "I will leave you now. I also have some writing to attend to."

A carillon began to play somewhere. It was a short hymn, and it ended with eight gongs. Mac would soon learn that this particular feature of the Rozengraacht neighborhood was part of Amsterdam's biggest amusement center, the "Nieuwe Doolhof," which was located right across the street from the houses of Rabbi Aboab and Rembrandt van Rijn.

Eight o'clock was too early for the amusement center to open, but the owner had the carillonneur begin to play at eight, before opening hours, as he believed that the citizens of Amsterdam might enjoy being reminded of the time and they may be encouraged to come to the park.

Mac was in the upper story of the house, high above the level of the early morning sounds. Besides the carillon playing, Mac could faintly hear—on the street way down below—the swishing sounds of the a street sweeper, the rattling hand-carts pushed by stoop-shouldered laborers, the clopping of wooden shoes and screaming seagulls scrabbling over scraps of food.

Mac unlocked his chest with his key and lowered the drop-down front. He moved the candle closer and saw that his journal was still in the chest where he had left it. It was a welcome sight for Mac's eyes to see it there, a thing so familiar, yet in such unfamiliar surroundings. Mac half-expected the journal to vaporize and disappear any minute, but it did not.

Mac sighed, and thought, *My imagination is running away with me.* He remembered the plate that was still in his outer coat pocket and he fished it out. He checked to see if the plate fit in his chest in the slot he had made for printing plates. It did. He took the pen from its place, opened the journal and began to write: *"November 2, 1660. Amsterdam. Faye, if you get this it will be another miracle."* He hesitated and wondered, *where to begin?*

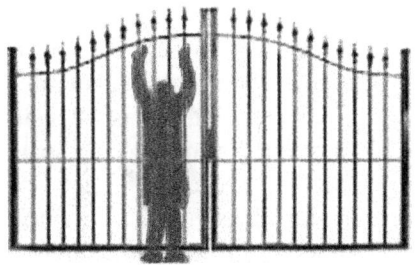

Chapter 17
Rembrandt Besotted

Three floors down on the cobblestone street, a heavily-shod dray horse clip-clopped past Aboab's house below the garret where Mac sat. The horse was pulling a fully-loaded beer wagon past the standing figure of a man, slightly hunched over and wearing a shapeless dark coat. The man had come out of the house next door, which was Rembrandt's house, and he stopped momentarily at the foot of the stairs to wait for the wagon to pass.

When the horse and wagon had rumbled by, the man walked slowly across the narrow street to the other side and stopped at the wide, locked park gates. The gates were fashioned as two iron-barred wings that swung open at the middle. The man leaned against the ironwork, reached both arms up high, gripped two bars to his left and right and then he sagged there. He pressed his aching forehead against the cold iron; and he stood there, as still as death.

If one were in a position to see the man from the other side—in the park and looking toward him, seeing him hanging by his arms at the gate—the viewer might be reminded of a man behind the bars of a jail cell, so like the image of a prisoner longing for

147

release.

Although his hair was an unruly mop and his clothes unkempt, he didn't look like an inmate; he looked like an ordinary middle-class, Amsterdam citizen out for a morning stroll and who paused to rest—and not one who was caged in a prison.

This was, in fact, Amsterdam's foremost painter, Rembrandt Harmenszoon van Rijn, and he was free to go anywhere in the city, more or less. There had been times, however, when it happened that successful people, even famous ones like Rembrandt, had ended up in debtor's prison.

Van Rijn had, so far, escaped debtor's prison, but narrowly; and, even in the open streets, Rembrandt recalled feeling incarcerated because he had been cornered for a long time by his creditors who demanded payment of huge debts. Once, not many years ago, he was rolling in money and his credit was unlimited; now van Rijn lived in uncertainty as to where he would find enough money for his family to live on.

Today he is worried. A major painting commission is being offered, and a successful, major painter such as Rembrandt might rightfully expect to win it; but, instead of the confidence that he used to feel, today he knows that it might be awarded to someone else—and probably a younger painter. The prize might go to someone from among his former apprentices, those who had become successful and who, today, compete with their old Master for work. It would not be the first time they beat him out; other prizes had been awarded to them. When this happened, often van Rijn wondered, *Don't they owe me something?*

Another thing that weighed on his mind was the latest published paper in which van Rijn was described as making crude paintings that looked like *drek;*[55] and also that he made impolite etchings unfit for viewing by the cultured, refined citizens of Amsterdam. This was not the first time that Rembrandt had been given bad press; but this was the first time the journalist suggested that he was "a madman."

If van Rijn had been driven to madness, then it wasn't any wonder, considering all that had happened to him in the past twenty years. There was the death of his first wife, Saskia, eighteen years ago; then came the loss of his fashionable home and, with it, the loss of his great studio just two years ago, and along with it, he lost his collections of art and antiques, exotica, and his printing press.

The present decline in interest in his painting was the worst thing of all. Although he was short-listed to compete for a major public art commission, which was to execute one of eight paintings for Amsterdam's New Town Hall, he was doubtful that he would win the award.

Rembrandt, once the painter at the top of the heap, had now been—for too long—at the bottom. Something would go wrong, once again. He knew it. He could feel it in his old bones.

The journalist's scathing criticism came back to Rembrandt's thoughts. *Mad? No, not mad.* To himself he was among the sanest artists of his generation and as good a painter as Peter Paul Rubens! While most of the other lowland artists since Rubens had been slavishly coveting art commissions and pandering to the city fathers, Rembrandt was true to himself, following his inner light, loyal to unseen realities in things, in every image, every action, and even in the

---

[55] Shit

nuances of words spoken in plain, everyday conversations that he could hear in the streets, marketplaces, the countryside and the dockyards.

To Rembrandt's way of seeing his world, everything in it had a potential to enliven a work of art, whether he was making a simple chalk sketch, a delicate silverpoint drawing, a great painting or an etching. He loved the potency of life, not only in what could be seen, but what could only be sensed. There are many qualities of life and existence to which most people had become dulled and unaware. Taking in the simple things of life filled him to overflowing with energy to imagine, invent, and create wonderful things. He wanted to discover new ways to see, and new ways to make art.

Rembrandt was besotted with life, with color, with texture, and the interwoven web that he believed related and connected everything. His love of the gifts of life, and his talent for expressing them in art, thrilled him. He lived to draw and paint; and, with fuming acid, he had etched into copper his crazy lust for life. With black inks he printed on fine, white paper. This was another way to prove his art—by using the craft, materials, and machines for printmaking. Van Rijn could proceed in the progressive steps of printmaking with an easy sense of the whole, mastering the plate-maker's art so as to form a seamless, creative process. Through the art of making etchings and printing them, he could express himself repeatedly in the same way that musicians replay their music and sing their songs—even make variations from print to print, performance to performance, and do it entirely in the complete, self-contained printing studio—furnished with a great wooden press—in his grand house on the Jodenbreestraat.

His studio experiences looped back and illuminated ordinary things. When Rembrandt pondered his favorite seashell (which was a chambered nautilus that had been cut in half to reveal its inner beauty) he was transported like a voyager visiting far off, exotic beaches that were the home of the nautilus. Van Rijn could be carried away as easily as that!

Moreover, he thought he could see—in the lines and swirls seashells—some deeper meaning which he would be able to use in composing his paintings and prints. How could he do it? No one could say; even Rembrandt would not say—even if he could. What? To try to put it into words might ruin the magic! No! Mad? No! Not mad. Besotted with life? Yes, to say that would be correct.

Rembrandt sensed, which is to say, *felt* more than he knew about faraway places and their people. Also he could read the harmonics of the man-made markings, carvings, and decoration on the things that he had collected when, in his times of riches, he had the money and he could collect whatever he fancied. He owned a veritable museum of resources for his art creations.

Those were the salad days of Rembrandt's life. In those times everything looked rosy. Saskia still lived, the money kept flowing in, and he commanded four and five-figure fees for his paintings. Those days were gone forever, and his collection of shells, birds, weapons and regalia from around the globe were gone too—not to mention the loss of his art collection, which was sold for a fraction of its worth to help pay his debts. Yet, that was not enough, and so he lost his house, too.

Was he being punished by God for his sins? He didn't think of himself as a deeply religious man. Any outward sign of his religion was, to him, part of being a fine artist; not that he was a charlatan or hypocrite. His religion was his work, not born out of fear or praise of the Almighty. He feared other men, it was true, and a few women; but not God.

With the variety and strength of the many conflicted religious confessions among the population of Amsterdam, Rembrandt figured that God must be kind. Or, maybe He didn't much care what inhumanity that mankind brought down on humanity.

As for Rembrandt's beliefs, he was a professional, and as a professional, Rembrandt played it safely. As religion goes, Rembrandt was like a chameleon, most of the time considering himself a Calvinist; but there would be days when, on one morning, he would win a painting commission by the good graces of a wealthy Catholic aristocrat, and on the following afternoon, he might be paid to paint a well-to-do Jewish merchant.

Rembrandt's clients came from many income levels and all beliefs. Thus, when it came to his work, he didn't dare mention God, or his opinions, one way or the other. If, as it sometimes happened, a sitter would pose a question or a hint about Rembrandt's religious beliefs or an offhand remark that had to do with the Almighty, then Rembrandt always diverted the topic with, *"Can you please raise your chin, just slightly? Ah, yes, there, that's better."* Any like comment that concerned the task at hand served, and, afterward, the sensitive subject would be forgotten. It always worked.

Maybe Rembrandt was a *Deist*, the closest confession that fit his beliefs. Or, possibly Buddhism (if his philosophical leanings had been recognized in European society of the day) as was practiced among oriental people, stories and news of which came to

Amsterdam borne on the ships of the thriving Dutch trade.

The rituals and strange ways of the "heathens and savages" of the Spice Islands were known to Rembrandt by way of fragments of tales told by masters and commanders of the great Dutch Merchant fleets. Rembrandt bought things from returning sailors—including pictograms and decorations on paper made from plant fibers. The practices they showed interested van Rijn, though he could not say much aloud about his interest in heathen beliefs.

Rembrandt knew about exotic religions through the stories that were connected to the objects in his collection. Discussing these foreign belief systems could lead to trouble in his society; one could be accused of heresy or idolatry. Rembrandt, a painter of the leading figures in Dutch society, had to watch what he said and what he wrote.

There was a clever way he had of working around any risks of expressing or documenting his thoughts. Rembrandt took up a practice of writing miniature notes. In tiny script, using a sharp-tipped silver wire on specially-coated paper, he described insights and ideas that were—sometimes—amazing even to himself. In the act of writing about ideas that popped into his mind, he was as if demon-possessed. Rembrandt had been afraid that the thoughts he wrote down could be incriminating and would be construed as proof of his being insane.

Where did these thoughts—so carefully inscribed on little cut-paper slips—come from? Were they from Heaven or from Hell? Or, was every man possessed with voices-in-the-head, as if he were being dictated to? No man but he would *write* such idiocies on paper; at least, Rembrandt thought that it was unlikely. As he was in his art—in his idiosyncratic act of writing things—he was probably unique in the world. Anyway, he could not stop himself. Van Rijn took the dictations like a mendicant, unable to refuse what his inner thoughts offered to him like alms to a beggar, or like sugar candies to a child.

In Rembrandt's judgment, too much of this kind of thinking is not good for the mind of a man; in the same way as sugar makes you fat and rots your teeth, so, also, too much thinking can drive you to madness.

Thinking strange thoughts is one thing, but writing down the products of such thinking might be worse. However, as van Rijn was unwilling or unable to stop himself from the practice, he had hidden his notes in a secret place. Now, he wished he had them; but they were out of his reach, hidden in the flooring in his old home.

If his notes were discovered, no one would be likely to understand the ideas behind them—his philosophizing—ciphered on tiny pieces of paper. Rembrandt was sure that discovery of his scribbling—if that should happen—would add to the mountainous problems that were already piled up on him today.

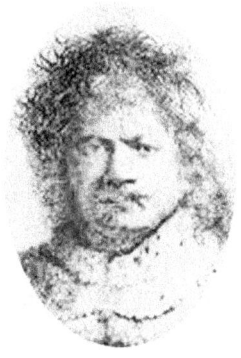

Chapter 18
Rembrandt's Secrets

A voice broke into Rembrandt's meandering inner dialog. "Excuse me, Meneer! We don't open for another hour!" Started, van Rijn dropped his hold on the bars and turned around. David Lingelbach, owner of the Nieuwe Doolhof, stood with the gate key in hand, waiting. When he saw to whom he spoke, he said, "Oh, goedemorgen, Rembrandt! I didn't recognize you from behind."

"Goedemorgen, Meneer Lingelbach. You find me daydreaming. Sorry to be blocking the way." Rembrandt stepped aside to let the owner by. "You are coming to work early, I see."

"Yes." Lingelbach said as he inserted his big key into the lock and turned it. He pushed in the gate to pass through. "There is no rest for the wicked," he quipped, "nor for Master artists, I see."

They were hardly acquainted, so had nothing more to say to one another. Lingelbach went in and shut the gate with a loud clang that made van Rijn wince. The park owner locked the gate from the inside and went on his way. Rembrandt's head throbbed as he watched him walk away and turn a corner. Van Rijn reached his hands up, gripped the bars and pressed his head against the cold bars and in this way recommenced his troubled meditations.

Van Rijn visualized objects he once had collected. It was sad that he no longer had them. In the decorated surfaces of shields from people of New Guinea, in the headdress of a Brazilian Indian, and in the carving on a deer bone from the American colonies, Rembrandt saw a commonality—as if these peoples' design ideas and artistry revealed knowledge of powers beyond the trendy Cartesian logic and religious dogma held in Amsterdam.

Sometimes, as Rembrandt worked at needling the coating on an etching plate, such thoughts would persist and become food for his notes. His hands would be busy with the *real*, and his mind would be busy with the *unreal*. His plates resonated with his imaginings like musical scores and testimonials. Printing them, he could make variations between each one, hand-wiping this one slightly differently than the next one and the one he had printed just before, and then go back into the plate with his needle— bypassing the slow etching steps.

That was at the time when he had his great wooden press, whose long arms of the wooden star-wheel he pushed slowly around, driving the press's purple-hued wood roller so that the entire printing table—wool felt blankets, dampened paper, and inky printing plate—passed through the groaning machine. The roller pushed the moist, pliant paper—so soft and fine—into the ink-filled lines of van Rijn's intaglio plate.

His press was gone now. How he missed his etching studio! Rembrandt visualized his press, where it had been situated, and how the blue-green glaze was worn off the tiled floor in places where he and his printer always stood as they gripped the press' star-wheel spokes.

Rembrandt's secrets lay under some of those tiles, laid with sanded grout. It was the only place he could think of to hide his notes. In solitude and in the night, van Rijn had painstakingly pried some out, gouged a shallow space in the soft wood underlayment, put his notes in and replaced the tiles.

His ideas came, unbidden, at the strangest times. Van Rijn recalled the time words appeared when he was sketching an old beggar, and another time when he was holding the spearhead from the new world, chipped from milk-white flint by a Native American flint-knapper. He would write with a point of fine silver wire on paper coated with white gesso.

The notes that he had left there gave him cause to worry and this mixed with his sense of loss; they nagged at him all the time. The notes' existence was a burden he could not unload— neither on his wife nor on his son as they doubted his reason already.

Van Rijn dared not tell anyone! He feared, too, that when he was in his cups—as he was last night— that he might spill his secret and that would result in incriminating evidence and more grief. For the poor, besieged van Rijn, things would be even worse if that happened. The only solution to the problem was to retrieve the notes before someone else did.

Sometimes Rembrandt would take a long walk and stroll by the mansion, hoping that—by some chance—he would find a way in. At other times he would hire a closed carriage and go park near the mansion, watch and ponder what to do. He spied from a safe distance, hoping for inspiration. He thought no one noticed him haunting the house.

Rembrandt wanted to see those notes once more,

but why? What was in those notes that had seemed important at the time that he was compelled to write them? Why this compulsion? For posterity? *Ha!* Or was it because, intuitively, he thought himself to be smarter with more poignant things to say than he would be able to in his old age?

Is it possible that, as a young man of a score and ten, he was of higher intelligence—or in touch with a higher intelligence—than today as a man of fifty-four? Van Rijn thought, *How long has it been since I had an urge to write down ideas that came cascading forth my mind? Too long! Much, much too long!*

Then again, maybe he did not need to worry about the notes' discovery because—even though he had wrapped the papers in oilskin under the tiles—the floor would no doubt be mopped and wash water would find its way into the packets. They would mold and rot. Eventually the old glazed floor tiles would become so badly cracked and worn that the new owners—the shoemaker and the silk dealer who had bought the house—would replace the tiles.

If that day came, then some workman would find his notes when he ripped up the floor. Rembrandt visualized the worker, chipping and hammering the tiles, discovering the oilskin packets in their little graves. As he would probably be unable to make out their meaning, the worker would think they served merely as padding and so he would fling the packets on a heap of broken tiles and dirt to be carried off in a wheelbarrow. Rembrandt's cornucopia of genius would help build up a new dike, or they would be dumped into the canal and float out to the sea.

Van Rijn felt his hands cramping and he realized that he gripped the iron bars of the gate too tightly and his knuckles were white. He let go and dropped his hands with a long sigh of resignation.

The carillon began to play, announcing the hour, and, further away, other bells rang out—but Rembrandt was not listening to what was going on in the outer world; he was thinking how to get his notes.

From behind Rembrandt, another man's voice spoke, and more loudly: "I say, Rembrandt, you're looking well, old friend."

Snapped back into the present, van Rijn turned. It was a familiar face but at first he could not think of the name; the man was from so far in his past.

"Don't you remember me? It's me, *Jan*. Jan Lievens!" he said. "Surely you haven't forgotten your old comrade-in-arms, van Rijn!"

Rembrandt smiled then. The artist certainly had not been forgotten by Rembrandt. They shook hands. He said, "No, I couldn't forget you, Jan, and never will I! I think about you often, in fact. It's good to see you." After their handshake Rembrandt added, "You're looking well. I understand that you live not far from here." While he spoke he was also calculating, *perhaps now that I am a neighbor, my old studio mate would help me*.

Lievens, who had first met Rembrandt thirty years before, appeared to be better off than Rembrandt if judged by his clothing, which contrasted with Rembrandt's. Everyone—including Jan—knew that Rembrandt could barely scrape by. Jan did well with his painting and lived in a fine house.

"Sorry I can't stay for a talk. My wife had me come and get a sugarloaf for breakfast, and I'm already late, you understand."

Rembrandt nodded and Lievens quickly turned and walked away, as he perceived that Rembrandt was probably about to hit him up for a loan. As he drew further away from his old associate, Jan thought,

Serves him right; he's his own worst enemy. From a distance he turned and, walking backward a few steps, he called, "Good day, old friend," and then he pivoted to continue on his way, his sugarloaf tucked under his arm.

Rembrandt watched Lievens' back for awhile and then he headed toward the *Blue Crown*. He glanced around and saw, coming down the street to his right that his landlord hurried toward him with evident purpose. Rembrandt pretended not to see and made haste to reach his door before his landlord got to him.

"*Meneer van Rijn! A moment, please!*" the man called. Van Rijn stopped, turned and looked around with mock surprise.

"Oh, *Goedemorgen*, Meneer van Leest, I didn't recognize you," Rembrandt lied. "What brings you out so early in the day?" The answer was obvious. Van Rijn's rent was overdue. Hendrickje had reminded him of that last night, and they had argued. Last night was a bad night at the van Rijns'.

"Your rent is overdue, as you know," van Leest said, "But there is another matter that I want to discuss with you—about printing *playing cards*."

Rembrandt frowned and wondered, *Did he say 'printing playing cards'? Did I hear him correctly?*

Rembrandt said, "Playing cards? You should know that I am an etcher, Meneer van Leest, not a wood block printer. And as for cards . . .."

Van Leest cut him off. "I will explain . . . inside." He was an ambitious entrepreneur and he had an offer to make to this renowned artist who—obviously—was down on his luck. "If you will, allow me to come in for a moment." He moved toward the front steps.

Rembrandt was about to fabricate an excuse. The last thing he needed right now was to talk about his rent and, on top of that, printing playing cards—the *speelkaarten* for which van Leest was famous.

It happened at this moment Rembrandt's wife, Hendrickje, open the front door of the house. She was taken aback; she had not expected to see the landlord. Yet, here was van Leest—and no doubt he had come for the rent money. Van Rijn skulked behind him. Her face fell in embarrassment but she managed a tight smile.

"Meneer van Leest! How good it is to see you," she lied; and although she was flustered, she collected herself. "Welcome. Please, won't you come in?"

Van Leest fleetingly thanked her, went up the steps ahead of Rembrandt and entered as Hendrickje held the door open. Van Rijn just stood at the bottom of the steps for a moment and bestowed a scowl on his wife. Then he followed.

***

Naturally Mac, writing at the desk high above in Aboab's upstairs garret, was unaware of the problems besetting the moody, grouchy, down-and-out, hung-over Rembrandt three floors below, as he reluctantly climbed the steps to the door behind the landlord. Even if he had known, Mac could not have guessed that the conversation between Jacques van Leest and Rembrandt van Rijn would, within an hour, determine events that awaited him.

Mac sat, hunkered over his journal in the warm wavering light of a single candle, and concentrated on his message to Faye, should he and his journal ever get back to the future. He tuned out the sounds of Amsterdam as the city came to life—the carillon, the church bells, and the voices of the people down on the street.

Meanwhile, the chambermaid tiptoed politely and

inaudibly up the stairs. She had a towel over one arm and she brought a white basin and pitcher of hot water. She passed through the narrow space behind Mac and walked toward a wash stand in the far corner. Mac sensed her presence and glanced around and saw the chambermaid's back. Aboab had told him that she would come. He returned to his writing so as not to lose his train of thought.

"I'm in a tiny room, and I mean tiny . . ." Mac ignored the girl and continued to write about the garret in a long, wistful message to Faye.

After the maid had set the basin and pitcher on the wash stand, she lingered. Mac was aware that she was still in the room, but the light was too dim to see her clearly or what it was that she was doing. She approached and stood closer to Mac and this drew him to distraction.

Mac wondered, *What is she doing? Waiting for a tip? Nah! Then what?* He turned to see what kept her and saw it was the girl who had been in his bed yesterday morning! Mac's mouth dropped open, struck dumb. She, however, showed no surprise at all at their meeting again and thrust a folded paper out to Mac. He glanced at it and then again at her.

"You!" he finally blurted. The girl flinched and looked down, embarrassed; but still held out the paper. She looked up at him, her eyes wide, and— with a gesture, she urged him to take her paper.

"You're the maid here? You are—*Mahault?"* he asked her, when he recalled the name.

She nodded her head shyly and now looked down at the note she proffered. Recovered from his initial surprise, Mac finally took it. He remembered Aboab had said that this girl could not speak. To read the note, Mac had to turn back and hold it close in to the light of the candle on the desk.

He unfolded it and saw that it was written in a mixture of English sprinkled with Dutch and appeared to have been written with a quill, scripted with a fine hand. The note was quite beautiful, not only for the penmanship of the hand that wrote the note but also because these were the first English words he had seen for days other than his own choppy handwriting in his journal.

The note read: *"This is Mahault. She is a good girl. She works for the widow, Mevrouw Schwarzesherz, but Mahault is not a whore. For Rabbi Fonseca she also works. Trust her. She listens but does not speak. I am her sister. She wants to thank you for the foreign coin. Our family thanks you. You are a kind man."*

Mac turned around in his seat to look back at the girl, but she had already left and without a sound. He wondered, *Didn't Aboab say that she would tell him if breakfast was ready? She's mute, though.* He sighed and thought, *Oh well, no matter.* Mac wanted to finish his journalizing so he turned back to the desk, and soon Mac forgot about Mahault and the note that remained on the desktop.

The natural light in the garret was improving and Mac went on with his message to Faye: *"Aboab, who took me in, is going to introduce me to Rembrandt; at least that's the plan. I guess Rembrandt is out of sorts. People seem to be unsure about him, like something is going on, as if he's in some kind of trouble."*

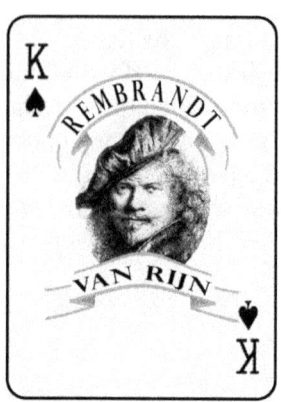

Chapter 19
An Offer to Refuse

At the moment that Mac wrote his thoughts about Rembrandt, down three floors and over in "The Blue Crown"—in the front room—the famous and worried artist, Rembrandt, scratched his head with vigor, his lips pursed, as he and his wife tried to comprehend the proposition that the visitor—his landlord Jacques van Leest, had just laid out.

Van Leest, Amsterdam's leading *speelkaartenmaker*, the playing card maker, had outlined what Rembrandt could only feel was a preposterous idea: *To publish playing cards with Rembrandt's self-portraits!* He was asking himself, *what could van Leest be thinking?*

Did the publisher think that Rembrandt was so far gone that he would resort to the designing of playing cards? To ask Amsterdam's foremost painter to illustrate playing cards would be the same as to ask the city's leading composer, Jan Sweelinck, the revered Oude Kerk organist, to play the carillon at Lingelbach's amusement park! The organist could no more be a carillonneur than Rembrandt could be a playing-card illustrator.

If Sweelinck were still alive, would Lingelbach insult the renowned composer in a comparable way as van Leest was insulting van Rijn? It made Rembrandt fume. He wondered, *What's the world coming to? Is fine art becoming nothing but commercial entertainment? Playing cards, indeed!*

On the other hand, there was the money to consider. If Rembrandt made van Leest's cards, then van Leest would have to compensate him, and it might pay the rent until van Rijn had a real art commission again.

Jacques van Leest's playing-card business' output was famous, and he produced standard cards by the thousands. They were based on the French Rouens and Flemish art, and they sold well; but van Leest wanted fresh ideas. It so happened that the publisher had come across a Rembrandt etching of a man playing cards. Since Rembrandt was known all over Europe (which owed partly to his engravings and etchings) van Leest glimpsed, in this chance encounter with the little card-player etching, an opportunity to produce Rembrandt designer cards. Perhaps, like his etchings, they would sell well also; and Van Leest would call them "artist cards."

Rembrandt and Hendrickje listened as van Leest rambled on enthusiastically and outlined his idea for artist cards. He had not touched the bread and cheese that Hendrickje had brought for him.

The artist raised his hand to his forehead and interrupted the businessman's sales pitch. "Wait, wait, wait," Rembrandt said, and van Leest quieted. "Your cards, Meneer van Leest, are printed with wood blocks. As I said, you need to know that I have only done etchings and engravings on copper plates, printed by the intaglio printing method. I do not carve wood blocks for relief prints. No woodcuts, no; and I am not about to begin now!"

"Yes, Meneer van Rijn, I thought of that and I imagined that you could adapt—"

Rembrandt exploded. "I don't want to adapt! And why should I? No! This is ridiculous!" His blood pressure rose, and his headache worsened. He put his hands to his temples and pressed.

Hendrickje, who had at this point taken a strategic position so that she stood behind van Leest where the publisher could not see her face-making and signals to her husband, vigorously shook her head to remind Rembrandt not to offend their landlord.

Now Hendrickje spoke up from behind their guest and quietly offered, "Meneer van Leest, would you like some tea? I can ask our assistant, Arent, to heat some water."

Rembrandt burst out, "Arent assists *me*, dear wife, and he is not your kitchen help!"

Hendrickje looked away, hurt.

Van Leest answered over his shoulder, "No, thank you Mevrouw van Rijn," and then the publisher tried another approach to the stubborn artist. "Then, make copper plates for the cards, as you wish."

Rembrandt had gained control over his temper and decided to try diplomacy—to play along with their landlord to see where a different response from him might lead them. If there was money to be made in publishing of any kind, it would help.

"Meneer van Leest, I take your proposition in good humor; but, if I did your 'artist cards' and I did them with the etching techniques with which I am most familiar, how would I then print them?"

This question stumped van Leest at first, and he hesitated. It seemed like a pointless question. Then he answered, "On your press, I suppose."

Van Leest's response was met with silence. Behind him Hendrickje took a deep breath and braced herself for the outburst which she knew would come. She had heard Rembrandt's lamentations and raging over his lost press so many times before.

In a frigid voice Rembrandt inquired, "Do you see a press, Meneer van Leest?" and, to underscore that rhetorical question, van Rijn gestured about the room. "Do you see a press?" He waited and van Leest looked confused. Van Rijn's voice rose in pitch as he cried, "I have not had a press for two years! No! No press!"

"I thought—," started van Leest. Then he looked up at Hendrickje and back at Rembrandt. "—I thought that you could keep your press, the means of your income." He looked embarrassed, as he knew that he had brought up memory of the famous bankruptcy and news of the losses that the artist experienced.

Van Leest was at a loss for words. "I am sorry," he said, as he stood up. "But, then again, in that case, maybe—probably there is someone who has a press that you could use. This would be a way to work around the problem!" He smiled at his solution.

Rembrandt snapped: "Do not think that I am going to go begging for someone to let me use their press so that I can print *playing cards*! They would laugh in my face! You insult me! Insult added to injury!" He leapt out of his seat. Instinctively van Leest leaned away and ducked as if he had thought van Rijn was so angry that he might strike him.

Hendrickje interceded, "Rembrandt, please. Be calm!" and she turned to van Leest.

"Meneer, we appreciate your offer, and, also, we apologize for being late with our rent," and then, brightening, she added, "Son Titus is, as a matter of fact, working to secure more business for my husband as we speak. He returns soon, from Leiden."

Rembrandt broke in. "I will do the talking, if you please, Hendrickje Stoffel, *I still wear the pants here*!" He again faced the publisher, and he was now calmed down, and addressed van Leest with measured words. "You know that I must maintain my professional position. Making such small prints . . .," he began, but van Leest interrupted him.

"You *have* made small prints! I have seen. In fact, just recently, at the home of a friend! That is what gave me my idea. It was a small etching, and it was of a man playing cards. You see what I mean? I took that as a premonition, a good sign and an inspiration."

Rembrandt frowned as he recalled the print. It was 1641 when he had made that one—the year Titus was born and about the time that Saskia took a turn for the worse. At that time, when he was making the plate, he broke some of the rules of etching. Van Rijn had scratched and burnished the copper—techniques that were faster than etching to achieve certain dramatic effects. Some people looked askance at his methods and spoke of them as being "unprofessional," and, worse, employed in the service of rendering subjects unfit for an artist of Rembrandt's stature.

If van Leest had heard the criticism, it did not put him off; he continued to describe his vision of the artist cards. "I picture your self-portrait on one side, and, the other side of the card, the . . .," but the artist stopped him.

"No!" Rembrandt retorted. "No, I say. It's inappropriate." Then, calmer and in a cold, professional tone, "Besides, intaglio printing is laborious and requires a master's touch. Your best block printers don't have it. As for me," and here he added weight to his statement in a mannered, hesitating speech: "No . . . Press . . . As . . . I . . . Said. *No press!*"

Van Leest would not be dissuaded. "It would not take a large press to print such small plates as I envision. Isn't there a small press that would serve?"

Before Rembrandt could reply, their conversation was interrupted by someone knocking at the door. Hendrickje stepped away from the two men to see who it was. The two watched her go to the front room.

Rembrandt continued with his lament. "*Large or small*, I have no press at all, nor do I have money to have a small one built. That is all. Good day to you, Meneer van Leest." With a curt, stiff bow, van Rijn turned away and went slowly through a door and closed it.

Displeased, Van Leest was left alone for the moment. Yet, he was not one to give up when he smelled a profit. He was staring at the ceiling, wondering how to salvage his plan when Hendrickje returned. He noticed that she carried a basket covered with a napkin of coarse linen.

Van Leest said, "Mevrouw van Rijn, will you see if you can arrange something? Explain to Titus when he returns, perhaps? Mine is a good business proposition which I have made to Rembrandt. As you are planning your art gallery, I suggest that you—all three of you together—reconsider my offer, and seriously."

At the outset of their rental agreement, van Leest had allowed a provision that the family could use the front room of the house as a family art gallery. Besides this accommodation, he charged a lower rent for the first year—only two-hundred twenty-five guilders. So, in his mind, he was not asking too much of van Rijn to collaborate in this publishing scheme.

He added, "As for the press, Rembrandt can surely locate one to rent, or get capital to have a small one built especially for printing artist cards."

Hendrickje appeared agreeable as van Leest listed ways to remove obstacles to his artist card proposal to Rembrandt, but she had no response. While he talked, the aroma of ginger and cinnamon reached van Leest's nose and became a distraction to him. He sniffed.

"Is this *suikerbrood* I smell? Forgive me, but I detect you have *suikerbrood*." His eyebrows raised, he sniffed again, and with a slight smile, he eyed the basket that Hendrickje held.

Hendrickje said, "Yes, Meneer van Leest, and I would offer you one if these belonged to me, but they are for another friend who kindly agreed to take in our daughter when I go on my errands. Little Cornelia is not well sometimes. Today she could not come to pay her respects, by the way. I am sorry."

"No matter," said van Leest. "How did you come by these loaves? They smell delicious."

"The baker, who lives just next door," Hendrickje replied.

"Oh, of course, Dieners van Catarina! Well, I must go and see if he has any left."

With that, van Leest was on his way to the door. "I'll see myself out, thank you Mevrouw van Rijn. Think on my proposal," he advised her and he added the encouragement, "We must endeavor!"

Once outside, van Leest went straight to Aboab's house and rapped the knocker on the door. In a moment Dieners' voice asked through the low grating, "*Wie het is?*"

"Jacques van Leest, Meneer van Catarina, owner of The Blue Crown next door." The door lock clicked and opened, and Dieners looked up at him, his face all surprise.

Van Leest said, "I learned that you have fresh *suikerbrood*. Have you any that I can buy?"

Dieners grinned. "For you, Meneer van Leest, yes, of course. Always! Come in. Come through to the back, if you don't mind," and he swaggered off through the hallway toward the kitchen.

Van Leest followed. He found Rabbi Aboab sitting at the table in the corner, reading. He closed his book and got up from his seat. "Meneer van Leest! A surprise! Welcome to our home," Aboab said, and he extended his hand and gave him a bow. "You honor our humble kitchen."

"The aroma of Dieners' baking beckoned me," van Leest said. "I was talking business with Rembrandt when Huisvrouw van Rijn received a delivery of *suikerbrood*. I couldn't resist coming to acquire some for myself and my wife."

"And how is Meneer van Rijn today?" Dieners asked from across the kitchen as he selected a loaf for his customer. Aboab shot him a warning look, but Dieners ignored it and dared to add, "Last night he was out of sorts," and he chuckled.

"He is somewhat churlish," van Leest allowed. "We had—I would not say an 'argument'—but a difference regarding a business venture involving printing. It seems the artist is without a printing press. It's so unfortunate, a fine etcher such as van Rijn. I had thought that he and I might embark on an enterprising collaboration." The publisher sighed and eyed the package that Dieners made ready for him. "Too bad. Such a good idea; still . . .," and his words trailed off as Dieners presented him with his loaf.

"That will be two stuivers, if you please," said Dieners. Van Leest produced his purse and paid.

171

Meanwhile, Aboab, with furrowed brow, pondered what he had heard the publisher say about Rembrandt's lack of a press.

"No printing press? Rembrandt has no press?" Aboab asked the publisher to make sure he had heard him correctly.

Nodding his head, van Leest replied, "He lost his press to creditors two years ago. But, you see, I didn't know that and I thought his small prints would make suitable . . . ," he hesitated, ". . . *cards*. As I am sure you know, I publish playing cards."

Dieners snorted as he thought, *He's joking . . . Rembrandt making playing cards?* Too late, he realized by the pointed looks that both Aboab and van Leest directed at him that the publisher was serious. The boy swiped at his nose to cover up his impertinence.

Embarrassed for Dieners, Aboab cleared his throat and redirected the subject. "We have a guest who is interested in printing!" he said, and thus deflected Dieners' slight. Van Leest looked at him and then at Dieners but his face was unreadable. It was quiet for a moment and Dieners turned his back and found something to do at his worktable.

"It is true," Aboab continued. "We are giving room and board to a visitor from the American colonies, a scholar of the printing arts."

"America . . . the colonies? Printing? Oh, well, I should like to meet him some time," said van Leest. "As for my business proposal, hopefully Rembrandt will find a suitable press, a small one, maybe."

Van Leest paused and, with a grin, he added, "Very small indeed. Playing-card size prints would not require a press the size of the one that he owned at his house on the Breestraat. I should think not, anyway! Now I must take my leave. I will be missed if I don't get back soon. Thank you for the *suikerbrood*, Dieners. Good day, Rabbi da Fonseca."

Dieners led the way to show van Leest out. As they reached the door, Mac was on his way down the stairs that sided the hallway. With surprise, van Leest noticed him and instantly realized that this must be the visitor from the American colonies. He did a double take and offered Mac a polite nod. Mac, also taken by surprise, stopped in mid-step to look down at the stranger, and then he nodded back.

Dieners, unaware that Mac was on the steps behind him, had by now opened the door. Van Leest hurried past and repeated his thanks for his purchase.

Dieners closed the front door, and, when he turned, he saw Mac as he was coming down the last few stair steps.

Dieners looked surprised to see Mac up and about and looking well. Their eyes locked a moment before Dieners spoke, unsure of his English so early in the day.

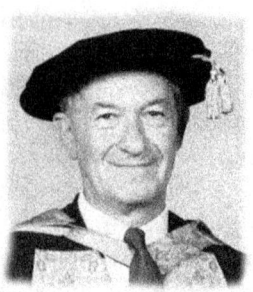

Chapter 20
Simon Says

"Well, here you are!" Dieners said. "Would you like to break your fast?" and, with an odd snicker, he asked, "How did you sleep? Well? I hope!" Without ado, Dieners waved for Mac to follow as the little man trotted through the hall to the kitchen.

Aboab heard their voices as they came. "Time for breakfast, Meneer MacRitchie," Aboab said with a nod toward Mac. "Please sit. Would you like tea?"

"Yes, please," Mac said as he took the chair Aboab offered. He felt glad to be among his new friends and looked forward to his first breakfast of Dutch home cooking. Mac hoped that he would get some of the special bread Aboab referred to, the "sugar loaf."

He was disappointed. Breakfast was not to be the soft-boiled egg and warm baked bread that he pictured a Dutch breakfast should be; and no sugar bread, either. Dieners served Mac a saucer of limp, gray pickled herring in puddle of fish juice, cheese, yesterday's cold bread, and tea. As he served Mac he carried on a conversation, in Dutch, with Rabbi Aboab.

Mac yearned for fresh hot toast and a cup of

Seattle's famous coffee. The smell of the pickled fish was all wrong to him. It was far from what he had been prepared for, and there was no sugar loaf in sight. He sipped his tea, braced himself, and made ready to sample the herring.

The Dutch conversation ended and then Aboab turned to Mac and said, "Excuse us for speaking in Dutch, but we needed to communicate a pressing matter. Something of grave importance has come up which I needed to clarify to Dieners."

Mac did not like to hear mention of the word "grave," but Mac waived the explanation away, saying, "No matter, Rabbi, I understand that it is tedious to use a foreign language when urgent or complicated things are in need of discussion." He wondered if the "grave matter" might involve him. He didn't need issues of gravity that added to his distress.

Aboab returned to his Dutch conversation with Dieners. Mac pretended nonchalance, tried the cheese and bread as he thought of a way to put off eating the pickled herring.

Their conversation came to a conclusion and Aboab said, "We had an unexpected visitor, Meneer MacRitchie. You saw him going out, I think. He is the owner of "The Blue Crown," the house next door, that is, Rembrandt's. The visitor came to buy a loaf of suikerbrood—the last one. Dieners mentioned your visit to him and he was interested in meeting you sometime. He is a publisher."

Mac stopped chewing his bread and wondered if that unexpected visit was what Aboab meant by, "a matter of grave importance." Aboab noticed the concerned look on Mac's face and he assured him, "It's nothing to worry about. However, I must exercise caution because, this man, Jacques van Leest by name, is well-known. He's a business man, a *speelkaartenmaker.* That is, he publishes playing cards. Do you know about such cards?"

Mac, his mouth still full, nodded to acknowledge that, yes, he did.

Now Aboab was silent and suspended his speech. Mac waited for him to say more; Dieners and Mac exchanged looks. It seemed at this moment that the rabbi was at a loss for words. His tensed shoulders dropped; then he took from his pocket the dollar bill Mac had given him and unfolded it, turned it over and over as if it might give him an entree for what he had in mind to say, the words that he knew must be said eventually.

Then Aboab refolded the paper and returned it to his pocket. He saw on Dieners' face the boy's concern. He needed to tell the boy the truth of Mac's origins—his story—and he needed to do it now. Yet, he wondered if he could trust the impetuous boy not to spread the strange fact of Mac's distemporal presence.

"What's the matter, father?" Dieners asked.

"There is something we, that is Meneer MacRitchie and I, have not told you, Dieners my son. Before we do, you must vow absolute secrecy. I dread to put it this way, but it is a matter of life and death. It might mean death for our guest if you tell others what we have, I mean to say, who we have in our home."

Dieners' widened, dark eyes twinkled. He loved intrigues and secrets. Dieners judged that the seriousness of the situation had risen to a climactic point as he watched the rabbi struggle for words to disclose something that must be of momentous importance, and he was about to be a party to it.

At the table, Mac decided this would be a good time to eat the pickled herring. Aboab had switched back to Dutch as he had prepared Dieners. He spoke in a tone like father-to-son, and Dieners nodded. The dwarf understood, and was inspirited to be part of an intrigue cooked up by the older men.

Dieners had known all along that something was up from the things that had happened since yesterday. First there was the bizarre way Mac had arrived, riding alongside the Black Widow, Vrouw Macia Schwarzesherz, in a common wagon. Add to that the so-called "print" that the American thought was worth room and board. Dieners thought that didn't sound like the night-soil collector outside last night, either, and there was the odd way Mahault had acted when she came this morning, and how she acted even more strangely when she left. Dieners had wondered, *What's going on?*

Aboab thought to prepare the boy for what he was going to disclose about Mac. He said, "Dieners, though it was ten years ago, I want you to recall the folk legends, the practices of magic, and other-worldly beliefs held by the natives of Brazil, and those of your African people enslaved there."

Dieners nodded. He remembered, and he answered, "I recall many things, and some were downright evil, too!" Mention of magic intrigued Dieners, and stepped up the boy's attention.

"It will seem—it does seem—that Meneer MacRitchie is the manifestation of such strange phenomena as those stories would have had us to believe," the rabbi continued. Now the rabbi switched to English to reveal Mac's distemporal existence to his unpredictable adopted son. "Dieners, our guest William MacRitchie is from another time. He's from another century. He came here from the future." Aboab had let it all out, at last, and he said no more.

As the two spoke, Mac had been gagging down the tangy pickled fish along with a bite of the tough bread. Then he heard Aboab tell Dieners in English that he was from the future and he was a little afraid how the impetuous Dieners would react to Aboab's disclosure. Would he run out of the house and call everyone to come and see the freak from the future?

Dieners looked over at Mac and Mac looked back at Dieners and Aboab. Smiling weakly, he didn't know whether to apologize for his intrusion into their life or to make excuses. Finally, he managed to say, "Good herring, Dieners!"

Their eyes locked. As Dieners stared at Mac he thought about the magic that he witnessed in Brazil in boyhood—magic of kinds both black and white. He was about to speak, but the moment was interrupted by the door-knocker rapping. Whatever it was he wanted to say would have to wait. The door rapped again but Dieners just stood looking at Mac, and Mac just sat and grinned back.

Aboab said, "Dieners? Do you hear? See who is at the door. Will you?"

Dieners broke eye contact with Mac, turned, and trotted away down the hall. Alone with Aboab for the moment, Mac wanted to sound the rabbi out on what he thought Dieners might do now—or what he might say to the visitor—whoever that might be. What if it was the Pereira brothers, back with a lynch mob to get the foreigner?

Plus, Mac wanted to ask Aboab about Mahault; but this might not be the right moment. There was also the matter of the peeping Pieter who Mac had seen the night before. *What was that about?* Mac wanted to know. On the other hand, Aboab appeared to not know that the Pieter incident happened.

"Rabbi Aboab," Mac began his questions, "The chambermaid, Mahault—she also works for Madam Schwarzesherz, does she not?" The rabbi had turned away after Dieners down the hall, distracted and only half-listening to Mac but also listening to discern who it was that called this early in the day.

"Yes," Aboab vaguely answered Mac. "She's employed at several houses, Vrouw Schwarzesherz', and also next door, where she is Huisvrouw van Rijn's kitchen maid on occasion." Aboab's attention was divided between Mac's inquiries and the conversation between Dieners and whoever it was at the door. "Why do you ask? Is something the matter?"

Mac said, "Probably it is nothing, but it is odd that I can't seem to get free of the Schwarzesherz' house staff—Mahault and, last night I saw her man, Pieter, looking in the window at me."

This got Aboab's attention right away! He was about to respond when they heard the sound of the front door close. Through the hall came Dieners with Rembrandt van Rijn following close behind!

Mac instantly recognized Rembrandt's face as glimpsed riding in the black carriage they met on the street yesterday—the man with the hat and frizzy hair. Awestruck, Mac stood quickly, then he thought to fall down and grovel at the artist's feet; Mac felt oddly vulnerable and thrilled at the same time. He suppressed an urge to gush and giggle.

Dieners announced, "Meneer Rembrandt van Rijn says he needs to consult with you, Rabbi. He says it is urgent."

Surprises came at the rabbi too fast, such as Mac's questions about Mahault and his mention of Pieter in his garden—looking in the window. Why would Mevrouw Schwarzesherz' man come around? Why was Mac interested in Mahault's employment? Why has van Rijn suddenly come?

Rembrandt had seldom visited before. Their

occasional encounters had always been cordial, but for reasons neither social nor for business. What important matter could it be that brought the painter to his house without a word sent ahead, and so early?

Aboab was befuddled but he maintained his outward calm and held back his questions as he remembered his oft-spoken axiom, *Hardly a day breaks that I don't find some amazing thing!*

He greeted Rembrandt in Dutch. "Goedemorgen, neighbor van Rijn! It's good to see you. Welcome to our simple home. Before I learn what matter brings you, allow me to introduce to you our very special guest, who comes all the way from the American colonies."

Mac was benumbed in Rembrandt's presence and ignorant of what Aboab said to Rembrandt in Dutch—although it implied that he was about to be introduced to the artist. Mac wondered if he should bow, but he need not have given it any thought because Rembrandt only glanced at him; he seemed impatient and indifferent and would have ignored Mac. However, out of consideration for Aboab, the artist acknowledged Mac and then stepped forward to pass the obligatory formalities hastily.

"Rembrandt van Rijn, *tot uw dienst*,"[56] he said.

"William Handyside MacRitchie," replied Mac. They shook hands. Mac couldn't find words. He felt he must look idiotic. He tried to say something in Dutch he had picked up in the last couple days, but all that came out of his mouth was, "Um, uh . . .."

Rembrandt frowned, thinking, *I know I've seen that face before*. He squinted at the American. *Maybe down in Leiden, or on the street—?* His gaze at Mac was hard. As they released from the handshake, Mac

---

[56] At your service.

notice that van Rijn's eyes didn't quite align, a condition called "strabismus." One Seattle friend, a painter with this condition, claimed that it gave her an advantage in her artistic style, a way in her vision that other artists didn't have, and she made the most of it. Could it have been true of Rembrandt, also?

"*Spreekt u Nederlands?*"[57] Rembrandt asked Mac, and then he said in English, "But of course, as you are an American colonial, you probably don't speak Dutch, I will speak English. I am at your service, sir. I hope you'll forgive me if I seem hurried. I came to get advice from Rabbi Fonseca. I didn't know he was entertaining."

He paused, then van Rijn feigned with, "I'm sorry. I am intruding, uninvited and unannounced. I didn't think. I can come back . . ." but it was obvious that he wanted to talk to Aboab and without delay. He had no intention of leaving just for the sake of the unexpected outsider, Mac.

Mac said nothing. He couldn't help but to feel that he was in the artist's way. Rabbi Aboab saved the awkward moment and switched back to familiar Dutch and addressed van Rijn.

"No matter, Meneer van Rijn. What can I do for you?" said Aboab, and then he added, "And let us speak English, for at least a moment, because it happens that Meneer MacRitchie is in Amsterdam for the purpose of arranging a meeting with you!"

Van Rijn looked at Mac again and, this time more closely assayed his costume. Mac felt undressed under his scrutiny. He wished for different clothing other than his Flemish costume. By now the expressions of all who regarded him had made Mac acutely aware its style was totally out of place. He

---

[57] Do you speak Dutch?

was embarrassed, especially now.

Rembrandt asked him in English, "Meet me? Who sent you to meet me?" Rembrandt was always on guard because angry creditors—people who never got their due from the bankruptcy settlement, still hounded him to this day. It seemed to Rembrandt that even total strangers looked for opportunities to pester him for money. Had news of his situation reached all the way to America? Was this a foreign agent or another opportunist come to harass him?

To Mac, the artist's haughty manner was like that of other painters he had known—the types that are overly-impressed with themselves. Mac had felt excited about meeting the great artist at first, but now his enthusiasm plummeted. Added to his first impression and disappointment, Mac was hard pressed as to how to answer van Rijn's unseemly question, *'who sent you?'*

Van Rijn tired of waiting. "Whom do you represent? *Who sent you?"* he repeated, and his tone of voice verged on the defensive.

Flustered, Mac chose to lie. He answered, "Simon Schama," and then he elaborated and gave the famed, 20th Century historian's full honorific title:

"*Doctor* Simon Schama, that is."

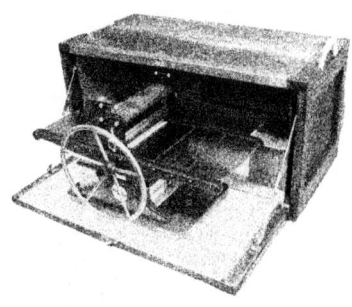

Chapter 21
For Want of A Press

The tone of Mac's reply, claiming that he had
been sent to meet Rembrandt by the renowned British
historian and star of BBC Television series, Simon
Schama, surprised Mac himself. Mac's sudden,
confident response had surprised Rembrandt, which
Mac enjoyed.

"Simon *who*?" Rembrandt asked Mac.

Of course, Rembrandt had never heard of Doctor
Schama—as Mac knew the name to be that of a
renowned history scholar, 300 years in the future.
Mac had read only two of Professor Schama's books,
but one of the books was about Rembrandt, the very
same man who stared—and with open skepticism—at
Mac at the moment of their confrontation.

"Doctor Simon Schama is a distinguished scholar
of history at the *new* Harvard University in
Massachusetts Colony," Mac answered, building on
his momentary advantage over Rembrandt in a game
of one-upmanship.

Rembrandt weighed what Mac had said for a
moment before he replied. "I haven't heard of him.
Scholar, you say? And he has a talent for history, you

think?"

He looked intently at Mac, who had trouble tracking van Rijn's eyes and he thought, *Rembrandt's eyes ARE special, just as Simon Schama mentioned in his book.* Then Rembrandt blinked. As for van Rijn's question of 'Doctor Schama's degree of talent,' Mac suppressed a smile. *I've heard that before. The audacity of some people!* Rembrandt frowned, but Mac sensed that he had gained a little traction in this repartee with Rembrandt. *Knowledge is power!*

Mac met the challenging tone in the artist's question of Schama's degree of talent. "That Doctor Schama has talent in his field would seem to be the case in the regard of the many in his peerage, yes. Yes, I would say that he is highly esteemed." Mac remembered that Schama's 700-page book, *Rembrandt's Eyes,* was regarded as a great achievement by his 20th Century contemporaries.

"*Schama.* Humph!" Rembrandt retorted. "And where is this place, 'Massachusetts Colony'? I've never heard of that, either." Van Rijn was not convinced that Mac was on the up-and-up, but he did not conceal his curiosity about this Doctor Schama, who sent an American colonial to him for reasons that had yet to be explained.

Mac answered, "On the Charles River, where it has been since 1645." He was on a roll, although not quite sure how the names and dates came to mind. In Mac's desperation, his intuition had dredged up the statistics from somewhere in his history lessons and a TV documentary; but if the places and dates weren't exact, it wouldn't matter; and there was a fact in Mac's ploy (if one ignored several hundred interim years) because Schama lectured at Harvard sometime during the 20th Century.

Rembrandt was at a loss, yet his suspicion

persisted. "Why did this *Simon Schama* send you to
me? What is it he expects you to acquire? What do
you want from me?"

Mac said, "Dr. Schama asked only that I deliver
his respects and good wishes, and I came to meet you
and perhaps discuss printing."

Aboab had watched this exchange in silence,
disarmed of his usual aplomb and he was inwardly
confused by Mac's authoritative demeanor, naming
Simon Schama, Harvard University, and such places
as Aboab had never heard of. He intruded carefully
into the joust going between Mac and van Rijn with a
cough and cleared his throat to get their attention.
Both van Rijn and Mac were relieved to disengage
and looked at the rabbi expectantly.

Addressing his neighbor, Aboab said, "Meneer
van Rijn, allow me to say that my guest has an
interesting print, given to me in exchange for lodging.
Let me show it to you." He withdrew Mac's one-
dollar bill and handed it to the artist who, by this
point in the goings-on, looked bewildered.

Rembrandt took the dollar, rubbed his eyes and
squinted closely at the paper bill. After a short time he
looked up at Aboab and then at Mac with wonder.

"This is not a print," he said. "It is too smooth.
Too shiny. Has no texture at all! The paper is too thin.
It may be Chinese, but I doubt it. I am not interested
in this kind of thing." He thrust the bill back to Aboab
as if it was un-clean.

Van Rijn issued a sigh and seemed to relent. He
turned to Mac and said, "We may talk later about
printing, if you wish, since you've come all this way.
I see no harm in talking. Nor do I see any profit, if
truth be told." He hesitated, and he turned to Aboab,
locked him in his gaze, and continued. "However, as
for me, I am no longer able to print, and this is why I

have come to consult with my knowledgeable neighbor here, Rabbi da Fonseca."

Rembrandt shut Mac out by switching to Dutch, as the artist explained the matter that he had come to discuss with Aboab. Coincidentally, Dieners listened in from the other side of the kitchen where he was quietly washing dishes.

Mac was effectively excluded, so he turned and edged toward the hallway. Whether Aboab or Dieners took note of his going or not, Mac did not know—and he did not care. Mac was crestfallen. Years of venerating Rembrandt did not shield him against van Rijn's arrogance and his easy dismissal. The great artist, so highly touted in history books was—in real life—like some other pompous artists that Mac had known in his own day.

He felt humiliated. Mac forgot for the moment that he was out of his time; also he forgot that he was out of his class. Mac was, after all, born a farmer's son and an out-of-work art professor. He had the audacity to worm himself into the good graces of the renowned Rabbi Aboab da Fonseca, and then—in the way of an ambitious opportunist—to try to get an "in" with Rembrandt!

In his game of one-upmanship with the famous artist, Mac had used Simon Schama's name and altered the timetable when Schama was at Harvard University—which was actually 1980. Who did he think he was? It didn't help Mac's self-esteem to remember that Rembrandt was himself low-born, the son of a miller, and therefore was really no higher-born than the farm boy, William MacRitchie.

Mac realized that he was put in his place and given the brush-off by Rembrandt. As he walked downcast from the kitchen to the end of the checkered, black-and-white tiled hallway, the floor took on the look of a giant game board and Mac the losing player. During his slow retreat up the stairway he rationalized: *So what if I met Rembrandt? Big deal!* Mac no longer considered it to be important; yet—like a dark cloud—a depression began to steal over him.

He had trudged only halfway up the first landing when, from the hallway floor below him, he heard Dieners hiss, "Psst! Meneer MacRitchie!" Mac stopped and looked down. The little man was hustling up the stairs to catch up. Mac waited.

"A word," Dieners whispered furtively when he reached Mac. "Let me have a word with you. Let us go on up to the garret and talk." The two went up the rest of the way. By now the light from the window was sufficient to see better, and Mac had not extinguished the oil lamp on the wall, although he had blown out the candle.

"Light the candle," Dieners said.

As Mac took the taper from its holder to light it in the flame of the lamp, Thomas Jefferson's famous words came back to him: "*He who lights his taper at mine, receives light without darkening me.*" Maybe now he could enlighten Dieners. Rembrandt's appearance at the door had interrupted the moment of disclosure regarding Mac's origins to Dieners. Now was the time to tell him everything. Mac made a silent promise to be free with his words to Dieners. Enlightening Dieners would not "darken" Mac—to use Jefferson's words.

The oil-lamp flame took to the candle and the room brightened—and Mac's outlook with it. In Dieners' youthful, impulsive acts, he was a lot like any 21st Century high school kid, yet he seemed much worldlier than any teen Mac had known. The knowledge that Mac possessed, and that he was now

187

prepared to disclose, would not cost Mac knowledge. He thought, *He's curious. Go ahead. Confirm to Dieners that you are a time-traveler. That's probably what he wants to talk about.*

"Explain to me," Dieners said, as Mac re-inserted the candle into the pewter holder on the desk. "Ever since you arrived with that wicked Vrouw Schwarzesherz, I have thought, 'yes I knew it,' you are not who, or what, you say!"

The boy-man gave out with a nervous laugh. "I think, in a way, you and I have something in common, as we are both out of our times and places, you and I, Meneer MacRitchie!"

"Thank you, Meneer van Catarina," Mac said. "I appreciate your friendly tone. You are perceptive. What Aboab told you is truth. Yes it is. Sadly, I do not belong in this time. Maybe it was by black magic or white magic, I cannot tell, I became distemporalized, out of my time and place by hundreds of years."

Dieners' face expressed no surprise, but showed his eagerness. "Then you can enlighten me! You can tell me the future!" Dieners acted more like a teenager who hungered for a good story, especially a story of the kind that foretold the future.

Mac empathized with Dieners; he had been entranced with science fiction and fantasy at Dieners' age, and fictional, fantastic worlds such as J. R. Tolkien's "Middle Earth" and L. Frank Baum's, "The Land of Oz." Those were stories about witches and wizards who had the power to forecast or dramatically change the course of history—all within the bindings of books. However, Mac also knew what the future held for the likes of Dieners and Aboab. It was not a pretty picture and not merely a harmless storybook fable.

Aboab had warned Mac last night—and wisely so, when he said he *did not want to know the future of humanity*. After the experiences that the rabbi had been through when he was a child in Portugal and, later, as a deportee in Brazil, he would rather not know from Mac anything of the future of his tribe.

Dieners was not as cautious as Aboab; and no wonder, considering that Dieners was only sixteen. When Mac was sixteen, he would have loved a close encounter of this kind—to suddenly find a personage who claimed to be a time-traveler would have been like meeting a sorcerer. One might become a sorcerer's apprentice! Yes, the young Mac, a teen like Dieners, would have greatly savored knowing what was yet to be.

However, this knowledge was not enjoyable to Mac and he wanted this experience to be over with. He wanted to go home. At this point Mac had committed to disclose all to Dieners in the spirit of "enlightening" him, but he chose to take a roundabout approach; Mac changed the subject.

He began, "I told you last night—when you were so eager to see what was in my chest—that today I would let you see. I would like to now show you what's in my chest, my *kist.*"

"Excellent!" Dieners had been unable to keep his eyes off the printmaker chest that was on the desktop. He reminded Mac of a kid on his birthday, with his eyes glued on a surprise package.

Mac reached into his costume pants for the key, and unlocked the drop-down door of the chest. His journal, which, early that morning he had returned to its place inside, fell out on to the desktop.

Dieners exclaimed, "A fine book! From the future! May I read it Meneer MacRitchie? I can read a little English. Will you help me?"

"No. It's my journal, my log, and contains personal things—nothing interesting. I'll show you other items, much more interesting ones," he promised. Mac then pulled aside some rags that he kept for cleaning and exposed the five-spoked, stainless steel wheel of his Mini Halfwood etching press.

Dieners gasped, "What's that?" and he climbed up on the chair to get a better view.

Mac answered, "What this is, Meneer Dieners, is my press, my etching press."

Dieners was fixated on the shiny wheel. The press was Mac's pride and joy, his stock-in-trade as a printmaker and teacher. To Mac, Dieners' reaction to seeing the press for the first time was a familiar one. This was the reaction of most people to whom he had shown his press at the dozens of school demonstrations and street fairs. He and Faye called the Mini Halfwood Press, "a traffic-stopper."

Moreover, the press—which was half-wood, half-steel, and precision-machined—was constructed several centuries beyond Dieners' time; therefore it looked all the more awesome to Dieners' eyes than it would to a 21st Century person.

Mac moved aside other contents of the chest so that he could get the machine out into better light on the desktop. The digital camera in its black fabric case was in there, as well as the box of chocolates. The camera reminded Mac of an idea which he quickly pushed aside and thought, *Don't even think of taking a picture! And don't mention the box of chocolates, either! Good grief, it's got Rembrandt's name on the cover.* Mac deftly closed the drop-down door.

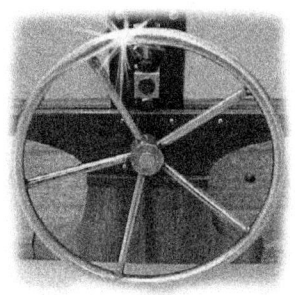

Chapter 22
Miracle Worker

Awed, Dieners opened his mouth and struggled for words as he was obliged to speak English to be understood by Mac, and he struggled to suppress his excitement when he saw Mac's Mini Halfwood Press. Dieners was at a loss, but not for long.

"Rembrandt is in need of a press! That's the reason Rembrandt came just now! It's what's being discussed between my father and Rembrandt downstairs at this very moment!"

"What do you mean?"

"When you walked away a minute ago, you didn't understand that Rembrandt said he came to consult with my father about getting a printing press. That's why he came! He needs money! *From Aboab—to buy a press!*"

"Oh?" Mac had heard them talking when he left them, but they were speaking in Dutch, and that had eliminated him from the proceedings.

"It's true!" Dieners continued. He was excited, and still standing on the chair he looked straight at Mac and said, "Meneer van Rijn needs a press! If that machine is an etching press, as you say it is, then you have to show it to him!" Dieners was gleeful. "He

191

will buy it if . . . ," and before he could finish, a loud bang resounded from downstairs. It was the sound of the front door slamming shut. Rembrandt had left the house, from the sound of it, and not quietly.

Mac thought, *That sounds to me like Rembrandt left in a great huff!*

A few seconds later, Aboab called upstairs from below, "Dieners, son, I need you."

Dieners hesitated and did not answer Aboab's call to come down right away. He was absorbed by the idea that Rembrandt would buy MacRitchie's press and he thought about what he should say or not say to MacRitchie. Dieners wondered if he should tell the rabbi about the press, and should they tell Rembrandt?

He wondered what Meneer MacRitchie was thinking. The American had some strange ways. The American might sell his press, but there was another problem. Everyone in Amsterdam knew that Rembrandt had no money, so the artist wouldn't be able to buy it. On the other hand, Aboab did have money. But why would the rabbi give money to Rembrandt, if the artist's credit was no good? Jews had no respect for people who didn't pay back what they borrowed. Aboab was no fool when it came to money; neither was Dieners. So, charity for Rembrandt was out of the question.

Aboab repeated, "Dieners?"

The press had captured Dieners' imagination. He wanted to learn more about it and maybe have a chance to play with the press. Mac, being from the future, made that prospect even more exciting. Dieners' boyish fascination for mechanical things was that of any teenager, or it was even stronger because Dieners was required to perform in the capacity of a grown man in order to survive in an often hostile world. Dieners sensed that something momentous was about to happen, something that would be set in motion by the appearance of this little printing press.

An opportunity was at hand, and how strangely this opportunity had come about. When Dieners first set eyes on Mac in the company of the "Black Widow," and dressed like a fool wearing that outlandish costume, Dieners had thought the foreigner stuck out, like himself as a dwarf; but the figure of Mac was more pitiable, laughable and, making it worse, he was a foreigner!

From below, and a little nearer, Aboab called again but Dieners was immersed in speculation. When Aboab had told Dieners that Mac was "from the future," it hadn't impressed Dieners all that much. Any time that Dieners' own origins were explained— that he was born in a Santa Catarina *quilombo* in Brazil—it was as if he, Dieners, was from another world and time, too.

MacRitchie and Dieners were not like each other in appearance, a dark dwarf and a regular-sized, old white guy, but what of their difference in appearance when it came to the their status as outsiders? In Amsterdam, if you looked like an alien and you talked like an alien, then you were an alien; and therefore you were regarded with suspicion.

There were footfalls coming up the stairs. Mac looked at Dieners and wondered where the boy's mind was, oblivious that it was dwelling on his presence and the amazing Mini Halfwood press.

Everything was different now because this alien, MacRitchie, had a mysterious object in his printmaker chest. This thing—this "Halfwood Press" as he called it—should eclipse his foreignness. And Dieners was the first one to see it! He knew that this was special.

Aboab would be proud of him. Or, might his

father be angry at yet another new development happening under his roof? Despite Aboab's long experience and wisdom in many things, Dieners knew the rabbi was burdened with responsibilities. The politics of Amsterdam were bad enough, but within the Jewish community there were compounding fears, jealousies and memories of wrong that could neither be forgotten nor forgiven.

The footfalls coming up the stairs were joined by Aboab's voice. He boomed, "Dieners? Didn't you hear me? I called you!" and suddenly there the rabbi stood, at the top of the landing. "I called you to come!"

He was angry, but when Rabbi Aboab's eyes fell upon the press his expression changed; he stared, his eyes fixed on the five spokes and polished, silvery-steel rim of the Halfwood Press. The wheel fairly gleamed like something precious. Instantly, Aboab realized that MacRitchie had opened his chest to Dieners without permission and showed the boy what it contained.

"Rabbi, I'm sorry . . ." Dieners began, and stopped. Aboab ignored him and had already forgotten the boy's delay to come at his bidding because now here was something more important that he would have to deal with! The wheel, a circle of steel with its five shiny spokes, was most compelling.

"And what *is* that?" Aboab asked Mac reprovingly, and he pointed with his long, index finger at the press. It was the first time Mac had been addressed by the rabbi in such accusing manner.

Quietly, Mac replied, "It is a printing press, Rabbi Aboab, and I was about to bring it down to show Rembrandt."

Aboab came closer to get a better look at the machine. Mac knew from his behavior that the rabbi

194

was apprehensive and angry, but when finally Aboab spoke again, his words did nothing to explain why he had reacted to the press in the way that he had.

"It's a good thing you did not. He wanted money, a loan to have a new printing press made."

Then Aboab came to the desk and looked down on the press. "I don't believe that to be a printing press. You confuse me, Meneer MacRitchie! You say that you are a scholar, a historian of printing. It seemed true enough to me; I saw that you have a printing plate. You also carry an extraordinary print—one with two sides filled with arcane symbols and text! Now this machine; it is too much, and you go too far to say that it is a printing press. I find it hard to believe!"

Aboab was exasperated. Dieners and Mac were silent, surprised at the rabbi's words and his distressed state. Aboab took a deep breath, pressed his temples with the tips of his fingers, and gained control of himself.

Aboab resumed speaking and in the way more typical of him. "I am sorry. It seems I am always apologizing to you, meneer, and it's not in my nature to speak as I just did. I forget myself." His gaze left off the press and studied Mac, marvel in his eyes.

"You are strange, Meneer William Handyside MacRitchie. Stranger than anyone I think I've ever met. You remind me of another man I knew who brought out my worst behavior." Aboab recalled a sad memory of the outcast Spinoza, whose name he could not say aloud; but he pushed it aside and went on. "You are from the future. To you, we must seem strange, too, as you seem strange to us."

The rabbi turned to Dieners and said, "Son, tell me, what has Meneer MacRitchie told you about this machine?"

"He said it is a printing press, but I think the machine is too small to be a press, father. Yet, Meneer MacRitchie says it is. Why don't we ask him to prove it?" They spoke English, but they talked about the foreigner and his press as though he were in the other room.

Simultaneously, the two looked at Mac and saw that he smiled at something—even though nothing they had said was anything to be smiled at. Mac smiled because telling him "to prove" the press was a welcome prospect: *Proof, that's the thing, isn't it? The word 'proof' describes every print a printmaker makes. It would be a trial proof, in this case, when you first try printing an as yet un-proven printing plate.* Mac was thinking it had never been so important for him to pull a proof as now. *This trial proof will be apposite, for I am on trial here, too,* he thought, and the prospect made him feel redeemed and happier than he had felt for days.

Mac asserted, "Yes, I can prove it." To be asked—indeed, to be *challenged*, to print, and thus prove what he claimed—what he and his new machine could do. Funny that it had come about this way, this stroke of luck. On this time-trip he had met with challenges by the dung boat skipper, then by that procuress, Vrouw Macia Schwarzesherz, and Rabbi Aboab, of course, and now Dieners. At last, he had a challenge he could handle with aplomb—show off his craft and his Mini Halfwood Press—like theater that he loved. It was a "command performance."

Mac had been intimidated by Rembrandt and driven to lie to gain credibility and the great artist's respect—saying he was sent by Doctor Simon Schama. *Indeed!* That was an embarrassment he'd never live down. What if Schama found out? Well, if Mac should live so long; it would be about three centuries until he could apologize!

Mac's Mini Halfwood etching press would be his redemption. All he had to do was to prove that it worked; he just had to show it in action. He had done it hundreds of times, sometimes for people who had never seen how a printing plate is printed by the intaglio method. To many of the people who saw this, the printmaking art was magical.

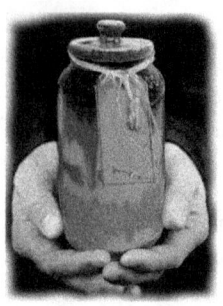

Chapter 23
Strange Gift

Mac was excited to begin. He nodded at his hosts, Aboab and Dieners, who waited for him to do something. He was about to open the drop-down door of the printmaker chest and get what he would need when, suddenly, there was a loud hammering on the door downstairs that startled all three of them. Someone was banging threateningly. The pounding repeated, louder.

Aboab said, "Dieners, go see, please."

Dieners did not move. Instead, he said, "Rabbi, the sound of whoever that is, it's something frightful. Will you please come with me?"

The annoying racket at the door came again. Reluctantly both Aboab and Dieners went down the staircase. Mac waited. He felt a knot of panic form in his stomach, sickening him and he thought, *Am I afraid, too? Or am I feeling that pickled herring I had for breakfast?*

Aboab and Dieners did not reach the door in time to see who had made the tumultuous pounding, which had stopped. They stood for a moment and waited because they had experienced disruptions like this in the past—events such as soldiers on purportedly official business.

There were times when Jew-haters brought impositions, and at other times people who bore a prejudice against the black dwarf descended on the house. In his wisdom, Aboab thought it better to be quiet and not to ask who was at the door at this time. Better to wait.

After some minutes' silence, it seemed safe to open the door. It was quiet. Whoever it was must have given up and gone away, but if Aboab stuck his head outside now, he might catch sight of whoever it had been. He opened the door cautiously and looked down the street, and then—up the street—he saw a wagon headed away. It was the same one in which Mevrouw Schwarzesherz had brought Mac; but it was not she who rode in the wagon this time. Aboab saw—beside the driver (easily recognized by a broad back) that it was Schwarzesherz' bodyguard, the young man Pieter de Wit.

Dieners, by now, had come out to look around. He said, "Father, look! A package!" On the top step was a small package wrapped in a coarse cloth and tied with hemp twine. Aboab hesitated to pick it up; he stood puzzled by the sudden appearance of Vrouw Schwarzesherz' man.

Dieners wasted no time. He scooped up the package and went inside. Aboab closed the door and followed Dieners to the kitchen. They put aside thoughts about the upstairs guest and his press. Mac waited in the garret and his ears strained to interpret from any sounds that he could pick up to signify what happened downstairs.

Mac held his breath. His imagination took flight and he thought, *It is so quiet now. What if someone got in and stabbed Aboab and Dieners?* Then he heard Aboab call up to him: "Meneer MacRitchie, please come down. Put out the candle, if you please, and come down."

Relieved, Mac exhaled and blew out the candle, with a glance at his press and said, "Sorry, Sweetie. I guess the show's been postponed." He still had his bad habit of talking to his press as if it were his pet.

Mac reached the bottom of the steps and went to the kitchen. His hosts waited for him beside the table, upon which there was an opened parcel. The fabric and the twine lay in a little heap, and a paper-wrapped object stood beside it. Aboab held up a gray paper note.

"This note suggests that Mevrouw Schwarzesherz remembers you," Aboab said. Mac wasn't glad to hear it.

Dieners interjected, "Don't trust her, Meneer MacRitchie!" Aboab shushed him, but Dieners had more to say: "She may be all sweet and generous-seeming, but don't fall for her words!" Again Aboab, with a reprimanding look, gestured to Dieners to be quiet.

As Dieners sputtered and fidgeted nervously with his beard, Aboab said, "The woman has sent you this parcel along with a note. I will read it to you, because it is written in Dutch, and she indicated that I should explain it." He glanced at Dieners and then he added, "You should interpret her meaning for yourself."

The rabbi began reading Schwarzesherz' note:
"Rabbi Isaac Aboab da Fonseca, please forward my warm greetings to your guest, William MacRitchie, and extend to him my apologies for my behavior when he was my guest. I acted out of a misunderstanding as to his desires. I meant him no harm, and wish him to hold me harmless. I have sent with my man Pieter a small gift of sweetened fig butter for Meneer MacRitchie, which I hope he will enjoy and remember

me with tolerance and forgive me, once again.
Signed: Macia Schwarzesherz."

"Shall we see the preserves?" Aboab continued, with a gesture toward the gift. Mac removed the paper wrapping. It was a small, brown-glazed ceramic pot, with a wooden stopper fitted tightly, sealed with wax and bound with woven straw.

"Dare I open it?" Mac asked warily. The question was as much to himself as it was for either Aboab or Dieners to answer. It seemed fishy to Mac that Madam Schwarzesherz would send a gift, and he could not easily ignore Dieners' warning.

"It is up to you," Aboab said, "Are you afraid?"

Dieners repeated his warning: "I wouldn't, if I were you, Meneer MacRitchie. The woman is wicked. Her reputation as a sorceress is well-known. I don't know how she has survived this long. Protected by a powerful client—that's what I think." Having had his say, Dieners stopped his invective.

Mac listened, but then said, "Fig butter is what we call 'jam,'" offered Mac, and he thought of it spread on a slice of Dieners' bread. Mac's sweet tooth urged him, *Go ahead!* Back home in his own time, he and Faye enjoyed sweetened fruit spreads on toasted home-made bread almost every day.

Aboab said, "Why not wait? Such a confection is something for reserve in the Jewish community. In Yiddish we say, '*Alevay zol men dos nit darfen,*' which in Dutch means, '*Mischient is er geen gelegenheid om het te,*'[58] and, English, 'may we not have occasion to use it,' because—among the less fortunate—such a delicacy is reserved for invalids."

He paused, reconsidered, and said to Dieners, "Why not store it away, I say. Or, why not use it in a

---

[58] May we not have occasion to use it.

filling for a pastry? We may soon have an occasion to celebrate." Mac studied the little pot and thought about his advice. For Mac the only cause for celebration would be for him to find himself at home.

Dieners asked, "What do you mean, Rabbi? Celebrate what?"

"Earlier, while you and Meneer MacRitchie were upstairs, I was talking with Rembrandt. He had come to ask for a loan—for a printing press. He's contemplating van Leest's business about the cards. I considered it, then I countered with an offer that he could not refuse. He will paint my portrait! And for a fair price."

"How much?" Dieners asked.

"Fifty guilders."

Dieners grinned. "That's not bad," he said. "He must be desperate for money if he's willing to paint for that."

"Yes, but he wasn't pleased by my counter-offer –for the portrait I mean. He left in a bad temper, displeased with the settlement. A short temper seems to be his nature, I have come to believe."

Dieners thought about it. "Fifty guilders—for a Rembrandt portrait? No, I imagine not."

Mac interrupted: "How much would he get, if . . . ?"

Anticipating the question, Dieners didn't wait to let Mac finish. "In better times, Rembrandt would be paid *hundreds* for a portrait, and for large commissions, a thousand." Mac had no idea of the worth of a thousand guilders, and he didn't ask. He thought, *Time will tell.*

They all flinched and turned as someone rapped on the door with measured, even cadence. Aboab thought he had never experienced so many disturbances and interruptions with such frequency in all his days before William MacRitchie appeared!

As it was Dieners' duty, he went to the door to see. He returned with Rembrandt again. The artist was quick to speak, yet humbled and embarrassed by what it was that he had come to say.

"Rabbi da Fonseca," he began, "I am sorry. Sorry for my bad manners and my quick temper when I went a moment ago, and I came back to apologize. Also I am sorry to have to tell you that I cannot fulfill the agreement we made. Hendrickje has wisely pointed out that my painting your portrait for fifty guilders will not be enough to get me a press as well as to pay for the materials and labor required for the painting—plus the etching. I'm sorry to have bothered you."

Having withdrawn the agreement, the artist was ready to turn and go; but Aboab asked him, "What will you do about van Leest's proposal, Meneer van Rijn?"

"Nothing! I will do nothing. Making artist's playing cards was a bizarre idea, anyway. I will cast the problem on to the shoulders of my dear wife, Hendrickje, as she still has hopes to salvage van Leest's absurd plan." Rembrandt was quite doleful, and again he started to take his leave. He paused, and added by way of an explanation, "She and Titus are to be the business minds from now on. I'm done! *Ik kan niet langer af te drukken.*[59] I am finished!"

Van Leest's artist's cards plan would certainly have ended then and there if Mac had not chosen this moment to intercede. Mac had picked up a few Dutch words by now—this being his third day in Amsterdam. Even though he could not understand the details, Mac thought that he understood the gist of it

---

[59] I can no longer print.

when Rembrandt announced, "*Ik kan niet langer af te drukken*," because he got one familiar word: *drukken*. Plus, Rembrandt's tone and body language said plenty—*he could no longer print!*—and he already knew that. To be more certain, and to wedge himself into the conversation, Mac spoke up and asked, "What happened?"

Rembrandt looked at Mac as if he hadn't noticed that he stood there, and he made no reply to Mac's question—like this was none of the American's business as far as Rembrandt was concerned.

Aboab answered Mac: "Meneer van Rijn says there is not enough money in the commission of a portrait of me for him to proceed with an etching project he contemplated. It requires a new printing press, but there is not enough money to have one made—even for a small one."

"He has no etching press?" Mac asked innocently—pretending that Dieners had not told him the facts just a little while ago. Mac made it a point to ask his question referencing van Rijn in the third person, but his eyes were fixed on Rembrandt's.

Rembrandt confirmed it, and he used English for Mac's benefit. "I have no press. I am finished, no longer to be an etcher or a printmaker." He was a little embarrassed to confess it to Mac.

Mac, having shown off his press to Dieners and Aboab a moment before, witnessed in those few minutes—he thought this for the hundredth time— that his Mini Halfwood Press could work magic. It was magic that would work here and now, too, even in such a place and such a time as 17th Century Amsterdam. Mac felt his first, off-putting impression of van Rijn change to empathy, and his emotions yielded to a higher level.

Mac bit his lower lip and calculated, but not for

long. He still held the little brown-glazed jar, Vrouw Schwarzesherz' gift of fig jam, and it reminded him of that woman's turn-of-heart and the warm apology she had sent to him. *Things are starting to go my way*, he thought. The indication of her turnabout boosted his self-esteem and gave Mac courage. The value of what he had to offer would be known, and Rembrandt would see it.

Mac was prepared to speak out and start on a new footing with Rembrandt. Van Rijn had no press and no options; but Mac had the perfect press for what the artist needed, and he was ready to prove to everyone in the house what it could do. Mac's bruised ego and his feelings of rejection by Rembrandt were eclipsed by the idea that Rembrandt's artist's cards could be made with his Mini Halfwood Press.

It was an audacious thought, but a voice inside said, *Go ahead! Make Rembrandt an offer. You will be a miracle worker!*

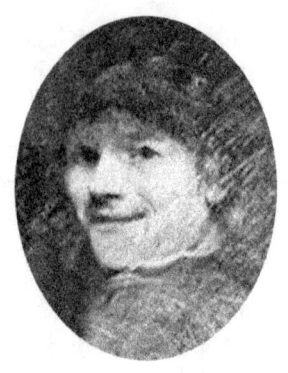

Chapter 24
Rembrandt's Apprentice

When Rembrandt's assistant, Arent de Gelder, was seven years old, his father—who was the papermaker for many of Amsterdam's printers and publishers—took Arent with him on a delivery to Rembrandt van Rijn's printing studio. In those days Rembrandt's press was installed in the basement of his fine mansion, No. 4, Jodenbreestraat.

While he was there, Rembrandt, who was in a benevolent mood, had shown Arent how he wiped an etched plate and printed it on the fine Van Gelder Zonen paper from his father's paper mill. In fact, Rembrandt gave Arent the print because Arent was so attentive. The boy even tried to turn the press' star wheel—something that took two strong men! Arent never forgot that experience. It was a magical, life-changing moment; and Arent still had the print—it pictured a man playing cards.

This print from Rembrandt's plate was one that he had etched in the early 'forties. The plate had been worn almost smooth from so many inkings and wipings, but it still printed. Arent learned that van

Rijn had rejuvenated the plate by scratching into it with a sharp needle in the places where the lines were worn down—a ghost of the original etching.

That was eight years ago. Arent became the artist's assistant when he reached thirteen years of age. His fifteenth birthday was last week and he was still with Rembrandt but his status was little more than that of an indentured slave. This arrangement was supposed to have been temporary. When Arent attained the age of sixteen, he could be one of Rembrandt's apprentices to become a painter—if he had talent—and if his father could afford it.

Although Arent's father was a successful papermaker he was not wealthy; but neither was the de Gelder family poor. When he was little, Arent remembered hearing his father charm his mother by crooning to her his promises of becoming rich, singing the words to her softly:

"*Ik zal van vodden naar rijkdom gaan,*"[60]

. . . which, in English, meant . . .

"*I shall go from rags to riches.*"

. . . and then they would both laugh.

The rags he sang about was linen stuff brought to his paper mill by rag-pickers from all over Amsterdam. The paper maker beat the linen rags to pulp in his wind-powered stamp mill. The pulp eventually came out as creamy-white, strong smooth sheets of paper for printing plates of every description. Thus, the *rags* in the elder de Gelder's little ditty were to bring him riches.

Alas, he was not rich. Not yet.

Some de Gelder papers were used for printing maps of the known world, and some were for reproductions of popular paintings. Rembrandt used

---

[60] I shall go from rags to riches.

the de Gelder paper for his copper plate etchings. At the time, the artist was still painting, printing and teaching in his grand house on the Jodenbreestraat. His prints were not reproductions; they were artworks in their own right.

For years after that visit in 1652, Arent would go to Rembrandt's house regularly and idle around the studio. By and by, van Rijn gave Arent odd jobs to do and paid him a few stuivers. However, when Rembrandt began losing his students and income from teaching—and his other sources waned—van Rijn usually paid Arent nothing.

Arent continued to hang around though, enamored of the lively studio at Rembrandt's house. He thought life there was glamorous and worth the possibility of not getting compensation; something might come up if he persisted long enough. Arent didn't care about money; it was not the most important thing to him. As he had got it into his head to become the heir apparent to the great artist, Arent vowed that he would be loyal to Rembrandt van Rijn to the end!

As the young de Gelder kept pestering his father to buy him a painting apprenticeship with the renowned Rembrandt, his father despaired. Painting was a perilous profession, so thought the elder de Gelder, while papermaking was a booming, growing industry with the skyrocketing publishing trade in books, maps and broadsides. The demand was growing for paper for reproductions of paintings by artists such as Bols, Ruisdael, Hals and Steen—not to mention paper for the unconventional and original prints of Rembrandt van Rijn. He was, at his career peak, one of de Gelder's best customers.

It was a sad day, two years ago, when Rembrandt had been forced to leave his great house and move his little family to the less affluent Rozengracht district. Arent had helped the van Rijn family pack what was left of their property after the insolvency case was finally closed. He had listened in as the notary argued with van Rijn about his last bundles of "Papier van Gelder Zonen." The notary had contended that the paper, along with everything else on his listed property, was to be seized to help settle Rembrandt's debts.

Rembrandt had argued that the van Gelder paper was for his livelihood. His drawings and prints required this fine paper. When Arent saw Rembrandt break down in front of the auditor and cry real tears, it was the best piece of acting he had ever seen anyone do. The official had given in, and they hauled the bundle of paper to the "The Blue Crown" in the Rozengracht.

These days, in their cramped quarters, Rembrandt was unable to find a place for Arent to do his practice work. Arent, by this time, had shown himself to be indispensible. Not having a space of his own in the van Rijn's present living situation made it difficult for Arent, but the de Gelder boy had the kind of patience that was required of a dedicated acolyte of Rembrandt.

Arent knew better than to complain. Years of service to Rembrandt taught him that van Rijn had a short fuse; and it was even shorter these days. Overstep the line and the artist might throw him out. Arent's parents, who were already dubious about their son's future as a painter, would certainly not be sympathetic. Better to grin and bear the situation, Arent believed. Rembrandt's financial affairs could only get better—that was his hope. When you reached rock bottom, the only way to go was up; and Arent would help. He would stick it out until the end, if that's what it took to be a great painter.

On this particular day—Tuesday—the whole van Rijn family was out. Titus, Rembrandt's son, was not yet back from Leiden, and Hendrickje had taken Cornelia to the park. Rembrandt was at the house of the next door neighbor—the Rabbi Aboab's. While everyone was gone, Arent was expected to scrub out the stone sink in the kitchen, but that chore could wait.

With the Master not watching him, Arent planned to get a little more done on his own secret project, which was to draw a still-life. It was not to be an ordinary drawing, however, because it involved a bold technical invention and, if it worked, the results should impress Rembrandt. He would take notice of the boy's genius if this experiment was a success. Maybe then Arent would gain respect from the master.

Rembrandt's method of silverpoint drawing gave Arent his idea. Silverpoint, used by most artists of the day, was nothing new. Drawing with a fine silver wire was a general practice in art studios all over Europe. To do it, paper was coated with warm gesso—which is a mixture of rabbit skin glue, powdered chalk, and white pigment. When the coating dries, an artist can draw on it with a silver wire.

By chance, Arent discovered that he could mark on the gessoed paper with a *copper stuiver*. That's when the idea hit him: *Draw with a copper wire point instead of a point of fine silver!*

Arent had followed the steps of preparing the paper when he was alone on Monday, yesterday. Now the paper was dry and flat so he was ready to make a drawing to confirm his theory. His drawing would serve as a demonstration and proof of his creativity and talent.

From the bottom of his tool kit Arent produced a wooden paintbrush handle, just like Rembrandt's silver point instrument, and in this the lad fixed the end with a copper wire. His drawing made this way would be called "copper point," of course, and Arent would be famous for its invention.

Arent's drawings, though never having received great praise in the past, might then be important as the first *copper point* drawings. Silverpoint drawings were cool gray when they were first executed. With the passage of time, the lines turned to a warmer tone. Compared to silver, the copper cast a greenish tone to Arent's drawing. This drawing would be different than the bluish, turning-to-brown-tones of the silverpoint drawings. "Different" was equated to "original," so, *different is good*. This is what Arent believed made good, original art.

Arent thought that someday his invention would be taken up by Rembrandt. If the master's drawings done in copper point were to receive good notice, then Arent would share in the credit and maybe van Rijn would also share the money when they sold. That would be fair and bring Arent closer to actualizing his life's dream of becoming Rembrandts' protégé. If that happened, it would then follow that Arent's paintings would receive their due respect. It could happen!

In the light of a candelabrum, Arent began to draw an image of a pewter tankard that he placed before him. He was startled when he heard the front door open and slam shut suddenly. Someone came in—it was probably van Rijn!

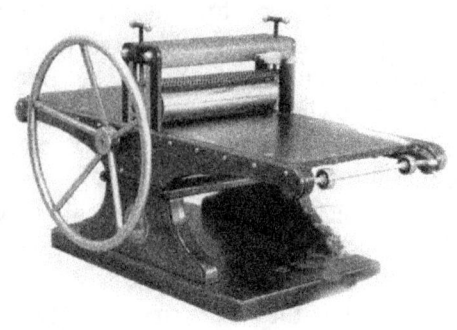

Chapter 25
For want of a Plate

It was Rembrandt, and he called out, "Arent? Where are you? I need you to prepare something!" and he hurried into the room where Arent had started to do his secret drawing. Arent covered what he was doing and fumbled around in his tool kit, trying to appear busy. Rembrandt didn't notice what his assistant was doing and Arent was relieved that his project went unnoticed, but he thought, *That's how it always is these days, 'ignore Arent' despite the advance money that Master van Rijn gets from my father for my apprenticeship, a whole year away!*

Rembrandt seemed to be in a hurry and he was giving Arent orders as he walked in: "We need paper. Some small sheets," he said as he scratched his head to think what he'd need at Aboab's in order to see the American prove his machine—which he claimed was a press—could actually do the job.

"Yes, small pieces—some scraps will do—about five *duim* by seven *duim*.[61] Quickly, now, boy! Cut

---

[61] Literally, "thumb," unit of measurement, about one inch.

them, tear them, it doesn't matter. Then dampen the paper with clean water."

"Dampen papers? What for?" Arent asked.

Rembrandt had seemed to be in a good mood when he came and started giving orders; but now he was suddenly changed. Arent's question had distracted van Rijn as he envisaged the preparations.

"*What for?* Don't ask what for! Just do as I tell you," Rembrandt barked. Then he remembered his indebtedness to the elder de Gelder and the money to be gained if Arent were to start his apprenticeship next year. And besides that, the artist still owed money to the elder de Gelder for paper. Rembrandt back-pedaled now, thinking, *The young de Gelder warrants a better response,* and van Rijn condescended to change his manner. "I mean to say, it will soon be apparent, Meneer de Gelder."

Arent stood up and went to the paper cabinet and withdrew a sheet of the printing paper and began to score, fold and tear the sheet into small rectangles. He was good at estimating the dimensions. Soon he had nine pieces from the original half-sheet.

While Arent was doing this, Rembrandt had disappeared into the back room. He came back demanding, "Where are my plates?" but the instant the words left van Rijn's mouth, he remembered where they had gone. He slapped both his hands to his forehead with a smack! He despaired as he remembered: *They are gone, taken in the bankruptcy settlement!* Over a hundred printing plates, all precious copper, and now they were likely sold to a metal smith's shop as junk.

Rembrandt's plates were probably beaten into pots hanging in someone's kitchen by now. This image made his head hurt. Some plates had been saved by his friend, Clement de Jonghe, but

Rembrandt would never print from them again.

"Argh!" he wailed. "My printing plates, all gone." It was a familiar refrain to Arent's ears. It seemed to him that almost every day van Rijn would remember a special item or a collection of things that he had once owned and that were now someone else's property. He was fond of those objects—all of them. Each one was special, symbolic, and rich with meanings.

Some of the objects might be inanimate, dead, metallic things to anyone else, but they spoke to Rembrandt and held vivid associations and brought stories to his mind. Some of the things had potential as props for paintings. There was an antique gold helmet, for example, various weapons and a pistol. He had a bisected chambered nautilus sea shell and a stuffed Bird of Paradise, and he had paid a lot of money for them.

Rembrandt especially missed his printing plates. The printing plates were not merely devices to replicate images; they were vehicles for ideas in ways that only Rembrandt could fully appreciate. He made them. Every line. Every scratch. Every texture. He invested his energy and alchemy in them. The plates captured time, gave form to periods past and had potential for printing again and again. Van Rijn thought the officials should have let him keep them. He had argued long and hard, but they had laughed at him. The auditor and the notary had said—they jeered—in unison!

"But you have no press, Rembrandt. You have no press. What do you need printing plates for if you have no press?" They thought he was joking and they had laughed at him! Laugh at Rembrandt, dare they? Irreverent fools! He wished he could destroy them all. Arent's voice interrupted van Rijn's inner ranting harangue.

"Master?" The boy had finished preparing the printing papers. He had soaked them, blotted off the excess water, and wrapped the damp sheets in oilskin so that they would not dry out. This "damp book" could keep for hours. Now, Arent was waiting expectantly before Rembrandt, holding out the pack of dampened paper for his inspection.

Rembrandt got hold of himself. He realized that he had lost control of himself in front of the boy as Arent looked at him in a perplexed way. Van Rijn wondered, *Did I blurt aloud my feelings? No, I did not. I must bottle up my feelings and say nothing more about my plates.*

Arent said, "Master van Rijn, I've done as you told me. The paper is dampened, and I have wrapped it." Arent couldn't help but wonder how van Rijn would be able to print without either a plate or a press. Maybe the Master had lost his marbles. What would become of Arent if Rembrandt was mad, as he had heard it rumored?

Arent recalled that Rembrandt had left the house in a depressed and short-tempered state a half-hour ago to see the neighboring rabbi. That was for the second time today—which was unusual. Not that van Rijn didn't like his neighbor—Aboab da Fonseca. Indeed not. As a matter of fact, Rembrandt had many Jewish friends and had painted the portraits of some; and many had posed for figures in Rembrandt's most celebrated religious paintings.

Then, upon his return from his second visit, van Rijn was a changed man, and yet still he was unpredictable. One moment he was excited and the next moment he was forgetful. He agonized over things he had lost and he gave bizarre commands to Arent—such as for him to dampen paper for printing

215

even though there was not a single plate and no printing press with which to carry out the process for which he was told to prepare the paper!

Early that morning, Mevrouw Rembrandt had treated Arent like a kitchen worker—having him make tea for their landlord, Meneer van Leest; and then she ordered him to clean the sink while she was out. As the morning progressed and regardless of these setbacks, Arent thought he could get something done on his drawing experiment. Not so, however. Arent discreetly wondered, *Am I to be a printer's helper for imaginary printing on an imaginary press?* Arent had heard of deluded people who were locked up in the insane asylum for having hallucinations. Maybe this was what was happening. Maybe Rembrandt had gone around the bend.

***

Arent would not find out until days later that, at Aboab's house, in that eventful half-hour preceding, Rembrandt had announced the end of his printmaking because he had no press, and how—at this news— Mac had hurried upstairs and had come back down to the kitchen carrying his printing press in his arms, cradled like a baby. Rembrandt had almost fallen on the floor when he saw the little press!

The Mini Halfwood Press was like nothing van Rijn had ever seen, in spite of his years of collecting mechanical things like automata, nautical, and scientific instruments (to which he thought the press bore a slight resemblance). To Rembrandt, Mac's etching press was like something from a ship navigator's store, with its precision ball bearings, fine-threaded tie-rods, and miniature brass screws set in dark, polished Brazilian hardwood sides. The design was similar to the style of 17th Century handcrafts, yet its engineering was ahead of the times. The press had none of the bulky weightiness of current industrial printing presses in the Dutch Republic.

Again, van Rijn was reminded of the treasured items he had acquired in his collecting days. How he would like to own this thing—this "Halfwood press"—as the American had referred to it. Rembrandt coveted the press; he thought, *With a press like that, I could take up my etching again!*

Then van Rijn remembered why he had come to Aboab's house earlier that day, which was about Jacques van Leest's proposal for printing artist's playing cards. Rembrandt told everyone to wait; he would not take long to get some paper that the American said he would need. Van Rijn's hopes were re-ignited and he went immediately back to his house to have Arent get the paper ready.

The three waited in the kitchen, expecting the artist to return any moment with the paper. Mac was nervous. He thought, *I haven't felt so full of anticipation since, well, since I was a college student in the 1960s!* That was when he initially pulled proofs of his first drypoint prints in Mr. Haines' etching class.

In those days—decades ago, Mac felt edgy like this before a critique by his art professor. He imagined what possibilities might open up in the critique, and his creativity brightened in the interaction with the professor and the other students. Those were heady days.

After college, Mac had become an art professor and specialized in printmaking. His years as an institutionalized artist jaded him as he felt obliged to play the role of art judge in front of cloistered art

217

students. He felt the core creativity of the printmaking experience fading because printmaking, which had been a creative process for him, had become constrained and predictable— neatly defined, packaged and bound by the university curriculum.

Having learned all the tricks of printmaking techniques, Mac had gone backstage, as it were, where he found that the mechanics of the institution "flat-lined" the highs that he had experienced as a young, *learning* artist and teacher. The magic was leeched out of discovery and teaching the art and craft of printmaking. In place of true creativity, teaching had become role-play. The realization had hit him one memorable day when he showed his class a portfolio of prints by his former students and one student had asked, in front of everyone: "How come your students' work five years ago is better than what we do today?"

She was right. He had experienced burn-out. That's what he thought it amounted to. He had attained the rank of full professor, true enough; but his teaching had peaked somewhere along the way. Teaching and research and sharing new things about printmaking with his students had been thrilling; but now the thrill was gone. He had frozen up inside and he thought, *You were a better teacher before. Better than you are today. "Before" was as good as it gets. "Before" was your Golden Age.*

Not long after the encounter with that prescient student, Mac left the university and became a press designer. Yet he still searched for the source of an original printmaking experience like that which had changed his life at an early age.

Mac had wondered, *Can I ever again find true art in printmaking?* Gone was the visceral *"Aha!"* of self-actualization that he experienced as a student in

218

his first printmaking class. Printmaking in the late 20th Century had become cultish, more focused on special effects, mechanical reproduction, consumer-driven, industrial-scale and dominated by people obsessed with money and power.

Then came computer graphics, and printmaking was subsumed into digital reproduction technology and became ever more commoditized and disconnected from old-world, hands-on, high-touch printmaking. What fun was that? Mac still thought that the ten digits of his two hands were capable of making more interesting things than what the trillions of digits computers processed in graphics and multimedia software—prints made with just one finger selecting a "print" icon on a computer screen.

Now Mac felt that he had fallen down a rabbit hole into a distemporal drama. His etching press sat on a table in the kitchen of a famous Jewish rabbi and with a sixteen-year old African dwarf watching; and—minutes from now—Mac would print a proof for their benefit and for the good of one of the world's most famous artists in printmaking history, Rembrandt Hermanszoon van Rijn!

This prospect made Mac's head spin. It sure wasn't an etching class critique! As he looked around and mentally prepared what he would need to get ready, out of the corner of his eye he glimpsed a movement outside the window.

Mac glanced up to see what the movement was, and he gasped at what he saw!

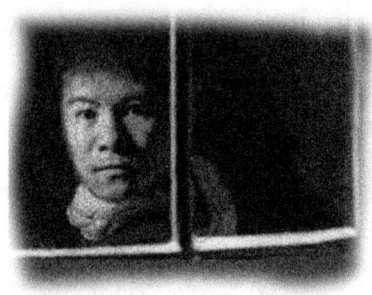

Chapter 26
Peeping Pieter

In the cold light of the day, there was no mistake this time: The peeping Pieter spied on them through the window as he had the night before!

Instantly Aboab noticed Mac's look of shock. "Are you all right, Meneer MacRitchie?" Aboab asked him. The rabbi stood with his back to the window, so he couldn't see until he turned and looked around. He saw Pieter, too, as the young man turned away to leave the yard. Aboab hurried to the door, unlatched the top half and swung it out. The half-door hit the wall with a bang. It was the first time Mac noticed the door was a real Dutch door that was divided in the middle.

"*Wat doe je hier? Wat wil je?*"[62] Aboab shouted. Pieter was already halfway along the garden path striding toward the back gate. He looked back and said something to Aboab, an answer in a tone which—to Mac's ears—sounded dismissive. Then, out the opening Pieter went and the gate shut behind him with a thump. Aboab stood, puzzled for a moment. With a sigh he brought the top half of the

---

[62] What are you doing here? What do you want?

door back, closed and locked it. His face showed concern as he turned back and spoke.

"This is not good," he said, to no one in particular. "He has seen what you are showing us, Meneer MacRitchie, your Halfwood press as you call it. He was sent by Mevrouw Schwarzesherz, I am sure. He would not have done this on his own." Aboab stroked his full, fluffy beard and pondered. "First Pieter delivers a gift, and next he spies on us. He will report what he has seen to the woman. I think she has a peculiar fixation on you, Meneer MacRitchie." Aboab tilted his head inquiringly and asked Mac, "Have you any idea why she is interested in you? Is it money? Or this machine?"

Mac speculated and accounted for his debt to the Madam. "It might be that she resents me. She found me in trouble on the wharf. She gave me a room for the night." Mac skipped the part about the girl in his bed. "And she fed me, twice, at her expense, and she brought me here. So, perhaps she wants compensation. But I have no Dutch money." Mac thought one other thing but did not add this: *This is not the entire story—more likely it's that stunt I pulled on her with my debit card.*

"She is strange in her ways. I think it is revenge that she wants," Mac allowed.

"Revenge? Really! You?" exclaimed Aboab, surprised to hear Mac's suggestion. "What for?"

"I frightened her," Mac said hesitantly, "with a realistic image of a bird. I scared her. She was making threats to me, since I had no gold," he explained. He could hardly keep from smiling at his recollection of Madam Schwarzesherz' reaction when she saw the hologram bird on his debit card.

"She thinks I am a sorcerer," Mac concluded. "And I led her on. I let her think I had magic powers and I took advantage of her superstitions. I showed her an image of a bird and she was terrified, something about, 'the hand that gives the bird.'"

Dieners snorted and interjected, "A sorcerer? You? Aha! These Ashkenazim are full of superstitions!"

"Enough of that, boy!" Aboab shouted at Dieners in an authoritarian tone that surprised Mac.

Dieners was about to say more when there came a clacking of the rapper on the door. This moment was charged with mysteries: the curious, peeping Pieter, Judaic cultural factors (which Mac did not understand) and Mac's persisting sense of distorted time and on edge; and then—as happened at regular intervals—someone knocks on the door! He hoped it would be Rembrandt returning. Dieners went to answer.

"Meneer van Rijn is back," announced Dieners as he returned with Rembrandt behind him.

"I have paper, as you asked, but I have no plate," said Rembrandt. He plopped a small oil-cloth parcel on the table and gave out with a long, dejected sigh. "No damned plate."

Aboab said, "Meneer MacRitchie, you have a plate, the one you showed me. Won't it suffice?"

"It will! I'll get it," Mac said, and he sprinted through the checkered hallway—this time feeling like a winner—and took to the stairs. Behind him he heard the rabbi and Rembrandt conversing in Dutch. As Mac climbed the stairs he mentally rehearsed his moves: *Ink the plate, wipe the plate—did he have everything he needed?* He couldn't remember for sure, but Mac's printmaker chest was supposed to have it all inside. *Ink?* Yes. *Tarlatan?* Yes. Mac was almost out of breath when he reached the garret as he had gone up the stairs so fast. He hadn't been so excited about pulling a proof since he could not remember when.

Mac knew that the old, blackened plate to which Aboab had made reference would not do, however, as it was still coated. Mac could not ink and print it in that condition. There would be no time to clean it even if he had some strong solvent.

To Mac, his printmaker chest—sitting on the desktop bereft of the press, looked forlorn. He rummaged around inside it and found that the only plate in the chest was one of his so-called "test" plates, which was a blank plate and not yet etched for printing! The edges were beveled, but the surface was as yet un-marked, polished smooth, ready for an acid resist for etching or to engrave directly. Its surface had no texture for inking and printing intaglio, no image, no anything. There would be no time for Mac to do a fast drypoint drawing on it, either.

Mac badly wanted to impress Rembrandt, and he didn't want to risk using the old, coated plate in its present condition. Mac never kept solvents in the chest because of the risk of its leaking. He wished he had some lacquer thinner now to finish cleaning the plate; lacquer thinner had probably not been invented, Mac figured.

Somehow, anyway, he must prove to van Rijn that his Mini Halfwood press really worked. "I'll have to wing it," Mac muttered aloud as he once again opened the drop-down door and took out one of the chest's small drawers that contained his test plate. "It'll have to do. I can make a monotype," he mumbled as he checked the tube of etching ink. "I won't take the chest, just this drawer, and not the camera! Oh! And, not the chocolates! What would Rembrandt think?" Mac's self-talk tended to get worse at times when he was under stress. "Especially not those things!"

Who knows what would happen if the three who waited downstairs saw the items that had crossed over 300 years of time with Mac? It could be catastrophic—even life-threatening. People of the 17th Century were, to Mac, full of dogmatic canon and mysticism and not long out of the dark ages and the Spanish inquisitions. He might be burned at the stake for the witchcraft they would find manifest in his digital camera! As for chocolate, it was known only to new-world natives of South America as a drink they made from cacao—not the dark squares of exquisite goodness in the fancy, bright red *Rembrandt's Chocolates* box tucked inside the chest.

Taking only the plate and materials necessary in one of the small drawers of his printmaker chest, Mac went downstairs to the kitchen. He thought of his slogan, *"Everything you need,"* and he felt like a sideshow magician as he started his printmaking routine.

He had done this so many times before. To Mac it was a feeling like getting ready to sing and play a favorite song that he knew by heart. Setting up to print was a habit with Mac. He put the polished, blank plate on the table and unscrewed the cap of the tube of his etching ink and squeezed the black ink on to the plate. To those watching, it probably looked like a fat black worm.

"My God!" exclaimed Rembrandt. "What is *that*?" In a flash Mac realized that lead tubes for paint and ink would not have been invented yet, and not for about two centuries in the future.

Mac thought fast and explained, "Colonial lead tubing." His words met with astonished silence and he added nonchalantly, "Good for carrying printing ink for use on ocean voyages. It was invented in the laboratories at Harvard." Everyone in the audience believed him and they were impressed.

"Meneer MacRitchie has many things that we, here in the Motherland, have yet to learn about," Aboab put in. "Apparently these American colonists have had to invent a number of things in order to survive in the new world." Cautiously, Aboab wondered aloud, "It makes me wonder, *Will they surpass us in printing technologies?*"

Mac was rubbing ink all over the copper plate, using a tightly rolled piece of felt, daubing the black, sticky ink and painting a tonal image of a face. He used the felt stump like a stubby brush and made lines in the tones with his fingernail. He started creating a likeness of Rembrandt, an image that van Rijn himself seemed to be fond of making—self-portraits that Mac had seen reproduced many times. He improvised his monotype, glancing at the famous man who was not four feet away from him. Mac was also going by memory of his portraits.

As Aboab, Dieners and Rembrandt watched intrigued, the carillonneur across the street began to play a hymn. The sound of the music transported the romantic Mac and he pictured the drama that unfolded. He saw himself as if in a movie. He was onscreen—not just watching from the dark with everyone in the audience—but as the star and the carillon music was the soundtrack. The famous Rembrandt, the renowned Aboab, and the garrulous, improbable Dieners stood by as, to Mac, the kitchen was transformed into a soundstage simply by the addition of song!

Heavenly music had set off a romantic specter and cast a dream-like setting over Mac's well-practiced printmaking act. Enraptured and lost in the moment, Mac unconsciously let his jaw go slack and—as can happen to anyone—Mac drooled.

"Oops," Mac said, with a hasty swipe at his chin to catch the spittle. The others politely pretended that they hadn't noticed. Unabashed, Mac announced: "And now I'm ready to print."

From out of the drawer-box Mac took out and unrolled two, foot-long felt blankets, stacked them on the press bed and tucked the leading end under the top steel roller. He twisted the press' adjustment screws which forced the top roller down on the felt blankets' end. Next he took the loose end of the felts and folded it over the wooden cross-piece above the press' top roller. Then he put his little monotype portrait on the press bed with the sticky ink-side up. All was ready.

Rembrandt anticipated what Mac needed next and opened his parcel of damp paper. "What kind of paper is that?" Mac asked Rembrandt casually.

"Van Gelder," Rembrandt replied. Mac knew that name. In the 20th Century, a *Van Gelder Zonen Paper Company* would be, in his time, one of the largest paper manufacturers in the world. In fact, Mac himself had used that paper; but, wisely, he chose not to mention it as he placed the damp, soft paper on the plate and laid the felts back on the press bed, covering the plate and paper. Finally, he took the wheel and began to turn it.

The mere touch of the steel wheel was a pleasant thrill and he recalled the many times he had turned it—his yet-to-be, his *future* life. While he continued to slowly turn the wheel, Mac's thoughts reached out and touched something in his true, 20th Century time; and yet, oddly, at this moment Mac was glad to be in the 17th Century.

One more turn of the wheel and a gentle thump indicated that the plate and paper had passed all the way under the top pressure roller and dropped off the plate's following edge. Mac lifted back the felt blankets and revealed the paper and the plate's embossment impressed in the paper. The others, full of anticipation, leaned in for a closer look.

He was about to pick and lift the corner of the paper to pull the proof when the door rapper echoed down the hall. Mac stopped and held off pulling the proof; he didn't know whether to go ahead and lift the paper or should he wait because—almost as one—his audience had straightened, turned their heads and looked toward the front door. It had broken the spell and the show was over, apparently, except for the climax.

"Who could that be?" Dieners said indifferently, and he turned back and watched for Mac to pull the proof. The boy was greatly intrigued and ignored the door.

"It's likely to be Daniel Pinto," said Aboab. "He sent word that he would be coming today, but I didn't expect him this early." Aboab gestured toward the door, "Dieners? Will you?"

Dieners, with evident reluctance, turned and strolled down the hall, disappointed because he would rather have stayed to witness Mac's moment of truth—the proof. He stopped when Rembrandt hissed at him and, in a whisper just loud enough to hear, stammered, "W . . . wait, *wait*, Dieners, if you will!" Dieners turned around as van Rijn, in a lowered voice and speaking in Dutch, asked Aboab, "You say *Pinto*? *My old neighbor from the Jodenbreestraat?* He's coming *here*?"

Aboab hesitated, then nodded and said quietly, "Yes, the same: *Daniel* Pinto."

"Oh dear!" said Rembrandt, in a nervous manner that suggested that Daniel Pinto was someone who van Rijn did not want to encounter.

The knocker rapped again. Mac was confused and unsure what to do—pull the proof or hold off? Would his monotype turn out like he expected? What's happening between Rembrandt and Aboab? What are they saying? He was shut out of their exchange.

Suspense reigned. Aboab wondered, *Why is Rembrandt suddenly acting so peculiarly at Daniel Pinto's arrival?*

From the other end of the hall they heard the knocker again, followed by Dieners' customary, "*Wie is het?*"[63]

---

[63] Who is it?

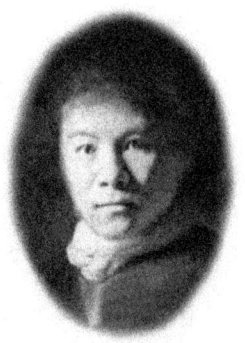

Chapter 27
House Call

Pieter de Wit hated his job. It was like slavery, as he had been indentured to Mevrouw Schwarzesherz at sixteen. He still had three years left to finish the old woman's dirty work and subterfuge—like the kind she had made him do today. He was ashamed of himself for spying on the good Rabbi Aboab.

He was glad in a way that Aboab had spotted him, because it meant that Pieter had been caught in an unlawful act so maybe the rabbi would report him and then Mevrouw Schwarzesherz would have to account for the trespass since Pieter was her responsibility.

It wasn't likely that the authorities would do anything, however. The Black Widow could get away with murder. He knew that. Oh yes, Pieter knew. He had eyes and ears and he could tell of her despicable deeds. No one ever asked him, however.

As Pieter made his way back to Mevrouw Schwarzesherz' home (her lair would be a better name for her house of dark repute), Pieter recalled all the good things that she had laid to waste; and he remembered that strange man the other day—that innocent, old one from Scotland—and Pieter figured that the foreigner was lucky to have escaped with his life.

Whatever it was that the Scotsman had said, or had shown to Mevrouw Schwarzesherz, it had scared her like never before. She had met her match that time! Pieter grinned at how she shrieked as he listened outside the door. What sorcery that strange little man must have demonstrated. Her wailing and carrying on about, *"The hand that gives the bird,"* showed Pieter that the woman was full of superstitious humbug.

Earlier, Pieter had glimpsed only odd, brightly colored cards the visitor had in his purse—nothing frightening or magical. He had not been the least bit curious. Now he wondered, *What was the power that could give the old witch a jolt and transform her like that?* He would like to know.

Pieter was not under the spell of Mevrouw Schwarzesherz as many other people were. He wasn't Jewish, for one thing, so half the time he didn't know what she jabbered about in that Polish accent of hers. So, whatever power it was that she had in the minds of her people meant nothing at all to him.

There were many times he wished her dead, and he felt no shame in thinking it. He had many opportunities to carry out the wish himself. He had the strength for it, as he had grown to be as strong as he remembered his father had been; but what use would it be if he killed Mevrouw Schwarzesherz? He would be hanged, and his poor, widowed mother would die of shame.

Pieter was stuck in the house of the Black Widow for at least three more years, and under her thumb. After that, he would sign up as an able seaman and sail away to the Spice Islands on a great Dutch Merchantman. That is what his father had done. He had been gone for ten years now, and everyone except his mother presumed that he was lost.

Someday, finished with Vrouw Schwarzesherz, Pieter would take his father's place on the high seas and he would bring riches back to Amsterdam for his mother and thus realize his father's dream. He knew he could, grown as big a man as his father.

Pieter was one of those young men who—even at sixteen when Mevrouw Schwarzesherz took him— was big for his age and he had the face of an older man. By the age of twenty, he weighed around two-hundred *ponds*[64] and was over six-feet tall. People went around him when they met him on the street. As he was self-conscious of his height, Pieter tended to walk with a stoop, hunched over, which added to his hulking, menacing appearance.

In actual fact, Pieter was a gentle soul. Nevertheless, no one challenged him. Not only was he big, but most people were aware that he was the property of Vrouw Macia Schwarzesherz. No one messed with The Black Widow or anyone or anything having to do with her. People took Pieter to be her bodyguard, and gave him wide berth.

As he returned to the Schwarzesherz house, Pieter decided that in his report he would not include every detail of his visit, nor that they had seen him when he looked in the rabbi's window. She wouldn't like it if Pieter told her that he'd been seen by the Scotsman and the rabbi.

Vrouw Schwarzesherz had acted strangely since Sunday. She was up to something and Pieter wondered what it could be. On Monday she had

---

[64] Pound, 500 grams compares to pound of 454 grams.

busied herself in her secret room full of bottles and jars, cooking up something. Then she had made a batch of sweet fruit preserves.

Today she had sent Pieter to take a package to the rabbi's door; and now she would be eager to question him and to know how they had received it. Pieter hoped that the rabbi would raise a stink. If he reported Pieter and sent the city guards to question Mevrouw Schwarzesherz, then she might get scared and stop whatever evil it was that she was about.

The Black Widow was an embarrassment to Pieter and his poor mother; but nothing could be done about it. He was resigned to comply. By the time he reached her front door, he was thoroughly depressed. When Pieter went into the house, Vrouw Schwarzesherz was impatient to get his report, as if it were uppermost on her mind.

"Well, Pieter?" she demanded. "What did you see?"

"Nothing."

"You saw something, surely! Tell me. Was he eating?"

"No. They were there. He was there. No package."

"How did he look?"

"Who?"

Pieter played dumb. At times like this it seemed to be his best strategy—to act dumb—a ruse that he often tried to avoid responsibility for the bad things Vrouw Schwarzesherz expected of him. She couldn't do anything about it if he was dumb, could she?

Vrouw Schwarzesherz shouted, "The visitor! You dumb-head! You know who—the Scotsman! How did he look? Did he look sick?"

She called him a dumb-head to his face many times—so many times that he wondered if he *was* dumb. When he asked his mother, she assured him, "No, Pieter, you are not dumb. You're as smart as anyone." She had told him many times, with an air of confidence that made him feel better. His mother always told the truth, and she was always right.

Pieter shrugged as he stood before Vrouw Schwarzesherz and stared down at his boots and recollected what he had seen through the window of the rabbi's kitchen.

"He had a thing. He had a machine. They were looking at it. That's all I saw," Pieter mumbled.

"A machine? What kind of a machine?"

"I dunno. A thing. A wheel thing."

"A wheel? Oh, what's the use! You are stupid. A wheel machine indeed! *A curse on him!*" Hearing this Pieter bowed his head and hardened himself—like a turtle pulls into its shell. The Black Widow always started out with those words, "a curse on him," when she was in a dark rage and readying to cast spells at someone. She was livid.

Pieter knew the routine; nervously he took a small step back and hoped that she would tell him to leave the room—leave here and spare him witnessing her Black Widow's obscene and unnatural rites. He hated being in the same room with her, but he dared not go without her permission.

But as she began, she forgot about Pieter. She closed her eyes and tucked her chin close to her throat so that she bowed her head at the floor. She began to rock slowly back and forth on her heels and toes. She flared her arms slightly out from her waist and locked her elbows, splayed her bejeweled fingers, and pointed them down. When she began to speak, she used a false baritone voice like a man's.

"I curse him! Cursed be he by day and cursed be he by night!" she started in on the hapless Scotsman,

Mac.

Pieter stared at the floor and looked hard at the details of the wood construction. He traced the grain of the wood planks and focused on the wood pins joining the ends of the boards and any other distracting detail he could see to help tune out her words. A tiny speck of a spider crept out from under the edge of a rug and Pieter watched its progress as it crossed the floor. All the while, the old woman droned on; and Pieter wished he were that spider.

"Cursed be he when he lies down and cursed be he when he rises up! Cursed be he when he goes out and cursed be he when he comes in! I will not spare him. I will smoke and drink against him and all the curses I know shall lie upon him. He shall die for pointing his evil image in my face! Eat what I have prepared, cursed man; taste the sweetness of my fig delight, then die with my curse heavy upon your soul!"

She ended with a low, "Hmmm." She took a deep breath in and repeated, "Hmmm." Then she stood still, deep in thought, her face waxen and unreadable. Her eyes remained closed.

Pieter frowned when he thought about the phrase with which she concluded her cursing. While this was not the first time he had heard the curse—and not the first time he had heard the Black Widow conjure injury or death for someone she had it in for—this time was different. He wondered, *What was this 'fig sweet' thing all about? What was that?* This was a new twist in her horrid lines that Pieter never heard before.

Finished with her throaty hum, Mevrouw Schwarzesherz opened her eyes, raised her face and found Pieter was yet standing there, still as a post. She had forgotten that he remained in the room and she scolded, "Get out, you dumb oaf!"

Pieter was happy to leave. He issued a long sigh into the dimly-lit hall as he shut the door behind himself. He turned and saw that the silent maid, Mahault, stood near the door. She looked frightened; her eyes were wide and apprehensive. She had heard the Black Widow, no doubt. Pieter pretended not to be concerned and he trudged heavy-footed to the end of the hallway, went down the stairs and retreated to his corner in the cellar. He wanted to withdraw into himself.

He wanted to sleep.

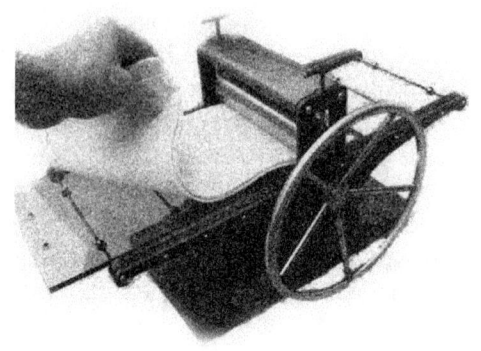

Chapter 28
Great Escape

Rabbi Aboab, with lowered voice, ordered
Dieners to stall awhile by asking the visitor to wait.
Acting quickly, the rabbi took a cloth covering from
the top of a hallway table and draped it over the press.
Mac's monotype, which he had not yet pulled, still
lay out of sight on the press' bed under the covering.
While Aboab was doing this, Mac and Rembrandt
stood aside and watched in wonderment.

Van Rijn was uneasy, and he glanced at the door
now and then. The rabbi shot a knowing look at
Rembrandt and lowered his voice as he explained in
Dutch, "Daniel Pinto sent word yesterday that he
wanted to consult with me on behalf of his neighbor,
Samuel Geerincx."

The artist nodded glumly at hearing it, his mouth
like an upside-down horseshoe. "Yes, Meneer van
Rijn, *that* Geerincx," confirmed Aboab, "The silk
merchant—one of the men who bought your house.
Now, your old neighbor, Daniel Pinto, is here as
Geerincx' agent, to discuss some business on his

behalf."

With a gesture toward the press, Aboab spoke to Mac in English, "As for this, it's best if the visitor doesn't see it. Nor either of you. So if you please, take a tour of my garden for a while. I will have Dieners let Pinto in and send him straight up to my study. Then both of you will leave out the front door when Pinto is with me upstairs."

Aboab gestured to Mac's setup and said, "And please take the press and everything with you and go next door and wait there." The prescient Aboab had thought and acted quickly and was shooing them out the back. Mac was mystified as he and Rembrandt slipped out the door.

With Mac and van Rijn safely out of sight, Aboab went to Dieners in the hallway and spoke quietly as he reiterated the plan for him. Dieners smiled and nodded—a twinkle in his eye. Then the rabbi turned and went upstairs. In a moment, Dieners would open the front door to the visitor.

Outside in the garden, Rembrandt and Mac stood off the pathway a little, out of sight of anyone inside who might happen to look through the window. Mac heard Rembrandt muttering under his breath, "*Drek, drek* . . .. "[65] Mac didn't understand the Yiddish obscenity, but he was getting the idea.

In the house, Aboab was already up in the study and he had closed the door by the time Dieners unlocked the front door and pulled it open. To the boy's surprise, there was not just the one he expected to see—Daniel Pinto—but, instead, *two* men standing on the porch. They were wearing long black cloaks and had on broad-brimmed Burgher hats. They smiled affably down at him.

---

[65] Shit!

"*Goedemiddag,*[66] Meneer Dieners!" said Daniel Pinto in greeting. "As I said, I sent word to Rabbi Aboab that I would be coming today. I trust that you have located him? I hope I'm not interrupting his prayers. Or is he otherwise occupied?"

Dieners was surprised to see that the rabbi's son-in-law, Daniel Barella, stood beside Pinto, but he quickly recovered from his surprise and answered, "No . . . the rabbi is not preoccupied. And, yes, I did locate him. I see Meneer Barella accompanies you! What a surprise!"

"Yes, Meneer Barella here has just come back from Tulpenburg, having taken his wife there to be with her mother," said Pinto. Dieners acted flustered, feigned dismay and stalled for a little more time to be sure that everything was set according to Aboab's plan.

"May we come in?" They were removing their hats as they spoke. They seemed not to be put off by Dieners for the time it took for him to open the door and oblige them.

"Yes, of course," Dieners said with a little bow. "I apologize for my slowness and keeping you waiting. You will find Rabbi Aboab in the upstairs study, the front room. You see, the door there was closed and he couldn't hear me. I went up and he told me to send you to him. He's waiting for you, Meneer Pinto. I'm sure he'll be pleased to see you also, Meneer Barella."

They entered and went straightaway up the stairs, with Aboab's son-in-law Daniel leading the way, since he was familiar with the house. In the study they found the rabbi waiting. Aboab registered surprise at seeing that Daniel Barella was with Pinto.

---

[66] Good afternoon.

"Shalom," Aboab said, "You honor me with your visit to my home. I am surprised to see you, Daniel, my son. But I remember, now, that you were going to Tulpenburg—you were to take Julia there to join her mother. How did you find my wife? Well, I hope?" He gestured toward the dark wood table. "Please hang your coats and make yourselves comfortable."

The two men found pegs on the wall on which to hang their cloaks, returned greetings in kind and took seats at the pedestal table. Their mood was warm and friendly, and Aboab's slightly nervous manner went unnoticed by the visitors during their congenial small talk.

"Mevrouw Fonseca is very well, she assured me, and sends you her love," said Barella. "Your wife and Julia are enjoying their holiday together and I believe they are expecting you to come, too, at week's end— to collect Mevrouw Fonseca. As for my being here, I just happened to meet Meneer Pinto at the market, and he told me that he was coming to visit you so I decided to come with him—even though you were not forewarned."

Pinto said, "I knew it would be alright that he should come along. As for what I came to discuss, it is a small matter and should take but a few minutes. As I said in my note, I come in behalf of my neighbor, Samuel Geerincx. He is in immediate need of temporary storage for some carpets and crates of silk, and he thought you might have a suggestion."

Pinto was being tactful, for he knew as well as anyone in the Amsterdam merchant's circle that Aboab had recently moved a shipment of tobacco which had been stored in his home. Surely he would have the space Geerincx needed.

"It happens I *do* have room—in my basement," said Aboab, "As I have just dispensed with a quantity of tobacco that the brothers Pereira had stored here. But, may I ask, why is Geerincx moving his carpets and silk? Has he sold them?"

Before Pinto could answer, the room door opened and Dieners appeared with a tray holding a pot of hot tea and dishware, fruit and nuts. He set the tray on a side table. They acknowledged the refreshment and Pinto continued his explanation while Dieners arranged the cups, plates and napkins and poured tea.

"Geerincx needs the carpets and crates taken out because he is having the floor repaired in the storage room," Pinto said, "It is the room where Rembrandt had his printing press years ago. The floor is tiled, and some tiles are loose underfoot. I'm told that it is unsettling to walk on that floor, so he's having the tiles taken up, cleaned, and reset."

Aboab thanked Dieners when he was finished with the tea setting, and the lad left the room, closed the door and went back downstairs. It was now Dieners' time for removal of Rembrandt, MacRitchie and the etching press from the house and hustle them over to The Blue Crown.

Outside, waiting in the backyard for Dieners' signal, Mac and Rembrandt had little to say to each other. It was awkward. The moody van Rijn was not inviting conversation, which seemed odd to Mac. Just seconds ago, the moment had been at hand to pull off a monotype, but now the proof and the press' working order seemed to be forgotten. In silence they stood and stared glumly at the rows of sad, wilted brown foliage of the garden. The darkness of van Rijn's mood was palpable. Mac shivered. He was cold and he felt disappointed.

Finally Rembrandt cleared his throat and said what he was thinking about. "Meneer MacRitchie, I am besotted with your press. Indeed, I will allow that

I am excited, even. And, these days, it takes a great deal to excite me. How much would you sell it for?"

"Sell?"

"Yes. Sell it to me. I need it. Surely you can obtain another one in America. How much?"

"I can't sell this press," he said. "I need it."

"What for? You're not a printer. You're a scholar, are you not?"

"I am . . . not only a scholar, sir. I am . . . I am also an engineer."

Van Rijn straightened and scowled at hearing this, and he thought it odd what Mac had said. No way could he sell this press! It was a special one, it was his original, the prototype, *number one*, the first Mini Halfwood. It was to be Mac's legacy! Mac fabricated a new story to counter this unexpected development.

"This particular press is an engineer's sample. I wish to establish trade between my enterprise . . . " but Mac's improvisation was interrupted by Dieners' opening of the door..

"Psst! Come now! Quickly! You're to go next door!" he said in a low voice. Mac and Rembrandt went back into the kitchen and Dieners closed the door and softly reiterated the rabbi's instructions for Mac and Rembrandt as he uncovered the press and put the fabric back on the hallway table.

"Take your press. The rabbi and his guests will be a little longer. You have time to continue with this printing business next door, after which you, Meneer MacRitchie, may return at your leisure." Dieners produced a bag, a coarse linen bread bag. "Put the press with this bag so no one outside will see it and get curious."

Mac scooted the press into the bag and picked it up in his usual way—like a babe-in-arms. Dieners preceded them to the front door. Rembrandt whispered loudly to Dieners when they were at the door: "What did Pinto come for?"

Dieners hesitated, and then answered as he started to open the front door. "I heard Pinto say they're going to store Geerincx' carpets and crates here while a floor is repaired—the printing room floor at your old house."

Rembrandt gasped. The thing he feared the most had come to pass! Dieners looked up at Rembrandt and asked him, "What's the matter?"

Van Rijn said, "Nothing! I mean . . . I had that floor put in. What's wrong with it?"

Mac was not part of the exchange between Rembrandt and Dieners because they had switched to Dutch, but he thought that Rembrandt seemed startled at something Dieners said. Mac cradled the press as they waited at the door, and Rembrandt held the box of supplies; his unanswered question hung in the air.

Dieners looked perplexed as he opened the door and held it wide for the two to go out; but Rembrandt didn't move. He waited for Dieners to answer his question.

"The floor, I asked you, Dieners—what's wrong with it?"

The little man furrowed his brow as he tried to remember the details. After a moment he said, "Well, Pinto said something about the tiles—they are loose. They're going to fix it."

"Who's doing the job?" Rembrandt pressed as he and Mac inched their way out onto the porch.

Dieners was confounded with van Rijn's interest in such trivia. He thought, *What concern is this to Rembrandt? It isn't his house, not anymore!* Dieners blurted out impatiently, "I don't know that! Probably I shouldn't be telling you these things." Then he was abashed as he remembered that it was not his place, especially as he was younger, neither to give, nor to withhold, information that was none of his business. Moreover, he should not make a show of disrespect for the great *fijnschilder* Rembrandt; nonetheless, Dieners was exasperated.

Rembrandt showed no indication that he took insult for the boy's outburst. Instead he surprised Dieners as he addressed him as an equal: "Meneer Dieners van Catarina, if you have an opportunity, then tell Rabbi Aboab . . . better yet, tell Pinto *directly* . . . that I know someone who can do the labor, and cheaply. It's my assistant, Arent de Gelder, who is always looking for ways to earn some money. Will you do that? Please?" van Rijn asked.

In fact, Rembrandt contrived the story about Arent looking for money; but right now van Rijn didn't care. The situation called for extreme measures, he knew, and God knew it, too.

All three were standing outside, Dieners even more perplexed. "*Gelder?* But I thought Arent . . . oh, very well," said Dieners. "Now you two must go. I should see to the needs of the rabbi's guests upstairs."

"Don't forget . . .." said Rembrandt, but Dieners had already gone back in and closed the door.

Mac and Rembrandt went next door to The Blue Crown and entered. Rembrandt said to Mac, "Come to the next room. I will introduce you to Arent, my helper." He shouted out, "Arent?" as he led Mac in.

Mac figured the teenager at the table was the helper and he was working on something; and now he was putting whatever it was away. The boy looked surprised to see that Rembrandt had brought in a stranger and he surreptitiously covered his copper point drawing with a paper sheet.

"Meneer van Rijn?" he said with surprise. He

stood up and, with a frown, he eyed Mac. For some reason the boy felt suspicious, as obviously the man was not from around here and was not likely to be an art patron—dressed as he was in Flemish-looking garb, and poorly-cut. It was even more peculiar that the stranger was carrying something bulky concealed in a bread sack.

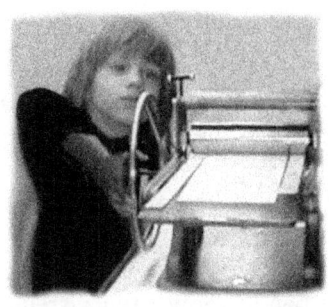

Chapter 29
Where There's A Will . . .

In Dutch Rembrandt said, "Arent, I want you to meet a visitor. He's come all the way from the New World. From . . .," Mac could tell van Rijn was stuck in the introduction by the way he hesitated, so Mac went to the table and set down the bagged press. He thought he would perform his own introduction, as it may be that the boy understood English.

Mac said to him, "William Handyside MacRitchie, of Se—of *Seattle*, recently of Massachusetts. I'm sorry that I do not speak Dutch." As he said this, he gave Arent a respectful nod. Mac thought he looked about fourteen or fifteen years old, a fair and open face which, at the moment, registered awe at his sudden encounter with an alien speaking English. The boy was staring at him open-mouthed, not understanding a word, and most likely unused to hearing an American accent.

Rembrandt hastily translated what Mac said for Arent's benefit. He garbled Mac's origin; he had already forgotten whatever it was—Harvard or Massachusetts—and Rembrandt thought that it didn't matter to Arent, anyway. The monolingual American wouldn't know about his error since he didn't

245

understand Dutch.

Van Rijn was, contrary to Mac's thinking, eager to see the monotype proof. After all the time of making their exodus, the monotype was still captive in Dieners' bread bag on the press bed, under the paper and felt blanket layers.

As it seemed like a good time to do it, Mac set the press in an open space on the table and removed the press from the bag to show Arent. Arent's eyes bugged out as he watched Mac fold back the felt blankets and gingerly pick up the paper by a corner, turn it over and lay it face up on the press bed.

"Not bad," Mac said aloud to himself more than for the two who watched. He leaned over for a better look and admired his little picture. "Not bad at all!" He was relieved, and he thought, *There's your proof*, even though it was not an etching.

Rembrandt joined him, looking in at the image. "*Niet slecht!*"[67] Rembrandt translated Mac's remark with a smile. He was impressed with the monotype, and did not mind saying so.

Arent studied the monotype and then looked at the machine. He thought that it must be a printing press, but not like Rembrandt's huge wooden one.

Hearing van Rijn's reaction, Mac beamed, looked up at the old Master and mimicked: "*Niet slecht!*" as he caught the meaning of the Dutch.

At Mac's mimicking, Rembrandt guffawed and repeated, "*Niet slecht*! Not bad!" He added, "*Wij zullen nog een goede Amsterdamer van u maken, Meneer MacRitchie!*"[68] Mac could only guess at van Rijn's meaning, but he laughed anyway.

Arent looked at one and then the other of the two

---

[67] Not bad.
[68] We will make a good Amsterdammer out of you, Mister MacRitchie.

246

older men carrying on—like someone watching a tennis match—and then again at the monotype. Regarding Mac now, Arent's expression said what he was thinking: *Who is this guy, anyway? What kind of print is that he pulled? And where did that machine come from?*

Rembrandt collected himself, turned serious and explained to Arent that this man was a guest who was staying next door, an American scholar . . . or engineer . . . who planned to sell these presses in the Dutch Republic, and he, Rembrandt, was going to buy the first one—maybe even become an agent of the American company! Mac was oblivious to what the story was that van Rijn told.

"Meneer MacRitchie, may I offer you something?" Rembrandt asked, suddenly hospitable as he switched back to English. Then, in Dutch he said to Arent, "Prepare some tea," and he added, "Oh, and another thing, I'm trying to get a job for you, some paying work!"

Rembrandt turned back to study the press and the monotype, but Arent didn't move. He frowned, troubled by the comment that Rembrandt planned to find him a job. Arent wanted to ask what Rembrandt meant by "a job" and why; but he decided instead to go into the kitchen and do what he was told.

He would ask later. He was worried. He hadn't bothered Rembrandt about money, so why was he sending him off to work somewhere else? It was depressing news and he was wondering, *Is there no end to the many obstacles in my path? The Master shows no interest in my work and treats me like a peon.*

Arent brightened as another thought occurred: *Just wait until he sees my copper point drawing. Then Master van Rijn will sit up and take notice!* For the moment, anticipation of *that* certainty restored Arent's spirit. He would bounce back. While he prepared hot water, Arent could hear Rembrandt jabbering to the outsider. For the first time in his life he wished he could speak the English argot.

In the middle room, Rembrandt made a new proposition to Mac for his press. Arent overheard van Rijn say something about playing cards— *speelkaarten*—and it made him wonder, *Could it be that the stranger is connected to the arguments he heard earlier when Jacques van Leest was here?*

Rembrandt was excited as he thought of alternatives to buying the press. He said, "I can give you a share in a project! I will make small etchings as I've been offered a commission by the world's most famous . . . " and he hesitated, " . . . do you know *speelkaarten*? It means 'playing cards.'

Mac shook his head; however, he had learned *speelkaarten*. In actuality, he had some thoughts of his own about playing cards.

"Have you heard of Jacques van Leest?" Rembrandt was eager to make a deal and he talked so rapidly that spittle flew out. Mac suppressed a smile at the specter of Rembrandt van Rijn frothing at the mouth he was so eager to involve him—an insignificant art professor—in a printmaking project.

In truth, the name van Leest was vaguely familiar as Mac had heard the name mentioned in a conversation earlier. Evasively, Mac replied, "*Jacques van Leest*? Never heard of him. Does he have talent?" Mac wanted to laugh at his wisecrack. It made Rembrandt pause and wonder what Mac could be thinking.

"Talent? No," he emphasized with a dismissive huff. "No, Jacques van Leest is a *publisher*, known for his playing cards. He said to me that if I print my

248

etchings on his cards, people will buy them in great numbers. My problem is that I have no press! Your press, I can see, will do the job. Is there a way that I can use it? For shares, perhaps, or a partnership?"

Before Mac could say anything, van Rijn had another idea to propose and, without a pause, he asked, "How long are you planning to stay in Amsterdam?"

"I don't know," Mac said, thinking to himself, *Maybe forever, for all I know.* He added, "I need to think about that."

Mac was, in truth, intrigued by Rembrandt's mention of playing cards. In the 20th Century, playing cards were mass-produced by machines and printed by the billions; casinos routinely drilled and discarded thousands of custom decks. Playing cards were to be part of a multibillion-dollar gambling industry. Added to that, sports cards and collectible cards came along in the 19th and 20th Centuries— which inspired new kinds of mass-produced cards, produced by the millions, and novel games—even major tournaments—that required them.

Mass production of playing cards was not the case in the 17th Century, however. Playing cards were produced a few at a time, by hand, on hand-operated printing presses. Such cards as survived had achieved the status of museum pieces by Mac's time. They were collectible art and antiques because they were hand-printed and therefore scarce.

Twentieth-Century artists had taken up making an unusual variety of custom cards that were widely referred to as *Artists Trading Cards,* or ATC. That's why Mac's test plate—still sitting on the press bed with Rembrandt's ghost image—was card-sized. Mac had designed his Mini Halfwood for printing several types of cards in mind; he was inspired by the quirky

ATCs; also artist's postcards—and even artist's stamps! The small size of it also meant that he could take the little press anywhere and print anytime. However, Mac never thought he would go as far away as Amsterdam, and certainly not back in Rembrandt's time.

Mac's thoughts were interrupted by Rembrandt as he repeated the question: "Well, Meneer MacRitchie? How long? Can you stay long enough for me to print the cards for van Leest?"

Mac thought for a second, and answered, "Perhaps. Would you be willing to endorse my press?"

"Endorse?" Never having heard of endorsement, Rembrandt was stumped and he looked quizzically at Mac for an explanation.

"Yes, you know, endorse the press. Put your name on it."

Van Rijn was speechless. He had never heard of such a thing. He scratched his head and seemed annoyed but he calmed and with diffidence he said, "I don't understand. My English—your use of words is confusing to me. *Endorse?* That's a word . . . that I don't know."

Arent returned from the kitchen with a steaming teapot and two heavy ceramic cups. Rembrandt dropped the two questions that were on his mind—one, *would MacRitchie stay, and, two, what was an 'endorsement?'*—and van Rijn switched to Dutch as he thanked Arent with, "Ah, Arent. Good boy!"

With a double-take on him, van Rijn saw that Arent sulked. "Say, Arent, you don't look pleased. Didn't you hear me when I said I may have found you a paying job?"

"I heard, master, yes, but I don't understand why."

"You need money! Isn't that a good reason why?"

"I do need money, but how would I work? I mean, how could I work with you, as your assistant— and what about my lessons?" The matter of his apprenticeship had not occurred to Rembrandt. He pursed his lips, puckered up and pondered the arrangements he made with the boy's father, the elder de Gelder.

"Oh, if the job materializes, that is—and I hope it does—then we can work it out. It's not a permanent job of which I speak." He paused, collecting his thoughts and reviewing the plan he had made up on the fly when Dieners informed on Geerincx. "My boy, do you remember the printing room at my former home?"

Arent nodded. "Yes, I remember it very well."

"The floor tiles have come loose. That silk merchant, who lives there—Samuel Geerincx—he aims to reset them. I volunteered your service—for pay."

As Mac couldn't understand the words in the discussion and as he was being ignored right now, he picked up the teapot and poured himself a cup of tea. Conversation between Rembrandt and Arent was gibberish to him and they did not take notice of the fact that the guest chose to serve himself. Mac's press had changed things for him; it gave him a sense of use and value. He was beginning to feel at home in spite of everything.

He thought that a piece of Dieners' bread with some of that fig jam that Madam Schwarzesherz had sent would go well with the tea; or, even better, spread on a slice of Dieners' sugarloaf! Mac swallowed at his thought and idly contemplated the blend of figs, ginger and cinnamon flavors. He wondered, *Would they go well together? Butter would*

be nice. Toasted sugarloaf and fig jam. Mmm. Mac
swallowed again and sipped his tea. He was startled at
the sound of the front door as it opened and closed
and a woman's voice called from the front room,
"*Hallo, wij zijn thuis.*"[69] A child's keyed up voice
chimed in, "*Vader, kom en zie wat ik heb!*"[70] Then,
suddenly, Rembrandt's wife, Hendrickje and their
daughter, six-year old Cornelia, were in the room!
The little girl's face was bright with excitement and
her smile displayed two front teeth missing.

They braked to a stop and Hendrickje exclaimed,
"Oh!" and then, speaking Dutch, "You have a guest! I
am sorry, van Rijn. What—who is this?" she asked,
her eyes set on the strangely-attired man standing in
her house, his mouth hanging open and holding a
mug.

Mac didn't need to understand Dutch to catch the
meaning of what Huisvrouw Hendrickje asked van
Rijn. The little girl had silenced, as glee over
something she held in her hand quickly turned to
shyness. She turned in to her mother's side and stared
openly at the stranger with Vader and Arent.

Rembrandt was effusive. "Hendrickje, a
wonderful thing has happened. This is . . . "

Mac set the cup down, turned to her and bowed.
His bow came naturally, which surprised even
himself. Hendrickje dipped her head politely. Mac's
impression of her was that she was taller than
Rembrandt, and that she must have been—at one
time—a beauty of a woman, and strong. Now she
looked comely, worn and tired. Hendrickje regained
her composure quickly after the surprise of finding a
stranger with her husband; and his clothes were as for
a costume party. She blushed after she looked him up

---

[69] Hello, we are home.
[70] Father, come and see what I have.

and down, and gave Mac a polite and gracious smile.

The Halfwood press caught Hendrickje's eye. Staring at it, she didn't seem to be listening as Rembrandt hastily filled her in on who Mac was, why he wore bizarre clothes, and about the foreigner's machine. She shot a look at van Rijn because of certain words he said—words Mac could not get, of course—but they were about his plan for buying the press.

"Van Rijn! *We can't buy that*! We have no money!"

This stopped Rembrandt. His face went hot.

Drawn to the press at the table's edge, their little girl lisped, "*Vader, wat ith dit?*"[71] Before van Rijn could answer, she gave the etching press wheel a good turn.

"Cornelia . . . *no!*"

---

[71] Father, what is this? (lisping the *S* sound)

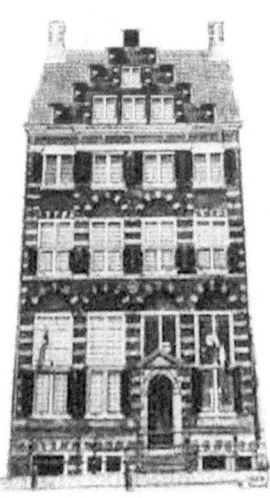

Chapter 30
'A Burgling We Go

Late in the afternoon, Mac followed Arent as they made their way alongside a canal to Samuel Geerincx' house. Mac thought he must look funny because he wore Rembrandt's borrowed clothes—not his Flemish costume. He was dressed for the role of a laborer—Arent's helper—and Mac looked like any other working-class Amsterdammer. The clothes were coarse and thick, and decidedly warmer compared to what he had been wearing.

Mac wore wooden clogs, called *klompen,* [72] that—even while they fit surprisingly well—made him clumsy and he tripped on the cobblestones now and then. Arent looked back to make sure that his helper did not wander off course.

An hour ago, when Rembrandt learned about

---

[72] Wooden shoes

Geerincx' floor tile project, it only took him two minutes to contrive a plan to get back his notes that he had secreted under the tiles. The floor's reconstruction which Rembrandt was afraid *could* happen was coming and the discovery of the hidden notes was imminent. He sent Arent and Mac, his "burglars," on their way to negotiate with Geerincx.

The key to his strategy was Dieners' willingness to be van Rijn's go-between and convey an offer of cheap labor to Geerincx by way of Daniel Pinto. Rembrandt and Pinto were not on speaking terms ever since—years ago—Rembrandt refused to pay his portion of the cost for fixing the foundation shared by their adjoining houses. There was a mutual animosity between them, even to this day.

Dieners explained to Pinto that Arent de Gelder, was available to do the project, and Pinto could tell Geerincx to expect a visit from Arent to settle the details that afternoon. A bonus in the offer was that Arent would include a helper to handle the heavy work. Geerincx would get two laborers for the price of one. He couldn't refuse. Dieners told Pinto that the helper was a foreigner, and mute to boot, but that he would follow orders and Arent would make sure that the job was done right.

When he had explained his plan to Arent in Dutch, van Rijn switched to English to describe the mission to Mac, who hadn't understood a word until after it was all settled. Since MacRitchie wanted Rembrandt's *endorse*—as the American had called it—van Rijn presumed that he could get MacRitchie's help without asking him first. Rembrandt figured correctly. As the Master had supposed, Mac was willing to go along with the scheme, even the part about playing "dumb." It made sense, considering the language barrier. He could be mute. It would be fun.

He had come this far so he didn't have anything to lose by playing Rembrandt's "Hidden Objects Game." In this case, the *hidden objects* were not merely *virtual* as they are in 21st Century video games, but *real things*. The hunt might be dangerous, since taking things from the job site amounted to theft, but worth the risk since Rembrandt might be more inclined to endorse his Halfwood press.

After Dieners made the offer to Pinto, the plan gelled quickly and a message came back from Geerincx for Arent to come before dinner. Rembrandt told his team to go right away to talk with Geerincx and scope out the job, and Arent should come back and report to him afterward.

Arent detected that there was something odd about Rembrandt's behavior. He sensed that van Rijn was hiding something but he didn't think he should ask questions. In Rembrandt's view, the impressionable boy shouldn't know, as the contents of the hidden notes touched on van Rijn's peculiar compulsions and were not part of Arent's training.

Rembrandt faced a dilemma in his telling to Mac why the packets hidden under the tiles were important and significant enough for the intrigue and the risk of trouble. He struggled to explain his reasons in English. Rembrandt was still trying to keep the facts of his personal musings to himself, and he was still not one-hundred percent convinced of Mac's motives for wanting to meet him in the first place.

But as Mac listened to van Rijn's halting, awkward summary about the notes, he understood him well. Note-writing van Rijn described reminded Mac of his *own* writing compulsion—absent, however, of the compunction that Rembrandt felt. The 17th Century was different from Mac's post-modern, science-and-technology-liberated, and enlightened, free-thinking times. Creative thinking in his 20th Century society was commonplace and unrestrained.

For example, as a young professor Mac had taken his imaginative musings and note-writing to extremes. He even categorized his notes. His epiphanies were *Flashes,* and when ideas flooded his mind they were *Cascades.* Unlike someone in Rembrandt's day, however, Mac did not have to keep his fanciful mind-games under the carpet. Mac lived into the Second Millennium, the post-enlightenment-information-superhighway-era. He showed his musings as Web logs and developed them as essays, full-length books and screenplays! Writing had become like a game to Mac.

Mac divulged his habit to van Rijn; he, too, was an inveterate note-writer. Rembrandt was pleased to hear him say this; he took it to mean that if it was be tolerated in the American colonies, then it was not madness. Mac thought to mention Ben Franklin, another avid note-maker; but Franklin was born in 1706, exactly 100 years after Rembrandt was born.

Van Rijn confided to Mac, "A philosopher told me you are not crazy if you can find one other person who agrees with you. So, I guess I am not crazy, Meneer MacRitchie, if you keep notes, too."

Mac told van Rijn that he had read the same thing in a book. Rembrandt was amazed.

"A book? Really? Who wrote it?"

"William O. Douglas," replied Mac.

"Never heard of him," said Rembrandt, as he turned and gave his attention back to Arent. In Dutch van Rijn elaborated on the plan. Their job the next day was to be kept secret. They should keep a lookout so that if Meneer Geerincx came to check, then they should act like they were on the job.

"No one must know about those packets!" Rembrandt warned. "Later, I will explain, but there is no time now. Trust me. Those don't belong to Geerincx or anyone else—nothing in it against the law. It is not burglary. It will be an adventure, and there is no harm in it or illegal."

Rembrandt's words and his manner towards Arent were a change from van Rijn's authoritarian style, and Arent was fortified with a feeling of importance as the Master took him into his confidence. That Rembrandt had the idea of sending him to work on such an unlikely undertaking showed that he trusted him. He was being given a man's job. To have Mac help was good, too. He might get to know the American, even though he would not speak.

Everything had been planned, and by mid-afternoon, Arent and Mac made their way to the canal called the *Houtgracht*. Arent knew the way, having been back and forth many times between Rozengracht and the Jodenbreestraat. The day was mild for November, but it was getting late and would be dark in a couple hours. Mac's walking skill in the clogs improved, but he lagged behind. Arent hid his impatience with Mac's slow progress.

There were numerous people along this canal. As it was long past the growing season, the flower market was desolate but tidy and the many little flower stalls empty and forlorn. Mac was impressed by the sight of neat rows of houses on both sides of the streets and canals and he rubber-necked in awe. The houses were all connected, with similar red brick and stone facades and steep pitched gables. Some of them had fancy carriages parked in front, their horses' heads drooped and their drivers dozed.

"Psst," hissed Arent, and made a funny, sign language gesture. Mac got the message. He shouldn't gawk as though he had never seen the city streets and buildings. If he acted like a tourist then he might attract attention, and they didn't want that.

Obediently following Arent like a dog, Mac tried to appear indifferent, but inside he was enjoying what scenery he could glimpse. A red wagon, piled with red-banded blue-painted beer barrels, trundled toward them drawn by four huge gray horses. This street was a little wider, but Arent and Mac still had to veer close to the houses—as all the pedestrians did—as the horses and wagon lumbered by. Mac could feel the ground vibrate in his cushion-less, wood foot soles.

Arent rehearsed what he was supposed to say to Geerincx. He wondered, *What if Geerincx wasn't interested?* But he was sure that was not likely to be the case. Yet, he worried, *How could Geerincx refuse such a good deal? He has to take the offer.*

"We zijn er bijna,"[73] said Arent to Mac, to let him know that they were almost there. He forgot that Mac was not supposed to be spoken to—plus the American did not speak Dutch. Mac looked up as he, too, forgot that he was supposed to be deaf. Mac recovered and looked around; no one paid attention.

Mac saw where Arent was heading as they got near the end of the block. Back from a row of trees by another canal were two stately houses standing side-by-side. Like most, they were joined by a common wall. Arent paused. Mac drew beside him and touched his arm; he gestured with a shrug to get Arent to tell him which one used to be Rembrandt's.

When Mac and Faye were on a working tour of Amsterdam in 1969, they visited the Rembrandt house, or, *Museum Het Rembrandtshuis*, and he saw the replica of Rembrandt's etching press made all of

---

[73] We're almost there.

wood. It was the seed planted in Mac's head that, twenty-five years later, would grew into his idea to use wood parts with steel in his Halfwood presses.

Mac couldn't remember which house it was because the building he remembered didn't look like either house. In a second Arent understood Mac's query and pointed to the second house from the corner, Number 4; he waived to Mac to follow him. When they got up to the house, Arent signed Mac to wait at the bottom of the steps while he went up the wide stairs and applied the brass door-knocker. In a moment a woman in servant livery opened the door.

Mac stayed below and he made his face look blank and vacant of mind. He could hear Arent speak briefly to the woman. As it was already planned ahead by the agreement, they were expected by Geerincx, and she turned and called for the Master of the house.

For his part, Arent had thought about what he would say and do as he remembered Master Rembrandts orders: *"Do whatever it takes,"* Rembrandt had instructed. *"Take whatever offer Geerincx makes. Don't haggle. Tell him you can start right away, tomorrow—Wednesday—preferably."*

Geerincx appeared and Arent started to introduce himself but his name and his good reputation had preceded him. Geerincx knew Arent's father and respected the papermaker's trade and the quality of his products. It pleased Arent to hear it. Also Geerincx knew why he had come.

While he talked with Arent, Geerincx glanced several times past Arent at Mac. Arent finished the work proposal, and then Geerincx stepped down to the street and looked into Mac's expressionless, unsmiling face. Curious, he gripped Mac's shoulder and felt for his bicep under Mac's thick clothing.

A shadow of doubt crossed Geerincx' face, Mac noticed, but maintained his deadpan expression. In Dutch, Geerincx called up to Arent, "Are you sure your helper is up to it? He seems a little old and puny to me."

Arent wanted to laugh and he wished Mac had understood Geerincx' slight; but he composed himself and responded that, *yes*, Mac was strong and able enough. Geerincx was satisfied. He liked Arent's offer. He left Mac where he was—no wiser of the merchant's insult. The owner went back up the steps and told Arent to come in with him to settle the details of their agreement.

Mac decided that now, with the two of them gone, he had a chance to get a better look at the Rembrandt's house. He went a few steps away to get a better view, stopped in the middle of the street, turned, and backed toward the canal so he could see all the house from the street to the top floor.

It was definitely different-looking from his recollection. Mac thought it was smaller than he remembered it from the 20th Century. It was about thirty-five feet wide—wider than Pinto's, Number 2, the house next to it. Number 4 was quite beautiful, rising up three stories with brick and inlaid stone on the facade. At the Rozengracht, the apartment was a come-down for the van Rijn family. Aboab's, even, was plain by comparison to this mansion.

Rembrandt's house had tall front windows with tops of half-moon stonework and inset red brick. High above, at the roofline, was a tall, five-stepped dormer with a double set of windows topped by another window set above those. To Mac, the only familiar features about the house were the windows with their half-moon stone arches.

It had a derrick system sticking out and,

silhouetted against the darkening gray sky, a pulley dangled. Almost all of the city's houses had these derricks and pulleys. Furniture and other large items could be gotten to the upper levels by pulling them up, as staircases were too narrow.

A passer-by stepped around Mac with a questioning look, as if to wonder what Mac thought was so interesting above. He reverted to his slouched, dopey look and shuffled, face down, to the sidewalk. He wondered what was taking Arent so long; then he heard Arent hiss from the stoop.

Aha! Mac thought, *Arent won't trick me into looking up. I'll act like I don't hear him.* Mac stared at the sidewalk. In a few seconds Arent came down and tugged Mac's arm. Mac gave him a quizzical, stupid look. Arent rolled his eyes and gestured for Mac to come along with him into the house.

Mac followed Arent up the steps and entered. It was as cool inside the home as out, but pleasant, and there was a faint smell of cooking coming from somewhere. Mac felt like he was in a museum loaded with highly polished, mint-condition period furniture and appointments. He wanted to linger and study the furnishings, the carpets, paintings and other luxurious embellishments of the silk merchant's home, but resisted. These weren't antiques, of course; everything was shining new. A candle chandelier provided a soft, warm light.

There were stairs at the left of the main entry that led down into the room that had been Rembrandt's printing studio. Geerincx had directed Arent to go take a look downstairs while the merchant tended to another matter. Arent knew his own way around the house. They went down the stairs. In the room, several lighted oil lamp sconces were fixed along one wall and augmented the meager November afternoon light coming in from a row of high windows at the street level. It was hard to see until their eyes adjusted to the gloom.

Arent found the studio strange as it was bare of furnishings. Geerincx' storage crates had been hauled out. The carpets, no doubt the ones he was going to store in Aboab's basement, were rolled up and stacked to the side so that the mottled, blue-green glazed tiles were all exposed and accessible.

A twinge of nostalgia struck Arent, but there was nothing about the room that reminded him of how it had been except for the ceramic tiled floor and sconces on the wall.

There must have been at least a hundred tiles. Each tile measured about six-by-nine inches. Mac tried to figure out where Rembrandt's great wooden press had been placed. He judged that it was probably in a spot near the wall that showed the most wear; the red of the low-fired clay showed through the flaked and worn blue-green glaze.

Arent paced around the floor and checked for the loose tiles; now and then he glanced expectantly at Mac. The silence of the room was interrupted when Arent stepped on one tile and it gave a telltale click. He stooped to see if he could lift it. They were startled by Geerincx' booming voice down the stairwell, "*Hebt u genoeg gezien?*"[74]

Arent called back to him that, *yes*, he had seen what needed to be done. The owner came in. More conversation ensued between him and Arent while Mac stood silently aside and studied the floor, curious as to which tiles covered Rembrandt's secrets and exactly what was written in those packets. Tomorrow, if all went well, Mac would find out.

---

[74] Have you seen enough?

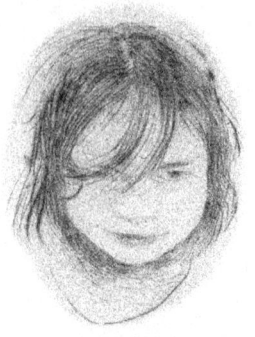

Chapter 31
Regarding Mac

Cornelia van Rijn pouted in the middle room. Her moeder[75] had scolded her for spinning the press wheel, but Cornelia could not see why she was not allowed. It was fun—as much fun as any of the attractions at the amusement park where she'd been. Her vader[76], too, had scolded her for no good reason.

After that unpleasantness passed, the grown-ups—including Arent and the man in the odd clothes who talked funny—had visited awhile until Arent took the man away. Where they went, Cornelia didn't know; and she didn't care. The funny man had left his machine, the wheel thing, on the table.

Cornelia sat quietly and thought of the charm which nice Meneer Lingelbach at the *Nieuwe Doolhof* had given to her. It was a tiny pewter windmill made to be hung on a necklace. She had forgotten about it in the excitement, but now she took the little charm from under her shirt and held it between two chubby

---

[75] mother
[76] father

fingers to study. She remembered her grootvader[77], because her moeder told her Rembrandt's vader had a windmill in Leiden; and also did Arent's vader have a mill. Cornelia wished the little metal sails on the windmill charm would go around like the wheel did on that man's machine, which sat on the table with no one using it. She longed to play with it.

Cornelia looked up at her father and mother as they bickered about the wheel thing. Moeder pleaded with vader and said things Cornelia didn't understand, but they had something to do with the machine. Cornelia hated when they argued; sometimes Vader shouted and Moeder cried.

Hendrickje said, "Yes, I do too understand, van Rijn—but what if the American doesn't sell it to you, and you promised van Leest, and you have already taken his money? What will you say? What will you do?"

"The American will sell. Already he has said as much. In America, they barter with a system called 'endorse.' All I have to do is put my name on it."

Astonished, Hendrickje stared at Rembrandt for a full second and wondered if he was serious. She burst, "Are you out of your mind? *Do you believe that?* He takes you for a fool!"

"Watch it, wife!" Rembrandt warned her.

Unfazed, she didn't stop. "No one is that stupid, giving to someone a thing for simply putting their name on it!"

Rembrandt glared at her. He thought that she may be right but he didn't want to give in. He turned away, his shoulders sagged and he let out a long sigh of resignation. As her husband deflated, Hendrickje felt sympathy for her downcast man.

---

[77] grandfather

She said, "Are you sure you understood him? Your English is . . .."

He stiffened. "I understand English well enough! *Yes!* Besides, consider the fact that he is a guest of Rabbi Aboab, who is honorable. He wouldn't open his house to a faker! He wouldn't invite a disservice to Rembrandt van Rijn!"

Hendrickje considered his reasoning as she looked over at their daughter, who sat quietly taking it all in while she fiddled with something in her little hands.

"Cornelia, please go to your bed and wait for me." The girl slipped off her chair and did as she was told. Hendrickje watched her and sighed, weary of argument. A moment later she said, "You do what you want, van Rijn. I'm tired." Dropping the matter of the press dealing, she looked at the clock and asked, "When will Arent get back?"

"Soon, I think. He went to look at the floor project and settle with Geerincx. He'll be back soon."

"And the American?"

"He will go back to the rabbi's." Rembrandt felt sorry for Hendrickje. She had put up with a lot, and she was so troubled. He made a mess of things, and knew it, but he could not make a clean breast of it. He said, "Hendrickje, trust me. I know what I am about. The rabbi wants me to paint his portrait. Van Leest wants small etchings for his *artiste speelkaarten*. The American is interested in—well, as I said—my *endorse*. If he stays long enough, I can probably use his press and not have to pay at all. He seems a little simple to me."

"Simple?"

"Yes," and he paused, furrowed his brow in thought before he continued. "He doesn't seem to know anything about Amsterdam. He doesn't seem to know much about anything. He hasn't learned to speak Dutch, either."

"That's understandable. He's a foreigner. From—where did you say he's from?"

"I forget, but I believe not far from New Amsterdam. New Netherlands, where beaver hats come from, I believe." Then he snorted, frustrated by her distracting question. "Oh, what does it matter? Anyway, you are right, it's no wonder he is ignorant, living in the wilderness, with the wild Indians."

Hendrickje thought about this. She nodded and said, "And yet, his machine is so fine." Silent, she stared sadly at the press on the table. Its dark wood and brass details were beautiful in the candlelight from the chandelier hanging above.

Rembrandt studied Hendrickje sitting opposite him. Noticing her face was lined and pale, he felt ashamed. He felt he had let her down. She looked up to meet his gaze and gave him a wan smile. Van Rijn was not good with tender words as he once had been. Yet it was an effort to hide his feelings for her. His next few words came really hard. He wanted to say something encouraging and give her hope; he needed to bolster his own confidence, too.

"Yes, and the new machine works. What's more, I know that I need it, Hendrickje. I think this may be the saving of my career. I have commissions both for a portrait and for etchings almost in hand. Titus will approve, I think, when he returns. Next month the damnable insolvency proceedings will be completely final, and then we—I mean, you and Titus—will get the business license for the gallery." He sighed and added: "Everything is coming together. That American's coming with his new machine is a Godsend, I do believe."

They heard knocking at the back door of the

kitchen and it brought Hendrickje to her feet to go see. It was Mahault de Witte. Hendrickje let her in and the girl went straight to work to help prepare the van Rijn's evening meal.

Hendrickje came back into the middle room where her husband was now contemplating the etching press, fingering the polished wood that clad its sides. He gave the wheel a spin as little Cornelia had done, mesmerized by the polished steel flashing and reflecting candle beams. He shouldn't have scolded Cornelia. She just wanted to play. She couldn't hurt the machine.

"I must go to help prepare for dinner. Cornelia will be hungry," Hendrickje said as she left him.

"Set a place for Arent at the table," Rembrandt called after her. "I want to be able to talk with him about the afternoon and make a plan for tomorrow." He looked around to the front room window and noticed that it was dark. "I wonder what's taking the boy and Meneer MacRitchie so long," he said to no one. Across the way, the carillonneur played the six-o'clock chimes.

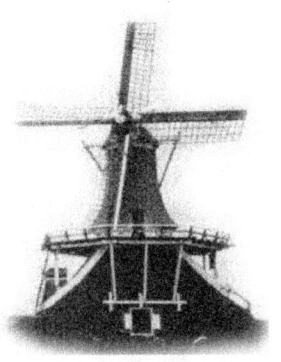

Chapter 32
Things that go Thump in the Night

On their return walk from Geerincx' house en route to Rembrandt's, Arent and Mac went the long way around that took them by the wharfs of Binnen-Amstel. Because Arent could not speak English to his workmate, he wasn't able to explain to Mac that he was going on an errand of a personal nature. He had no choice but to drag Mac along as he dare not send MacRitchie back alone. It was somewhat embarrassing to have the American tagging along, but unavoidable. The fool would get lost if he told him to go back on his own, and Master Rembrandt would not like it.

As they walked, Arent felt good about the prospect of making some extra money, and so he was going to stop on their way and pick up a sugar loaf for his mother. She would be surprised and pleased. He would have to hurry, though.

The route to the bakery took them through the shipping district of Amsterdam. Mac got a feeling that

269

he had been in this neighborhood before, but in the dark he couldn't be certain. Boats and barges were tied up at the wharfs to unload, and much of the area was given to warehouses and lumber yards.

This was also the center of the wood trade. The signs were meaningless to Mac, but translated to English they meant, "New Wood Market" and "Long Wood Street"; and there was a canal named, "Wood Canal." They came to a bakery; it was the one where Madam Schwarzesherz had bought Mac brunch on his first day here. The establishment was called *De Vier Suikerbroden,*[78] or, "The Four Sugar Breads," and it was renowned for its sugar loaves.

Mac's stomach growled loudly. Arent heard the sound and grinned. The stomach spoke the universal language of hunger. As they entered the bakery, they were immediately enveloped in the warm fragrance of the shop.

Mac humbly waited at the side while Arent got in line, and when his turn came, he ordered a sugar loaf and two *gevulde koeken,*[79] which Mac would learn are soft almond-filled cookies, like a dessert biscuit. The clerk tending the counter wrapped a sugar loaf in gray paper for Arent, who paid her with several copper coins.

Back on the street, Arent gave one of the filled cookies to Mac, who smiled and nodded in gratitude. He liked the kid. Too bad they couldn't talk.

A lamplighter ahead of them lighted a street lamp. While Mac took his first bite of the cookie, he could smell fresh-cut wood carried on the cold breeze as they walked by warehouses where fir, oak and beech logs were being made into ships' parts.

He passed a shop window and Mac could make

---

[78] The Four Sugar Loaves
[79] Filled cookies

out fancy furnishings on display that were probably meant for ships' officers' quarters. He stopped. There were fine wood-crafted things like binnacle-housings, cabinets and instrument cases. He was drawn strongly to them as they were the very objects he had in mind when he designed the Halfwood press and printmaker chest.

Arent had gone ahead as Mac studied things in the window. "Psst!" Arent hissed at him to come along. Mac assumed his convenient, deaf mute act and continued to feast his eyes and memorize details of the things arrayed in the shop window.

Soon Arent was beside him and tugged at his arm, impatient to be on their way to the de Gelder paper mill. Mac went along, but he looked back and made a mental note of the name on the overhead carved-and-painted trade sign that hung over the shop front: *Marine Hout Handwerkman van Hooft.*[80] It was futile to memorize the long words.

They walked on. Darkness was complete. Mac heard a booming sound coming from the direction they were headed. The noise made Mac curious. He had heard it before. Arent suddenly stopped at a door. It sounded like there might be a giant garage band inside playing amplified drums with such great pounding force he could feel the ground under his clogs vibrate with each riff. He thought, *It's like that effect in "Jurassic Park" when the T-Rex was coming, and coming at a gallop!*

They had arrived. Knowing not a word of English, Arent made no attempt to explain to Mac about his parents' great paper mill home—neither their business nor what made the rhythmic, heavy booming that resounded from within the building.

---

[80] Marine Woodworker van Hooft

Arent slammed the black iron knocker on the door. He had to bang it loudly in order to be heard over the pounding. A creaking and swooshing noise overhead caused Mac look up into the night, and he realized the building was the base of a windmill! He could make out the taught canvas sails stretched on the windmill's huge arms as they swept around, turned by the evening breeze.

Arent started to knock again but the door opened. There stood Arent's father. The gentleman was surprised when he saw his son—and a foreign-looking stranger with him.

"Arent! *Wat doe je hier?*" he said, surprised, and, as he regarded Mac: "*Wie is dit?*"[81]

Mac had by now learned the words meant, "Who is this?" Arent started to explain, but his father stopped him as if it were of no matter, and said in one breath, "*Kom binnen,*" and—to Mac: *"Welkom!"*[82] as he held the door open wide.

Immediately they were in the main room of the paper mill. The rhythmic, beating sound was deafening. The air in the room felt humid and heavy with rank smells. Mac realized that the thumping sound was from a stamper, its hammer-like arms booming relentlessly on a plank. Repeatedly the heads on the arms fell, driven by a turning cylinder with cogs. The iron-bound cylinder was powered by a huge wood cogwheel, which in turn was connected to the windmill's turning mechanism.

A vertical timber, thick as a man's chest and like the mast of a ship, towered up through crisscrossing beams and disappeared amid an arrangement of cogs and pulleys, barely visible in the dark, where it connected to the windmill sails.

---

[81] What are you doing here? Who is this?
[82] Come inside! Welcome!

The stamper heads lifted and dropped repeatedly on a solid, dark reddish wood plank. A worker shoveled rags onto the plank for the next drop of the hammers. The rags must have been processing for quite a long time because they had already turned into mush by the beating.

It was hard to imagine that the muddy gray sludge swirling around the water vat would, eventually, be molded into sheets of beautiful, white printing paper that could last hundreds of years.

Mac was engrossed. He flinched as he felt a shiver—not from the cold in the room—but an epiphany, thrilled as he made the connection to Arent's family name, *Gelder*. This would be *Van gelder Zonen,* or Van Gelder Sons, the paper company that would last over three centuries and become known worldwide. He was standing in the birthplace! At least, this is what Mac assumed. He himself had used the Dutch etching paper in the 1970s, and he was Seattle's importer of the paper until the company closed down in 1980.

Mac idly watched the workers and stared long at the vat man and the coucher as they plied their trade. The latter noticed, and with a frown he made an unfriendly gesture at Mac. He looked away as Arent tugged at his arm and indicated he was to follow him with his father to a door that opened into another room. It was evidently the family's living quarters, warm and cheerful, but noisy.

As Arent closed the door, Mac took another look back at the stamper. He wondered, *Why doesn't this jibe with what papermakers use to make pulp in Seattle? Their pulp-beaters don't look like that.*

In Mac's time, handmade papers would be prized by printmakers and other artists, craftspeople, and designers. Most of the western-types of papers were made using the *Hollander Beater*-style of machine. Mac thought, *I'd sure like to visit a mill with a Hollander Beater like the ones I've seen.*

With the door closed the noise became somewhat subdued. Arent's mother was in this room, surprised to see her son and the more so to see the stranger with him. The three chatted in Dutch and then Arent presented to her the paper-wrapped sugar loaf. She held it up to her nose, took a sniff, and squealed with delight.

"Suikerbrood!" she exclaimed, and then turned suddenly shy and, with a giggle, covered her mouth— embarrassed for acting childish in front of a stranger. Mac grinned at the loving display.

There was much to be said among the family members, and they babbled rapidly to catch up on the day's events. They expressed disappointment when Arent explained that he had to go back to van Rijn's. There was too little time for more family news. Soon Arent and Mac were on their way again.

Mac made a mental note that this was a place he'd like to revisit; and he would draw a sketch of the Hollander Beater to show to the elder de Gelder, and then he could direct Mac to where he could see one. If anyone in the city knew where he could see a Hollander, it would surely be Arent's father.

After a long walk they were back in the Rozengraacht, nearing the houses of Aboab and Rembrandt. There were no lamps. From the darkness they heard a man's voice demand, *"Wacht!"*[83]

With a slouching, slow gait, a figure approached. As he came closer Mac saw that it was Pieter de Wit! Arent didn't know him and showed no concern; but Mac froze in his tracks and wondered how fast he

---

[83] Wait!

could run in the bulky wooden clogs that he wore. Pieter stepped up to them and thrust something at Mac, and Mac automatically took a step back.

Pieter snorted and smirked because he was not threatening. He said, "*Neem dit*,"[84] and he again thrust what he held out toward Mac. It was a covered basket. Pieter wanted Mac to take it, but Mac just stood fast not sure what to expect. Pieter sighed and set it down at Mac's feet. He made a *tsk-tsk* sound and shook his head at Mac's unneeded fear.

Pieter turned to Arent and explained what it was and who it was from. Mac relaxed as he realized that, this time, Pieter meant no harm. He had been instructed merely to deliver the basket as another peace offering by Madam Schwarzesherz. Mac thought, *She must really be worried!*

Pieter finished his brief explanation to Arent and then he looked straight at Mac and repeated, "*Neem dit!*" a little louder this time and pointed at the basket—as if shouting would translate his words into English. Mac was supposed to take it.

Pieter's loudness must have worked because Mac took "*neem dit*" to mean "Take it," and Mac picked up the basket. Pieter, satisfied that his mission was complete down to the last detail, turned on his heel and was gone.

---

[84] Take this!

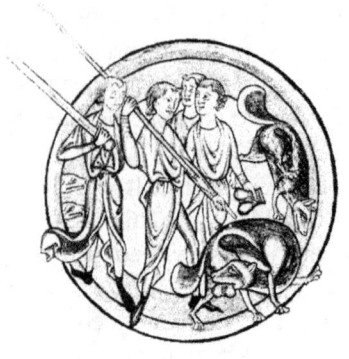

Chapter 33
The Shadow Knows

Mahault de Witte studied some writing on mottled, yellowish vellum—neat lines in small, delicate, forward-slanting script. Someone had written it with a quill—in a hand somehow feminine. She peered closely to make out the words and read by the light of a single, fat candle.

Who would have suspected that Mahault—Vrouw Schwarzesherz' mute, busy housemaid and kitchen helper—was the Black Widow's shadow? Was reading the Latin script difficult for Mahault? Yes, somewhat, but even more difficult in the wavering candlelight.

In this dungeon-like chamber in the basement of Vrouw Schwarzesherz' house, Mahault perched on a high stool and studied a certain entry in a thick, ancient-looking book. This room served as the Black Widow's alchemy laboratory and it was here where the old woman made perfumes and other "essences".

When Mahault's father died she was ten years of age. She had been indentured as a housekeeper to Vrouw Schwarzesherz who, when she first interviewed the silent little girl, detected that she had a sharp mind. The woman thought that Mahault would be an apprentice candidate someday. Her being mute was no handicap; and she didn't mind if Mahault spent time in the room to clean and straighten up as part of her chores.

Mahault was now fourteen, and what Vrouw Schwarzesherz did not realize was the depth of this girl's curiosity, genius and learning—which, because of her Catholic upbringing, included Latin.

Latin, of course, was the primary language in which the text and formulae in the Black Widow's precious book were recorded. This heavy book of thin vellum pages was bound in leather, ivory and wood. Vrouw Schwarzesherz acquired it just before she fled Poland. It was a prized tome of alchemy, medicinal and perfumery lore, and lent to her hasty flight from Poland ten years ago. Getting it nearly cost her life. Now she had a lucrative practice, and two young, unquestioning slaves—Pieter and Mahault—to do her work.

On days like this one, when Mahault was finished cleaning and putting things in order, she studied the labels on the bottles and packages that crowded the shelves. Her curiosity was piqued by what the labels read: *Candied rose petals, "Oyl of Sulphur," cherry syrup, alum, almond oil, Aurum Potabile (made with gold), peppermint schnapps*, and *dried earthworms.*

Among the bounty of interesting things in this room, the book was the best thing Mahault discovered. It was inside a chest in a niche high in the wall it and contained all the potentials of the ingredients that were stored here. To match the Latin text with the labels on bottles and packets had become her favorite game.

The newest additions to the stock were wrapped

up in a package that Vrouw Schwarzesherz had carried home last Sunday night. The new supplies had been wrapped in heavy, oiled paper bound with coarse twine and sealed with blood-red wax—protection for the green bottles and packets sent from New Amsterdam. That was the night that she dragged home the drunken foreigner that she found on the wharfs of *Binnen-Amstel.*

Among the new items was a bottle labeled, *castoreum.* Mahault wondered, *What is it, and what is it for?* Macia Schwarzesherz' best-known product was perfume, and this *castoreum* sure wasn't perfume. Perfumery was not the Black Widow's most lucrative trade. She made other things by alchemy, too. Mahault was certain the woman also made poisons, and this frightened the girl. Mahault took her meals in the same house, and she knew what might happen to her if the woman decided she was disposable. Mahault was always extra nice to the Black Widow, and careful to conceal her growing understanding of alchemy.

When Mevrouw Schwarzesherz told her to open and shelve the contents of the package from America, she grew curious about the bottle labeled, *castoreum.* So she looked it up in the big book. The page Mahault now studied had a colorful illustration. It was a simple woodcut—as most pages in books were these days—but painted in by a masterful hand. It pictured a hunter, his spear raised, its sharp point directed at a hapless, cowering brown-furred creature with a broad flat tail, the actual source of *castoreum* is the beaver.

Below the imminently tragic tableau was the name: *Castor Canadensis.* There were details in the drawing which—when she looked closer—made Mahault blush when she saw the private and potent male parts to which the text—below—directed the reader to note.

The text read: *The beaver, Castor Canadensis, also called Pontic dog, is named from being castrated. Besides for their skins, male beavers are hunted for their testicles and castor sacs. They exude a yellowish secretion which, in combination with their urine, beavers use during scent-marking of territory. The dried sacs are good for medicine, perfumery and also, when mixed with certain substances, poisons. When a hunter comes near, the male beaver bites off his own testicles to save himself. The beaver shall be found in the British Isles and in vast numbers in the New Netherlands of North America.*

Mahault read and re-read the phrase, ". . . *when mixed with certain substances, poisons.*" She raised her eyes to the green glass bottle with the wood-stopper which sat on the shelf above the work counter. She re-read the words written on the bottle label to be sure that they matched the text in the big book: *Castoreum.* She checked again the paragraph and the phrase that described uses of castoreum: ". . . *for perfumery and poisons.*"

With this explanation, Mahault began to understand the odd actions of Mevrouw Schwarzesherz. Since Monday, after that hung-over "Scotsman" made his escape, the woman had returned home—soaked, and mad as a wet hen. Ever since, she was preoccupied and short-tempered. For the past two days she had acted like a mad woman, rancorously mumbling Polish and Yiddish words that Mahault did not know.

Just two days ago, in the kitchen, she had told Mahault to make sweet fig paste. Then she added some of the beaver extract plus a white powder that she did not name. Mahault thought, *strange ingredient indeed!* and her curiosity grew. Sweetened fig paste did not need enhancement. Everyone knew that; and what *was* that white powder?

Then, on another day, she told Mahault to make fine pricks in the skin of some apples and marinate them in a brine of lemon juice to which she saw Schwarzesherz again add powder. This was not to make the apples more delicious, Mahault deduced; there was another reason.

Mahault could not report to anyone about Vrouw Schwarzesherz' misdeeds. This was an important advantage favoring the Black Widow: Vrouw Schwarzesherz figured that if anyone ever investigated her pursuant to allegations that her practice went beyond perfumery and questioned the girl in due process, Mahault would never, *could* never, utter a word against her.

Nor could Mahault report the Black Widow's attempt to prostitute her—ordering her to bed with the drunken Scotsman that she brought in! Mahault couldn't tell her frail mother or crippled sister. They would die if they knew, and they were helpless.

Mahault suspected that danger awaited the Scotsman, who she thought was probably a good man in spite of what had happened. There was something evil that lurked in Vrouw Schwarzesherz' mixtures that contained castor's essence; and by the time the girl finished reading about the uses of this compound from unfortunate *castor Canadensis*—a poison *or* remedy—Mahault had a premonition that this knowledge would come in handy someday.

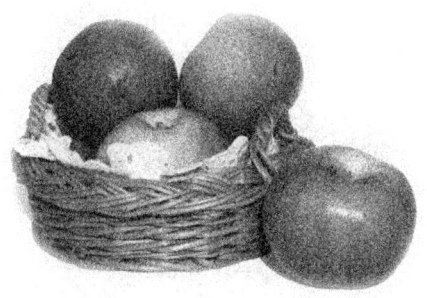

Chapter 34
Quest

Pieter, stepping out of the darkness as he and
Arent were returning the night before, had given Mac
quite a scare; but Pieter only handed over a covered
basket. Mac saw the basket as another goodwill
gesture from Madam Schwarzesherz.

It contained four apples. Mac thought the apples
were of the MacIntosh variety. His Highland Scottish
clan name derived from the MacIntosh clan had
scared Madam Schwarzesherz and this, Mac said,
accounted for his extraordinary powers. He thought,
*How clever that she sent MacIntosh apples! How
thoughtful!*

In the exchange between Pieter and Arent, Mac
overheard the woman's name mentioned. Whatever it
was that they said, Mac believed that the apples
expressed her sincere wish for reconciliation.

Arent did not try to tell Mac what was said,
simply mumbled something in Dutch that might have
meant, "Good night," and then the boy left him at
Aboab's and went over to Rembrandt's house.

For Mac it was another dinner with Aboab, a little
wine, and another night was over. The morning of the

next day—Wednesday—the apple basket from Madam Schwarzesherz rested on the floor in a corner of the kitchen—across from the breakfast nook. The fruit would number with the fig preserves that were stored in the larder. The combination of the apples and fig jam reminded Mac of Faye's apple-fig pie.

Mac, Dieners and Aboab were quietly having breakfast at the table. Mac was thinking, *I must ask Dieners to make a Dutch apple pie like Faye's with Madam Schwarzesherz gifts.* He would think of cutting out a piece—that would be a piece of a "peace pie." He smiled at his own clever play on words and wished he could tell Faye about it.

The three were silent as they ate breakfast, each absorbed in his thoughts. From outside there were the usual street noises: horses' shod hooves and wagons with steel-rimmed wheels that made a racket on the stones of the street. Mac was barely aware of the sounds, however, as by this time he was acclimating to his surroundings and paid only slight attention. Even the carillon did not draw his notice.

He thought about home cooking, about pie made out of apples and fig jam. Mac remembered the humor in the episode of the credit card hologram. He recalled the woman shrieking, *"Evil is the hand that gives the bird!"* He smiled again, visualizing himself offering her pie with the same hand—his hand—and saying to her, *"Here, Madam, have a piece of apple-fig peace pie."* Mac paid no attention to his hosts since they conversed in Dutch.

Dieners had asked Aboab, "What time do you expect Rembrandt, rabbi?" Aboab had been out walking early and had already had a meeting with Rembrandt so he knew the artist's full agenda. It would be a long day, from the sound of it, as he gave Dieners an accounting.

"He told me that it would be around nine-o'clock," said Aboab, and switched to English and related to Mac: "Rembrandt is coming today to make sketches for my portrait."

His mouth full of cheese and bread, Mac could only nod as Aboab waited to see what Mac's reaction might be. After Mac swallowed hard, he said, "Good!" and asked, "Do you think I might stay and watch? I'll be quiet."

"I think not, because van Rijn has planned to send you with Arent this morning. You do recall the floor plan?"

Mac nodded. How could he forget the floor tiles, and his continuing role-play as Arent's deaf-and-dumb helpmate? Except for the possibility of finding the stockpile of Rembrandt's hidden notes, Mac wasn't looking forward to the job. Learning the old master's secrets made it worthwhile.

Aboab had more instructions, so he elaborated: "There is more. At midday, you'll be going to help Dieners to get etching supplies for van Rijn. Rembrandt plans to begin his printing project this afternoon, and so he needs things from the chemist; and, also, from de Gelder, the paper-maker, and then finally the metal smith—because Rembrandt needs copper plates."

Mac was cheered at the prospect of going shopping for printmaking supplies and getting away from the floor project. He looked forward to seeing more of the city, plus Mac might find out from Arent's father where he could see a Hollander Beater—the paper maker's machine that Mac thought must have originated in Holland and, most likely, here in Amsterdam.

With breakfast over, Aboab and Mac helped Dieners with putting things away. Dieners spoke in

Dutch to the rabbi as they finished up and confided that he was really bothered by the apples in the basket that sat in the corner under the larder.

He said, "Father, I am troubled about those apples that Mevrouw Schwarzesherz sent. It is odd that she is so generous toward our guest, sending little gifts of sweets and fruit. On that day she came—delivering Meneer MacRitchie—she was in a foul mood. *Most foul*! She was eager to be rid of him, I thought. Now, the old crone has turned all sweetness and nice."

Aboab swiped a few crumbs off the bread cutting board into the palm of his hand as Dieners spoke his mind. Dieners continued: "I verily believe that she had something against the American when she brought him, and to my mind she probably still does. Do you know what I think, Father?"

Aboab made no answer, but folded his arms across his chest and waited for Dieners to finish.

"I think we should throw those apples of hers to the pigs." Dieners' wastefulness surprised Aboab.

"Throw away good apples? No, Son. I think not. I have already apprised our guest regarding this matter of the Vrouw Schwarzesherz," replied Aboab. "She may have been angry over some misunderstanding with our visitor at first; but see how she seeks forgiveness now? So, we will let it be."

Dieners persisted: "Those apples are covered with a *pox*, as if an insect has been at them," he pointed out, and he went to the basket and picked up one and held it out to the rabbi to show him.

Head tilted, Aboab took the spotty apple and turned it around and around. He saw that Dieners was right—the apple's skin was freckled with little sting-marks. He said, "These fruits came from her basement, no doubt. They are only insect stings. That is all," and he handed the apple back to Dieners. "We should not waste . . .."

"Still . . .," Dieners dared to cut him off. He would not let the matter go, and it tested the rabbi's patience.

"Enough, Son! It is my contention, my belief, that all matters of the world hang in the balance and anyone—like yourself, you personally—can tip it either way with your words. You must think kindly, even in these trivial matters, as we have more pressing things with which to concern ourselves."

Aboab looked over at Mac, who was oblivious of the nature of the debate between himself and Dieners. He noticed that their guest had moved to the window and he gazed outside. Mac appeared to be daydreaming, so Aboab turned back to Dieners, who had clammed up and now sulked.

Aboab continued ingratiatingly, "For one thing, we need to decide the question: *Are we to tell van Rijn about the true nature of our guest?* Of course, I refer to our guest's being 'from the future'?"

There was no response from Dieners, smarting from Aboab's admonishment. A few seconds passed in silence. Mac noticed the break in their conversation and looked around. Both Aboab and Dieners stared at him.

Aboab translated for Mac what he said about telling Rembrandt of Mac's true origins: "We are wondering, Meneer MacRitchie, if we should tell van Rijn the truth about you, I mean, of whence you came. Tell us, what is your opinion?"

"No, I think not. I know too much, and it would not help matters . . .," Mac was quick with his reply but the knocker banging on the door stopped him.

Dieners went to see and returned to the kitchen; and Mac thought, *Speaking of the devil!* as Rembrandt followed him in. Van Rijn's stride was brisk and purposeful—like a business man on his way to work. He carried a pack of paper and clutched some drawing chalks in his hand. He wore a beret today, his untamed hair sticking out like a wreath around his pudgy face.

He was the image of one of the etchings Mac remembered. Here was Rembrandt in the flesh, and in the same second Mac flashed back on the image of the Rembrandt self-portrait wearing a beret. It gave Mac a feeling similar to when he recognized that face in the carriage on Monday! The artist noted Mac's astonishment. Rembrandt smiled and chuckled.

"Well, my American friend," he said, "you look as though you've just seen a ghost!" In Mac's mind the image persisted of the man in reality and in the same moment Mac's memory of van Rijn's world-renowned self-portrait.

Mac was mum. The Old Master's jocularity ended as quickly as it came. He was in a hurry to get the niceties out of the way, so he turned to the business at hand and spoke thoughtfully to Mac.

"How is my good neighbor, the Rabbi Fonseca, treating you? Well, I trust?"

Mac gave a weak nod. Van Rijn continued. "I have spoken with my wife, and she agrees that we must invite you to dinner. Sometime. Soon." With this non-committal, vague invitation having been made, van Rijn changed the subject. He turned to the business at hand, for there was much to do.

"All right!" Redirecting his attention, he spoke to Aboab and, in an almost saccharine manner, he began: "Rabbi Aboab Isaac da Fonseca, my most renowned and esteemed neighbor, leader of the Brazilian mission and worldly voyager, are you ready to sit for your portrait by the *great* Rembrandt van Rijn?" He laughed as the famously humble rabbi nodded, unused to such praise and not sure how he should react to van Rijn's theatrics and vanity.

Mac thought Rembrandt's comic was overly familiar, but the rabbi did not seem to mind. The rabbi smiled and humored the artist and replied, "Yes. It will be an honor," and he started toward the stairs. "We should go up to my front room. The light is better, and we will not be disturbed by anyone."

But Rembrandt wasn't ready quite yet. He turned his attention to Mac to make more arrangements. "Meneer MacRitchie, I could do with more of your help. I have another need to be fulfilled in addition to the floor work that you saw yesterday," he began.

He looked Mac up and down. "I see you have found my clothing suitable, and that's fine. Not a bad fit, I might add." He sniffed and swiped his nose before continuing. "My clothes look better on you than that mad Flemish attire you were wearing when first we met. I confess that I took you to be a jester!" He gave Mac a friendly punch on his shoulder in good fun to make his point.

Rembrandt was being especially nice to Mac, a contrast to the initial minutes when they first met yesterday. He thought, *Yes, my little press does work magic sometimes!*

Rembrandt was in a rambling good mood, now that he was employed and he could set his mind on applying strategic solution to his problem of the notes, solutions that required stealth and intrigue over and above artistry. His eyes were bright as he listed the items on their day's agenda.

"You must go again, Meneer MacRitchie, with Arent, to the floor project at Geerincx' house. You will leave with Arent directly. Then, at midday you will be joined by Dieners."

He paused and gave a nod to Aboab, who listened

from the end of the hallway where he waited at the foot of the staircase. The rabbi acknowledged with a nod of his head since they had worked out the arrangement where Dieners fit in as he had a part in Rembrandt's plan.

"For *your part*, the work on the floor project will take you about two hours, I estimate. You should be able to fulfill *your part* in that time." He laid emphasis on the two words, "your part," to make sure that Mac remembered his special role.

Mac nodded, *Yes, he got it*. The reason for collecting the notes was a secret between him and van Rijn; the rabbi and Dieners would not know about Rembrandt's motives. It came back to Mac, too, that if Aboab or Dieners had revealed Mac's distemporality to van Rijn behind his back or in Dutch, then Rembrandt either didn't believe it, or he was unimpressed; unimpressed or in the dark, either was plausible. Mac had made up his mind, for Rembrandt's own good, that he should never know.

It was to be a full day for Mac of burgling in the morning and going on a shopping spree in the afternoon. Everyone had a task on Rembrandt's list.

"At midday, Dieners will come and tell Geerincx that Arent's helper is needed elsewhere, and Arent will stay there and continue working. Dieners will have my shopping list and, my good patron the rabbi willing . . .," and again he and Aboab exchanged knowing looks to reaffirm their earlier negotiations, ". . . you will have a purse with some money for to buy me etching and printing supplies."

Rembrandt was focused on Mac. "In shopping, there may arise a need for technical clarity. I will rely on your printing knowledge, Meneer MacRitchie, to make substitutions if necessary."

He puckered his lips as he reviewed the plan. He

held Mac in his gaze, and Mac had trouble knowing for sure which of Rembrandt's eyes to focus on, A feeling of *déjà-vu* came as he watched van Rijn screw up his face in concentration like one of his famous face-making etchings.

"Remember, you are not to speak. *Nod and point.* I do not want anyone to know that you are involved with me, you understand. No one will expect you to say anything, as a deaf mute. Don't forget!"

Rembrandt was a man used to giving directions. Had he been born 300 years later, he would probably have been a successful movie director like Steven Spielberg. In the 17th Century, painting was the equal of blockbuster films in the 20th Century, almost the only major public art form, up there with architecture and the opera.

Finished with the recital of his agenda, Rembrandt shuffled off to join Aboab at the foot of the stairs. Midway, van Rijn stopped and turned to add, "I will be here, with the rabbi, to make my sketches."

Aboab started up the stairs as Rembrandt followed him, and the artist continued to recount his schedule, raising his voice to be heard by those below: "When I have finished, then I will lay the oils on the panel that Arent has made ready this morning, after which I will be painting and then do my etching between painting sessions." All this Rembrandt said as he was going up the stairs.

"Arent has the shopping list I made for Dieners. Understand, Meneer MacRitchie?" and, with that final piece, van Rijn was done giving orders.

Below, Mac digested the plan and memorized it. He was thinking about his ball point pen to write it down, how it would be handy but impossible. On the stairs, Rembrandt had stopped halfway up to wait for

Mac to respond; but he hadn't replied.

"Well, Meneer MacRitchie?" Rembrandt barked.

Startled, Mac shouted back, "Okay!" and there followed a moment of stony silence. Dieners stared at Mac, awed at the word, "*Okay*." Rembrandt took three steps back down the stairs.

He said to Mac, "What was that you said? '*Okay*?' What was that supposed to mean?"

Momentary panic gripped Mac. He hoped it wasn't an explicative in Dutch, like *Hell no!* Or Worse! Mac covered quickly.

"'Okay?' That's an expression I learned from . . . from the Indians. It means *'good*' or *'Yes'*. So, I meant, 'Yes, I understand.'"

His explanation satisfied van Rijn. He mulled over the interesting new American Indian word, "'*Okay*.' Hmm. Well, I happen to be interested in the American Indians. So . . .," and van Rijn hesitated as he pondered this tidbit of insight.

To say the least, he *was* interested. Rembrandt had once collected things from both North and South America that were made by the natives. He asked Mac, " . . . You have *talked* with Indians? Yourself?"

"I have done," Mac replied. It was true. He grew up on the Yakama Nation Reservation, but he didn't dare elaborate on this.

Aside, Dieners said to Mac, "I'm impressed. They're not dangerous?" he asked. He was enchanted by this news.

"It depends . . .," Mac began to explain.

Rembrandt interrupted him: "Not now! We have work to do. Some other time we can talk about these things, so, if you please?" and he continued up the stairs.

Dieners issued a sigh, resentful that he was going to miss out on the art session. He would like to have watched Rembrandt in action. Also, he would like to have discussed Mac's adventures with the wild Indians; but Rembrandt was right, they had much to do.

***

A half hour later, as Mac and Arent searched under the loose tiles at Geerincx' house, Mac thought it was like an Easter egg hunt. Surely, Easter Holiday was observed in the 17th Century; but Mac wondered, *Do they hunt colored eggs now*? He had to be silent, or he would have asked his young supervisor, Arent.

It would be interesting to speak English to the kid. It might even be fun! Mac had to keep his sense of humor in check, however. If Geerincx happened to overhear, the ruse would fail and no telling what would happen then.

As they could not speak, they nudged and pointed. Arent had a leather pouch into which they dropped the packets they located. Arent decided on an efficient system to make sure that they had checked every tile in order to locate the right ones. He directed Mac to work from one corner and fan out from there, like the method of an archeological dig. The artifacts were Rembrandt's secrets.

While they made progress, Mac would have given anything to know what was in the notes, but he was mindful that they were none of his business. He wondered if Arent was curious. Mac perceived that the boy wasn't as curious in the same way that he was. Arent was well-disciplined, Mac gave him that. What arrangement there was between Arent and van Rijn was not clear. Mac had only a vague idea about apprenticeships.

After an hour's work, they heard voices up stairs.

One of Geerincx' servants came down and spoke to Arent, who then relayed through his sign language to Mac that he was to go upstairs. Mac's work here was done. Someone was waiting for him outside. Mac felt reluctant, but he expected it to be Dieners because it was about time to go shopping for Rembrandt needs for etching and printing.

As Mac expected, it was Dieners waiting and the aspect of shopping in 17th Century Amsterdam was stirring. Without a word or hesitation, the unlikely pair headed out on the first leg of their shopping spree. Dieners kept a tight grip on the purse strapped to his side. It held money to pay cash to the merchants of paper, chemicals and copper plates.

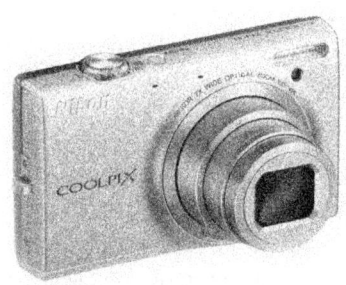

Chapter 35
Printmaker Chest

Mahault spent part of her every day working for Aboab and Rembrandt. The agreements with the two houses in the Rozengraacht were made years ago, when Vrouw Schwarzesherz took Mahault into servitude. Although it was unfair that Mahault had to turn over the greater part of her wages to the Black Widow, the girl preferred it to spending the entire day in the old woman's lair.

At ten o'clock, Mahault came to the rabbi's to do the chambermaid's duties. She let herself in the back way. The house seemed empty, but as she reached the second-floor landing on her way to the top-floor garret, she could hear from behind the closed door the voice of the rabbi; and she recognized Rembrandt's voice, more strident, too.

Mahault went up the stairs and set about doing her work. Having put the bunk bed clothing in order, she noted that Mac's Flemish costume and hat hung on a peg on the wall—unworn today. The chest was still set on the desktop. Its drop-down door hung slightly open, inviting opening.

Resistant to temptation, she turned to her tasks. Mahault set the covered chamber pot on the floor by the top landing of the stairs, a handy spot for when she was ready to take it downstairs. Next, she brought the used wash basin, cloth and the water pitcher and set them alongside the pot. She was about to take all the toilet articles downstairs when, again, the printmaker chest attracted her attention.

She was warned never to snoop in the employers' homes, but she went to the desk to see closer and remembered how avid was Vrouw Schwarzesherz' obsession with the Scotsman's *kist*. The Black Widow could have opened it with Mac's key Sunday night when he was unconscious; but too superstitious and afraid that it might be a trap. Here it was—unlocked and partly open.

The chest was made of a light-colored wood she had never seen and put together with tiny round, black pegs, each one marked with X-shaped notches. Mahault wondered what could be the meaning of these symbols. Maybe these explained Vrouw Schwarzesherz was afraid. They might be warnings but Mahault had no fears. The unlocked drop-down door beckoned to her. If she was careful and peeked to see what was inside, no one would know. The rabbi and Rembrandt, in the room a floor below, would not notice.

With hands that trembled, Mahault lowered the door. She saw wonderful things inside, of which the most attractive was a beautiful, bright red box tied with a gold string. She slipped out the box and recognized the name stamped in gold on the top: "Rembrandt's". But she had never seen the second word: "Chocolates." She tugged on the gold string. It was surprisingly springy and stretched like a silken cord; and yet it shone like real gold.

The cover came off and inside was a piece of delicate, snow white paper and, under that, two neat rows of cubes like polished dark wood. A fragrance, unlike anything she had ever smelled before, wafted by her nose. She picked up one and held it to her nose and sniffed. *Nice!* She sniffed again.

As the cube had started to feel slippery in her fingers, she put the piece down quickly. Where she had held the piece between her finger and thumb, there was a sticky residue. The cube melted—like butter! Mahault started to wipe the dark smear on her white apron, but thought better of it and licked her finger instead.

Pursing her lips, she thought it tasted pretty good; then she licked her thumb. The taste was better the second time. A fleeting, strange sensation came over her. Time seemed to stand still. She stared at the cube and realized that the stamped texture on its top was not merely decoration but a man's face— resembling a nobleman or a burgher—with a flowing wig and great hat. It was a familiar face, somehow.

Mahault dared to pick up the chocolate again, sniffed it once, twice and a third time. Her tensed shoulders dropped, her resistance fell away and, with her eyes slightly closed, with her teeth she tested the cube's hardness. She could feel it beginning to melt again in her fingers, but Mahault was unstoppable.

She bit off the corner!

Her tongue met and melted the tiny bite of chocolate instantly and a spontaneous, perfect, *"Oh!"* escaped her. The rare, spoken word reverberated in her head and shocked her. Panicked, she dropped the chocolate back in the box and licked her fingers.

Eyes wide and staring at the chocolate, Mahault was dazed, partly frightened and partly thrilled, as the combination of fear of being caught and the thrill of the incredible, new taste had worked its magic. Swept away, Mahault wept.

In a minute she sobered and looked at what she had done. She began to shake. Hurriedly she replaced the white paper and the cover and tried to fit the stretchy gold string back in place. With the red box back inside the chest, Mahault calmed.

Next to the red box a black, bulky pouch—like a coin purse with a black strap wrapped around it— caught her notice. She took it out of the chest. This bag was made of a finely-woven, hard fabric. Memory of the penny Mac gave her came back and she wondered, *Could this be a pouch full of coins?* But it was not heavy enough to be full of coins.

A short black metal tab dangled from its side and invited her fingers to take it. Marveling at the ingenuity of the thing, Mahault unzipped it, smiling at the sound it made. She zipped and unzipped it several times. *Zzzip! Ziiip!*

Inside the pouch there was a hard, pewter-colored object. This was Mac's, like new, digital camera, a thing completely alien to the girl's wondering eyes. It spoke to this curious and imaginative girl, as if to say: *"Take me out, take me out!"*

Her encounter with the chocolate magic made Mahault more daring and, although she knew that she should not, she *did* take the camera out of its case. She turned it over and over, studying all of its features. Even in the half-light of the garret, the object's surfaces shone like silver and other silky-smooth, precious metals of kinds that she had never seen in any of the homes where she worked.

On one edge there was a small, mirror-finished

silver bubble and it urged her, *"Press me, press me!"* When Mahault did, she nearly dropped the camera because it awakened with a soft, purring and clicking sound; when it stopped, an obscene extension had insinuated itself out its side.

She smiled at the treasure she held, thinking that it must be an automaton like the mechanical toys at Meneer Lingelbach's *Nieuwe Doolhof* across the street. This was different and much better, although she could not imagine its use.

Turning it over she was astonished to see that a tiny, bright, shimmering painting had magically appeared on the side opposite of the protruding turret, and the picture moved each time she moved. It was like a tiny, bejeweled mirror that changed with even the slightest movement.

Mahault was mesmerized as she slowly moved the camera this way and that and watched the little picture change. She looked again at the silver bubble she had pressed first that set it in motion. She saw, too, that besides the one she pressed there was a second, larger bubble that she hadn't noticed.

She pressed it. It made a noise like, *"Kuh-lick!"* and again it startled her but she held it tight, emboldened by the experience of the moment before. Mahault waited to see what the automaton would do next.

She waited.

And waited.

Nothing happened.

She realized now why Vrouw Schwarzesherz was obsessed and muttered endlessly about the Scotsman's *kist*. Was it this automaton that was the object of the Black Widow's dark desires? Or the seductive, dark cubes with their wonderful flavor? How could she know? She could not have guessed in a hundred years because the magical things Mahault saw were far and away more powerful than anything known by the possessed Vrouw Schwarzesherz.

Thirty seconds passed with Mahault immersed in the miracles when, suddenly, the metal thing vibrated in her hands and, with a quiet sigh—as if tired of waiting for Mahault to do something—it withdrew its turret. Awed, she watched as the extension tucked itself back into its hard shell like a turtle pulling in its head.

Mahault put the object into its pouch and—as she was already expert in using a zipper—she zipped it shut and put it back into the chest. She thought everything looked the way it had been.

Now there was no doubt in Mahault's mind. She was convinced that the foreigner was a true sorcerer, and—in her mind—probably a good one.

It would be too bad if he had to die.

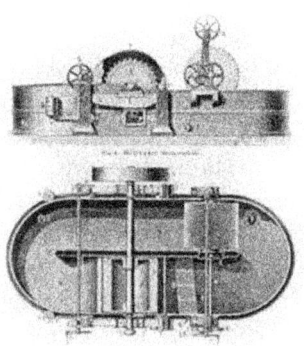

Chapter 36
Papermaker Revisited

Dieners' and Mac's first stop on their shopping trip was the papermaker's. When he opened the door, Arent's father was impressed with the fact that he was to meet Mac for a second time. De Gelder thought that, despite the poor man's handicap, the mute foreigner had an intelligent face.

The previous night, when Arent showed up with Mac, there was no time for de Gelder to learn anything at all about the foreign-looking stranger who, today, was accompanied by Aboab's African helper, Dieners. The unfriendly coucher, who Mac had seen the night before, now sat at rest and bestowed a bigoted glower on Mac and Dieners.

Mac could only smile as all the while Dieners did the talking. De Gelder knew Rabbi Aboab's dwarf assistant by reputation, and he also knew the fact that the Fonseca house neighbored Arent's master's house—his former customer—the debtor Rembrandt van Rijn. Dieners offered that de Gelder's son was away working on a special project in the

Jodenbreestraat and, coincidentally, Mac had been helping him that very morning.

He got down to business and said that they came to order paper for Rembrandt's new project, a type of paper that would be suitable for printing playing cards. He allowed he thought the paper would be different from paper that de Gelder usually provided publishers for prints, books and maps.

This posed no problem to the papermaker—renowned expert in his industry—because he made playing-card paper for Jacques van Leest. The problem was—and it caused an awkward moment—Rembrandt had never paid de Gelder what he owed for paper years ago!

The coucher, who still sat on his stool and had put his head in his hands, overheard Rembrandt's name and he stood up and barked, "Har!" and spat. "Master de Gelder, don't listen to these two foreigners—the little African and the stupid one—everyone knows Rembrandt does not pay!" he said.

Dieners straightened and he seemed to grow two inches taller; but he said nothing. As for Mac, he didn't know what the coucher had said in Dutch but it didn't sound friendly. They glared at each other briefly; but Mac looked away and wondered, *What's going on?*

De Gelder hesitated. He knew the coucher had a hangover and was in a foul mood and rude, but he had to agree that the coucher was right. When he asked Dieners if Rembrandt expected to order the paper on credit, Dieners unstrapped his purse belt and handed over ten guilders. Then he answered the coucher with a dirty look.

De Gelder's manner changed quickly and the transaction was settled without further ado. Rembrandt would have his paper. Thus did de Gelder tell the coucher to make up a package of sheets of a certain paper. Still sullen, the coucher went to another room to do as his employer ordered.

There was yet another matter. As they had walked along on their way to the paper mill, Mac cautiously asked Dieners a favor—one to which the boy had agreed before they got there. It was a request that the papermaker give them directions to a paper mill where Mac could see a *Hollander Beater*.

Dieners' description of the machine no doubt suffered in translation; and what followed was comical because Mac accompanied Dieners' Dutch words, miming with gestures, grunts, facial expressions and signing.

De Gelder watched the show, open-mouthed, and he slowly shook his head in disbelief. He didn't understand. Dieners' description of the machine made no sense to the papermaker, and he knew machinery well.

Eagerly, Mac offered to draw a picture of the machine's workings. With a piece of brown chalk and paper, he drew a diagram and pointed out comparisons to the stamper that constantly rattled and banged away in the background as they tried to communicate what it was that Mac was eager to be shown.

Mac churned his fists to imitate the rolling, grinding action of the cylinder that he remembered the macerating action of the Hollander Beater's he had seen in his day. It took a great effort for him not to explain what he meant. Dieners made an effort, too; but the boy neither understood what he himself was talking about, nor why Mac wanted to see this incredible thing.

De Gelder listened to Dieners, shook his head and—awed by Mac's weird show—gave Dieners a look that suggested his helper ought to get a doctor's help. Anyway, he said, no such machine existed in Amsterdam.

Mac judged that their effort was of no use and maybe he had pressed the man too far. He smiled and, as Dieners took his arm, Mac backed off with a grateful nod to de Gelder. He had tried; but it was no use.

The coucher came back with the sheets wrapped in a heavy gray paper and tied with rough string. His mood had not changed, and he looked doubtful as Dieners reached for the package, but relented and handed it down whereupon Dieners smartly hoisted it over his head like a great hood and turned toward the door to go.

Mac followed, and gave a backward glance to see de Gelder scratch his head in bewilderment at Mac's schematic he still held his hand.

They closed the door behind them and Mac followed Dieners' lead as they headed to the alchemist's where they were going to buy Rembrandt's necessary etching chemicals.

For a few minutes after Dieners and MacRitchie were gone, de Gelder continued to study Mac's sketch. The coucher sidled up beside him and with a disparaging remark, he asked to see it.

"Ach!" he said, and by habit he turned his head to spit. "That foreign dolt's scribbling is garbage—better to make that paper useful and throw it back into where it can do some good!" With that he snatched the paper and started toward the tub.

De Gelder stopped him and retrieved the drawing to give it more study and figure out what the mute foreigner had meant to show. He understood that the mute wanted to see a machine like it, whatever *it* was. De Gelder wondered, *But why ask me?*

A minute passed. He was absorbed by the drawing. One might say the wheels were going around in his head. He was silent until—thanks to his mechanical acumen plus his lifetime spent in beating rags into paper pulp—his engineer's mind gave him to realize how the machine in the drawing worked.

It came clear to him in a flash! The beater's shafts and cogs would be powered by his windmill and the spinning, tooth-ridged, cylindrical drum rolling against a hard platen would pulverize and macerate the rags. In the whirlpool of water and rags in an oval tub, the linen fibers would be reduced to mush much faster than in a stamp mill!

"*Eureka!*"

The elder de Gelder let out with a shout so loud that he could be heard over the din of the stamp mill. The coucher stepped back aghast and the other mill workers looked up. De Gelder scared his wife in the other room and she came to see what happened. Excitedly, her husband showed her the drawing. She looked at it and then at her overwrought husband. Worry lines crisscrossed her face.

Was he crazy? Later, his wife would understand from her husband's explanation what Mac's drawing described. The *Hollander Beater* would become the name by which the machine was known for centuries to come and it would revolutionize the papermaking industry worldwide. The de Gelder couple would—in the end—*go from rags to riches,* and big time! It would be just as de Gelder sang to her to charm his dear wife.

De Gelder's shout of *Eureka,* while it was loud, was not loud enough to reach Mac and Dieners' ears. The two were too far away by now.

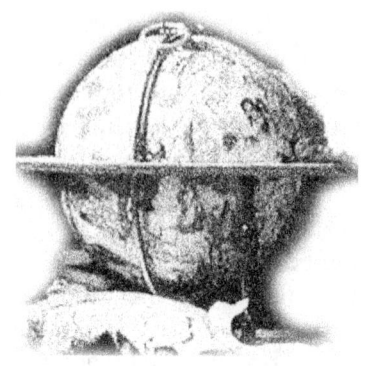

Chapter 37
Toxic Printmaking

In the alchemist's shop, the extensive collection of jars, boxes, barrels and bottles astounded Mac. At first glance, he might have thought it was a spice and tea shop; but then his nose met with the acrid smells. It was a store that sold an array of chemicals for industries of the day such as ore-testing and refining, metalworking, production of gunpowder, ink, dyes, paints, cosmetics, leather tanning, ceramics, glass manufacture, preparation of extracts, liquors, and so on.

This shop was the source of ingredients for Rembrandt's etching solution, too. The solution would be known by Mac in his day as an "etching mordant." He once used a green solution in his studio called "Dutch Mordant," and he remembered that, to make it, he mixed hydrochloric acid and potassium chlorate in water. This mordant was especially good for etching copper plates, but it had a nasty, irritating chlorine smell. Mac hadn't used it for years. He preferred to use ferric chloride, which was just as good—if not better—since it is a mineral salt and not a corrosive acid.

Dieners called out and the proprietor came in from the back. He wore a heavy, grimy leather apron. He had the look of one who had been too long around dangerous substances. His hair was patchy; he squinted and blinked frequently and also he twitched as he peered at the two. Mac thought, *Life among chemicals must be hard on a man. This one will die young, probably, from exposures to the things that he has had to deal with daily.*

The fellow had a fidgety manner as he assessed the unusual combination of a dwarf African and a foreign-looking person who, to his eyes, appeared to be not quite right in the head.

When Dieners read from Rembrandt's scribbled shopping list, it was evident that there must not be much call for the etching ingredients because the shopkeeper shrugged and shook his head. Maybe he didn't stock the chemicals. More likely, it was because he was too distracted by the odd-looking pair in front of him. To the shopkeeper, the dark dwarf and mute old man didn't look like they *really* could know what they were asking for. They weren't the type that usually came in his shop.

After Dieners made repeated attempts to convince the shopkeeper that they *did* know what they were about, he turned to Mac and signed for him to hand over the blackened etching plate Mac had in his pocket. They had brought this plate with them as they might need to explain that the chemicals were going to be used to eat lines in copper.

"*Voor het in eten van koper,*"[85] Dieners told the man. Mac caught the word "*eten*" and he thought how similar the word sounded to the English word,

---

[85] For to eat copper.

"etching." He took the plate out of his pocket and handed it to the chemist. The man took it, looked, squinted and held it to study—so close that it almost touched his nose. So it happened that bringing the plate was a good piece of foresight, because the man nodded, handed the plate back to Mac and went into the back room where he kept the most potent stock.

Mac pocketed the plate, thinking, again, *This plate proves that fate works in strange ways!* The touch and feel of the plate took Mac back to his home in the 21st Century, and how curious it was—in Mac's home-time—that the old plate had traveled all the way from the Atlantic Northeast to reach him out in the Pacific Northwest. Mac had been asked to clean and print it for its owner because the Easterner didn't own an etching press. This was what Mac had in mind on Halloween night in Seattle as he started to clean off the black, hard coating. He had planned to print the plate the next day.

Instead, the plate had brought him here! That's what Mac had meant when he told Aboab the first time that they talked as he said, "That plate transported me." Mac evaded Aboab's questions and stalled so as to avoid the real truth of how he had landed on a dung boat at dawn in Amsterdam. The plate was a kind of magic carpet like something out of *The Arabian Nights*—a magic plate.

While the shop's proprietor weighed portions of the chemicals, Mac looked around and spied a world globe that sat atop a huge wooden barrel and he went to get a closer look. The globe was like the replica of an antique one that Mac had seen in a mail-order catalog that came to his home. This world globe, however, was not a replica of the 17th Century model; it was the *state-of-the-art* thing, the real 17th Century world as known today.

Mac saw that there were spaces on its surface that did not show extant islands and the correct shapes of continents. The land masses looked distorted, out of proportion, and they had strange names. Seattle was not on the globe, of course, and California was shown as being an island.

There were images of exotic animals, incredible sea monsters and dotted lines that ran from Europe and crossed the oceans and marked ships' courses indicated by the famous voyagers' names—Magellan, Drake and Loyola.

Presently the alchemist returned with two earthenware jars plugged with wood stoppers. He covered the tops in oilskin and tied string on them to make sure that the oilskin stayed in place. He was continually talking to Dieners while he kept an eye on the African's manservant, Mac. Dieners shelled out several gold coins from his purse and then directed Mac to gather up the jars.

The shopkeeper said, "*Wacht een minuut,*"[86] and he gave Mac a small basket for carrying chemicals.

Outside in the damp, cold air again, Mac issued a snort to try to clear his irritated nostrils; and Dieners—his nostrils bothered likewise—rubbed his nose vigorously. The air of the shop was contaminated with particulate toxins and noxious vapors.

Dieners led the way toward their next stop—the metal smith's shop. Mac carried the basket with the containers in his left hand. After a little way, his free, right hand felt cold and he automatically shoved it into his pants pocket for warmth. There his hand met the sharp edge of the plate.

As Mac and Dieners walked toward a small

---

[86] Wait a minute.

drawbridge for pedestrians that crossed over a canal, Mac's index finger—as if it was curious and had an idea of its own—sought out the partly-cleaned spot on the plate and felt for the texture of the etched face there. Mac was not aware of doing it, but he teased at it with his fingernail.

In mid-step, at the moment that Mac reached the steps to the footbridge, a Boeing 787 "Dreamliner" roared overhead and Mac met a rush of many voices. The street and the drawbridge on which Mac was about to cross was filled with 21st Century tourists rushing around him. Everywhere there were reflections on chrome, gaudy street signs and neon lights. Mac turned in a small circle taking in a 360-degree view, then spun back around as a car horn beeped on his left and startled him as a silver-and-purple SmartCar whizzed by. The driver and the passenger craned their necks and the passenger gave him the finger and laughed. Mac tottered and stepped back toward the bridge steps as a bicyclist in red-and-black spandex ding-dinged his bicycle bell, and headed right for him. Mac leapt toward the bridge steps and, in the next instant, the roar of the jet, the bike, car, people, signs and the cacophony of noises switched off!

The mirage of noisy, 21st Century Amsterdam was gone as fast as it came. Mac jerked his hand out of his pocket and grabbed the drawbridge handrail to catch his balance. There he stood for a second by the railing. He felt dizzy and he hung firmly to the wood rail with his right hand and on the basket in his left hand.

Dieners, already partway across the bridge, noticed that Mac was not with him. He looked back for his helpmate and saw Mac, who held on to the railing, his mouth open and with a lost-look.

The shock Mac felt was gone in a twinkling, and the hallucination left no more of an impression on him than if a shadow of a plane had passed over on a sunny day. It vanished from his thoughts, like it never happened. Yet, still, Mac remained rooted to his spot by the steps of the bridge.

Dieners came back to where Mac stood and nudged him. Mac looked down at Dieners and blinked wonderingly as if seeing him for the first time. Dieners looked around them to make sure that no one was watching as he took Mac's arm away from the handrail.

Dieners muttered out of the side of his mouth, "Don't overdo it. You're only mute. You don't have to look like an idiot!"

With the basket in his left hand, Mac walked on and let his right hand ride along the smooth, worn wood railing and resumed his place a few steps behind Dieners. They stepped off the bridge on the other side of the canal and, a little way farther on, they went toward a side street which would take them to the metal smith's.

At the opening of the street, Dieners paused and looked up at a certain house. He beckoned for Mac to take note and whispered hoarsely, "This is where Rembrandt lived when he was first married to Saskia. He became successful, and then they moved to the Jodenbreestraat." Dieners nodded in the direction that they were heading. "Not far from here is where he got copper plates for etchings," he added.

Two people approached and looked curiously at the odd pair. As they saw where Dieners and Mac stared, then they, too, looked up at the house. There was nothing remarkable about it; and when they looked again at Dieners and Mac, the two were already off to their next destination.

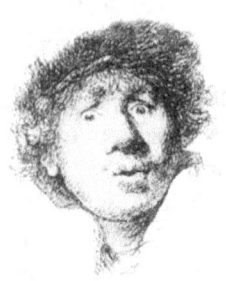

Chapter 38
Kitchen Etching

There would be no lunch today at Rembrandt's for the Master of the House was busy at his art and craft. Rembrandt took over the kitchen when his drawing session next door with Aboab was finished and the paper samples, chemicals and copper plate arrived, brought home to The Blue Crown by Dieners and Mac.

The shopping trip had been a success, and van Rijn was generous with his compliments for his two helpers. Dieners had left immediately, as Rabbi Aboab was behind in his Synagogue duties and needed Dieners to help him catch up.

All was quiet at the Rembrandt household, and in the kitchen Hendrickje looked over van Rijn's etching things that cluttered her otherwise orderly domain. She asked, "How should we prepare dinner with all these things taking up the room?" She spoke softly so as not to annoy her husband, as Rembrandt had begun to get back into his old familiar etching production mode after a long time of neglect.

In his former home, van Rijn had ample space,

plus windows that opened to let out the smells of his mordant solution and those of spirits, warmed ink vapors and burnt linseed oils. Here, he had to make do with Hendrickje's kitchen; and then, later, he would print in the middle room. He was resigned that the kitchen would have to serve, she guessed, and did not persist any further. She could wait.

He was busy opening the parcels from Dieners' and Mac's shopping. Checking the contents, Rembrandt picked out the samples of de Gelder paper and tested one, feeling it with his fingers. He held the sheet up to the lamp as if to see through its substance; then he stuck out his tongue and touched the paper's edge with it to estimate how much sizing was in this paper. He nodded. He found it acceptable.

Concentrating on his preparations, Rembrandt hadn't answered Hendrickje's question about space for cooking. Knowing better than to say more, she quietly withdrew, leaving van Rijn alone with his single, attentive audience member, the American colonist.

Out of the blue, Rembrandt asked Mac, "Where did you learn about etching?"

Mac told a lie built on his best guess of any American center for learning etching that was likely to have been in existence in the year 1660. "At Harvard. They etch to make decorative work for name plates."

Mac avoided reminding Rembrandt of the printed dollar bill since the etcher had flatly denied its being an authentic print. Either van Rijn accepted Mac's as a Harvard-trained etcher or he wasn't listening to him, immersed as he was in making preparations for his drawing on his new copper plate.

Mac was agog as the way Rembrandt prepared the new plate was so different from the way that he was accustomed to doing plate making in his 20th Century days. For almost a generation, Mac had taught etching at the University of Washington. At that time, etching materials and supplies came in boxes, cans and bottles, already made up and ready to use. Little preparation by the students was required, nor was it expected of them. The techniques that Rembrandt knew and practiced constituted a lost art.

Mac never had to mix his own etching grounds or grind pigments in oil to make printing inks. When students had asked him how they could make their own inks, etching grounds and engraving tools in the old world manner, Mac had diverted their earnest curiosity. He would not admit that sometimes *he did not know the answer!* Instead, he would say something vague about "professional practices," or respond with a clever dismissive, such as, "You don't want to know."

Students *did* want to know, however. In fact, one former art student, after art school and on his own, dug through antiquated books, tried some old ink formulas he found, and proceeded to build a company around ink-making with the slogan, *Life is short. Art is long.* He had a passion for old printmaking techniques so he had begun with etching ink; as his company grew he added paints and pastels to his company's offering.

However, there was a shred of truth to Mac's snide answer, *You don't want to know.* Printmaking materials and supplies of certain kinds were actually toxic and hazardous and required special precautions in their preparation and use. Bright-colored pigments frequently are oxides of heavy metals—bad for your health if you inhaled the finely-ground powdered pigments. Fumes from heated etching grounds are carcinogenic—a few seconds' breathing them equaled

312

smoking a pack of cigarettes. Solvent fumes could cause fainting spells.

In Mac's time, the Occupational Health and Safety Administration—OSHA—had established stringent rulings about the ways that institutional employees were to handle liquid etching grounds, Dutch Mordant and even lampblack pigment. Books were published on the hazards of art materials, and Mac had seen most of the toxic compounds used by the old masters, like Rembrandt, replaced with nontoxic substitutes. The things spread around Huisvrouw Rembrandt's kitchen were forbidden in the art school studios of Mac's day.

Mac was among the last, diehard holdouts for old-world techniques and he advocated the use of archival papers, inks and oils in printmaking. The smells in the kitchen inspired nostalgia and desire for honest-to-goodness, original etching methods and materials for printmaking that were the almost-forgotten ways of the old masters. Therefore, the scent was like printmaker perfumery to Mac.

He was surprised to see that Rembrandt was *not* using a *hardened* acid resist on his plate such as Mac had taught his students to use. The coating that van Rijn applied was soft and pasty. He applied the resist using a soft, flat brush with the sureness and dexterity of a painter. His strokes were sure and even, and what resulted was a smooth, black coating on the copper.

Almost without stopping in the coating process, Rembrandt picked up a stylus and was about to apply it to the plate when they heard the front door open and then close. Mac could hear Hendrickje and Arent's voices from the other end of the apartment.

A second later, Cornelia bounced into the kitchen from the other room. The little girl excitedly announced Arent's return, lisping her *"S"* sounds.

"Vader, Arent ith terug. Hij heeft wat bij zich en hij ith ook vuil!"[87]

Mac smiled at her excitement and her wispy-sounding words, even though Mac didn't understand what she said. Rembrandt grunted, acknowledging his daughter's news, but he remained attentive on his drawing on the plate.

The artist spoke to Mac without looking up: "Meneer MacRitchie, my daughter just said 'Arent is back,' and 'he has something,' and she also said, 'he's dirty,'" and van Rijn chuckled.

As Rembrandt had finished the translation of Cornelia's outburst, Arent appeared in the kitchen doorway. Sure enough, he *was* dirty—his clothes dusted with whitish grit; his hands were grimy and little patches of dried blood showed where he had nicked himself. He looked dead-tired from continuing alone on the floor project for the hours after Mac had left him at Geerincx' house. Arent put the leather pouch on the table, bulging with the collection of Rembrandt's notes.

Mac was keen to know what the notes inside the pouch said. He wondered, *How could Arent resist sneaking a peek? If I were a Rembrandt student, I would sure want to know my master's inner thoughts! Therein would be the core of his creative genius, his secret, inner visions—a goldmine of ideas!* Yet the aspiring young painter appeared to be indifferent to the treasure he had collected—his face as nonchalant as if he had been out picking up litter.

With a single, sweeping glance, Arent took in the collection of etching miscellany arranged around the kitchen work area; he sidled in closer to see his master's actions. As he stood close to Mac he could

---

[87] Father, Arent is back. He has something with him and also he is dirty! (Lisping her *S* sounds)

smell the boy's hours of sweating away at the hard work he had been doing.

Without looking away from his plate, Rembrandt spoke to Arent in Dutch:

"How did it go?"

"Fine."

"Did you get everything?"

"Yes."

Arent said no more. He was engrossed in Rembrandt's drawing. With only the low light from several candles, it was hard to see but for the glint and copper sparkle of delicate lines Rembrandt scratched through the thin coating of etching ground.

A face was taking shape under van Rijn's stylus. He started with a nose and forehead; and then began scribbling many curling lines for hair—a lot of hair! Mac and Arent were silent, aware that they were in the presence of an imaginative genius at the work of invention. This etching would be yet another Rembrandt self-portrait—suitable, perhaps, to his idea of an artist's playing card.

Mac happened to look at Rembrandt's face and was surprised to see the artist grin, then scowl, and then he opened his eyes wide with an exaggerated look of surprise. His forehead wrinkled in a washboard of furrows; then his forehead went smooth. He sucked in his cheeks, puffed them out, and his mouth twisted and leered in an amusing range of theatrics.

Without the aid of a mirror, van Rijn documented the plasticity of his own face on the copper plate. At one point Rembrandt chuckled, although no one had said anything funny. He seemed to be enjoying the moment, as if he had abandoned the world and all his problems for a precious few minutes. As Rembrandt's current reality was broken, the act of drawing a caricature of his own face—all happy and gay—might actualize a better reality for him.

With a giggle Cornelia said, *"Vader, je gezicht ziet er grappig uit!"*[88] She had slipped in between Mac and Arent to see what her father was doing; but she only watched her father's face, not what he drew. So Cornelia told him he looked funny and laughed at her father, and this broke the spell that held van Rijn and mesmerized Mac and Arent.

In Dutch, van Rijn responded to Cornelia's witty remark, "Yes, Little Cake! Vader *is* making faces just to see you smile!" and with that he set down the plate and his scribe, reached his arms up high and, turning to her—his face all twisted and fearsome—he wriggled his fingers, claw-like, and grappled at her threateningly. He snarled, "And now I am hungry and I see a delicious Little Cake! I shall gobble it up! Here I come!"

Cornelia squealed, leaped and stepped backward toward the middle room. Rembrandt strode stiff-legged after her, fingers high and wiggling. Terrified and delighted by her father's sudden, scary act, Cornelia turned on her heel and—with an ear-piercing shriek, she ran to the other room and the safety of her mother's arms.

Arent and Mac winced as Cornelia's screech hit a high note and the two exchanged grins. Mac could not know how long it had been since Rembrandt had shown joy like this, the delight that he showed in those few seconds. Arent knew, however, and he thought, *The American has no concept of what Rembrandt has gone through for the past few years.*

Simultaneously, Arent and Mac turned back to study the plate that was lying where Rembrandt had

---

[88] Father, your face looks funny!

316

set it down. He had drawn a good likeness of his face, wearing a fur cap. The bright, coppery lines showed him scowling out from the black. This face was ready to be bitten into the metal by the acid mordant.

"Arent, prepare the etching bath!" Rembrandt said, as he returned to the kitchen. Mac heard Hendrickje laugh behind him in the other room and she spoke softly to her daughter. Cornelia giggled about something her mother said.

With no hesitation, Arent got busy and took a glazed shallow stoneware dish from a shelf. He poured water into it from a pitcher and gingerly opened the string-tied-and-stoppered earthenware bottle that Dieners and Mac had brought from the alchemist's.

Van Rijn went again to be with his family as Arent dribbled the liquid into the water. The penetrating smell of chlorine told Mac that this was the hydrochloric acid. How they made it in these old times was a mystery to Mac. If anyone had asked if they had this acid in the 17th Century, Mac would have guessed, "No." While Mac had used Dutch Mordant to etch copper in his studio—and also at school, but rarely—he never knew why they called it "Dutch Mordant" until now. He supposed it had been invented here.

Arent opened another of the bottles that contained a crystalline powder which looked like lumpy table salt. He shook some of the crystals into the water-and-acid solution and then Arent rocked the pan back and forth so that it would dissolve faster.

Mac remembered the formula by this time. He thought, *That's the potassium chlorate! Who would have thought they had this stuff this far back?* There was a lot that Mac didn't know about the Lowlands' branches of alchemy—the *protoscience* of the Dutch

Republic's Golden Age.

Rembrandt came back into the kitchen. "Bath ready?" he asked Arent.

"Yes, Master," his assistant replied, as he stoppered the bottles and methodically re-tied the oil cloth over the corks.

"Good. You'll be a fine etcher someday yourself, Meneer de Gelder."

Although Arent's chest swelled with his master's compliment, inwardly he knew that his fame would be for painting, more likely. He didn't like all the messy chemicals required in the art of etching—the pungent fumes of the mordant and the irritating black dust of the pigment for the inks. They all seemed poisonous to his way of thinking.

Also, you had to follow the system through several steps without seeing your results right away like you can in drawing. The job of grinding dry pigments and oil for painting were nothing by comparison to etching. Also there was Arent's secret copper point drawing that was a better use of his time and creativity. Painting and copper point drawing— *Yes*! Arent thought, *These will be my claim to fame someday, not etching. Not likely will I be remembered for etching.*

Rembrandt continued to bestow credit on Arent. "Also, you did a good job preparing the panel for the rabbi's portrait. I've already made progress with the under-painting." A second later, van Rijn gave him an affectionate look and added, "Thank you, Arent," as he went to the table where Arent put the pouch.

Arent glanced at Mac to see if the foreigner was as surprised as he was at the changes that had come over Rembrandt this day, his ebullience and play with Cornelia, and his generosity with praise and gratitude. He was a different Rembrandt compared to a few days ago. He saw, however, that Mac only stood there looking at the copper plate. The boy thought, *No, he has no idea how different the Master has become. The fool can't even understand Dutch!*

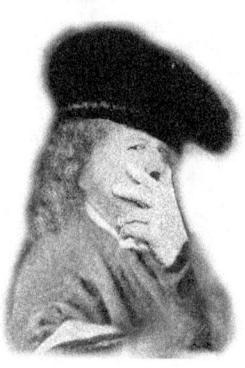

Chapter 39
Mac Beware!

At the table where Arent had put the fruits of his labor that day—the pouch—Rembrandt fiddled with the buckle on its closing strap; but whatever he intended, he changed his mind and set it aside. He returned to his plate, carefully picked it up and let it slide off his fingers into the fresh etching bath. The copper lines instantly turned to neon blue-green in the mordant. It was quite beautiful to see.

"Now, let me have a look at what you brought back," said Rembrandt, and he turned again to the leather pouch. He removed the strap from the buckle, opened the flap and reached in. As he retrieved one of the packets, Rembrandt shot a furtive look at the door of the other room where Cornelia and Hendrickje could be heard as they talked and played a game. Mac noted that if Arent was curious about Rembrandt's obvious secrecy, the boy's face sure didn't show it.

Mac knew why Rembrandt acted sneaky, however, because he shared something with van Rijn. It was an unspoken awareness of the importance of those packets' contents—Rembrandt's data mine.

Mac thought that those writings must be the genius' observations about reality, thoughts on creativity, theories about where ideas come from, notions about faith and religiosity, spirit and life and death. Heavy stuff—these were the kinds of things Mac—in his egg-headed, professor's arrogance, had thought about and, he assumed, so did Rembrandt.

Mac availed himself to 21st Century, hand-held digital devices, scanners, optical character and voice-recognition software on computers and wrote and collected thousands of these sorts of notes. He understood Rembrandt's compulsion to set his musings to paper. Would Rembrandt share his writings and his thoughts with Mac? Would he let Mac read his secrets? And would these tiny notes, over time, become resource material for historians' eyes so that they could write accurate, detailed accounts of Rembrandt's ideas and so publish them over the ensuing centuries?

Mac couldn't recall if his favorite authority on van Rijn, Simon Schama, provided direct quotes from Rembrandt's notes; Mac thought, *probably not*. Could it be, then, that this treasury of notes did not survive? Mac thought about all these things while Rembrandt unsealed the packet that he had taken out of the pouch.

"Would you like to know for what you worked so hard to bring back to me?" he asked Arent in Dutch. He repeated the question in English for Mac's benefit. "Would *you* like to read one, Meneer MacRitchie?"

The two both nodded—Mac first and with obvious enthusiasm. Rembrandt smiled at him and withdrew a small piece of paper from the packet—it looked like a modern matchbook to Mac, only thinner. Van Rijn carefully and slowly unfolded it. Once opened, he read it to himself first, holding it close to his eyes to make out the tiny, silverpoint handwriting done so many years ago.

"*Cum autem peregrinus incerta futuri nescia,*"[89] he droned, and then bestowed a broad smile on his rapt listeners, pleased with himself.

"Arent! How's your Latin?' he asked, and, then in English, "Meneer MacRitchie, I don't suppose you read Latin, do you?"

Mac shook his head and admitted that he did not. He mentally calculated where he might find a Latin translator if he could somehow get those notes back to Seattle in the 21st Century. Probably he could use an Internet translation service, in fact.

Rembrandt handed the little paper to Arent as it fell to his assistant to decipher the meaning of the note. Arent read it and his eyes wandered to the ceiling and he recited, translating into Dutch: "*Als je een buitenlander bent . . .,*"[90] and he stopped, shrugged.

"I don't think I know the rest," he confessed and looked to Rembrandt for the remainder of the translation.

"The rest is: '. . . *onzekere toekomst, niet wetende!*"[91] van Rijn related in Dutch. Then, in English for Mac, "'*If you are a stanger, the future is uncertain but it is not unknown!*' Ha! I remember writing that! But what was I thinking? What a load of *drek*!" van Rijn disparaged loudly over his portentous scribbling.

His explication could be heard in the next room, and Hendrickje objected, "Rembrandt! Please! *Your language!*"

---

[89] When you are a stranger the future is uncertain but it is not unknown.

[90] When you are a stranger . . .

[91] . . . the future is uncertain but it is not unknown.

"Ach, yes. Sorry. *Sorry*," called van Rijn, loudly enough, and he addressed Cornelia and added to his apology in Dutch, "Little Cake, never say that word!" and he smirked at Arent.

Mac was not privy to van Rijn's self-deprecation in the Dutch language; and neither did Mac understand the explicative, *drek*; he knew not what transpired between Hendrickje and van Rijn, nor did Rembrandt bother to translate anything.

Rembrandt left the pouch for a moment and went over to examine the progress of his plate that lay immersed in the mordant. Mac and Arent were quiet, afraid to speak as the artist's manner had turned somber while he gently rocked the tray back and forth and gazed into the greenish solution at his etching.

Deep in thought and, as though he was alone in the room, van Rijn muttered low, " *'If you are a stranger, the future is not certain but it is not unknown.'* Indeed. Stupid! Yes, I was stupid." In saying this, he spoke English so as not to drum too strongly into Arent's memory his words of self-contempt. Mac got it, and he thought wonderingly, *I don't understand why he is so hard on himself.*

Rembrandt concluded his pondering over what he would do since, at long last, he had the worrisome secrets back in his hands. He switched back to speaking Dutch and said, "Arent, forget those words. They are foolishness. The bag is full of that . . .," and he lowered his voice, ". . . *drek*." He added, quieter, still speaking Dutch, and with gravity, "I want you to take it out and dump all that *drek* in a canal—a canal far from here."

Arent thought Rembrandt must be kidding, but then he could see by his master's face that he was serious. He said, with his voice lowered in keeping with Rembrandt's confidential tone—almost whispering—"Dump it? Throw the packets away? After all that work I did to get them?"

Rembrandt nodded with earnest. Then he turned back to his acid tray, picked out the copper plate and rinsed it in a bowl of water in the sink nearby. He turned back to the work table where the light was better and peered at the plate closely.

Arent had not moved. After a while he said, "*Dump* them? All that work for nothing?" Arent repeated. He was incredulous.

Rembrandt nodded again and—without looking up, said, "Dump them, yes. Let them float out to the Zuider Zee. Let the herring read them! Food for thought! Ha ha!" He laughed. Then he silenced and continued to examine his printing plate.

Even having been told a second time, Arent did not move. After a minute, Rembrandt explained, "Already, I feel somewhat relieved since you retrieved those, young de Gelder, and I will be completely relieved when they are food for the fishes."

He respected Arent's reluctance, and he repeated Arent's words back to him: " '*All that work,*' you say? '*For nothing,*' you say? Geerincx paid you, yes?"

"Yes."

"Then it's not a wasted effort, is it?"

"Well, no. But—"

"No '*buts*' about it, boy. Go. Dump them. Dump them all. Far away. And now!"

Mac observed all this. While he could tell by the tone of their exchange that it was some kind of an altercation happening between van Rijn and Arent— or maybe a work assignment Arent didn't like—but whatever it was, the dialogue made Arent disconsolate. He glumly picked up the leather pouch and turned toward the door.

Mac couldn't have understood Rembrandt's order, or where Arent was off to when the boy left the kitchen. He heard Arent say something to Hendrickje on his way out and then he heard the door shut. Mac thought, *Maybe Arent went home, or maybe Rembrandt ordered Arent to read the notes—a homework assignment. He seemed depressed, to have to read all that Latin! Too bad for Arent—he'll miss seeing how the plate looks when Rembrandt clears away the etching ground!*

The note that was left out of the bag still lay on the table where Rembrandt had left it, so it was not with the others that went with Arent. Mac was tempted to snitch it, but he resisted.

To Mac, part of van Rijn's aphorism was a riddle, even after he had translated it into English for Mac: '. . . the future is not certain but it is not unknown.' Puzzlement, yes; yet Rembrandt's words seemed profound and this would bear thinking.

Mac wondered why van Rijn added the dismissive '*Indeed! Stupid!*' because he thought that what the great artist had said was a good thing to say. Apropos to Mac's way of thinking—*really it was!* Thinking about the words, Mac concluded, *Those were the words of a genius—and I was there!*

So inspired was Mac that he decided to try to express his admiration for him. He summoned up his courage to interrupt the master, and said, "Meneer Rembrandt, I am full of admiration for what you have accomplished."

At Mac's praise van Rijn stopped his study, raised his eyes and looked at Mac with a quizzical frown as though he didn't understand the American. Studying Mac, his eyes shifted left and right and wondered, *Did he mean this little plate?* Without a word Van Rijn returned to his examination of how deeply the lines were etched in the plate.

Finally van Rijn responded: "But this is nothing. A trifle! It's an absurd, little man's face and good for nothing more than to titillate card-players. It's for a commission I am forced into—more or less. Didn't I tell you? Didn't anyone tell you about van Leest and his artist playing cards?"

He continued his inspection of the plate, grumbling under his breath in Dutch, his mood darkening. "This is no accomplishment. It is *drek* compared to what I could be doing." He didn't bother to translate his disparaging words. He didn't want to talk about it. It hurt.

Mac sensed that he had said the wrong thing and he wanted to try again to communicate what he felt.

"I mean, not that *one* etching—although I've never seen anyone draw directly into the plate with such confidence and surety of hand. What I meant was my admiration for . . . all your accomplishments . . . and . . . .." Mac stammered and his words trailed off.

Rembrandt looked up from his plate and stared at Mac; his eyes bespoke a warning. Mac sensed there was danger here and, finally, he managed to squeak out the words, ". . . your life." The way he said it made it sound like a question to van Rijn.

Too late! Rembrandt fixed his strabismus eyes on Mac, and not in a friendly way. As soon as Mac said it he realized he had ventured close to Rembrandt's life's province which—as an American colonial just arrived in Amsterdam—he could not know about in such a short time.

Mac could not take back his words. Rembrandt had detected a sense of prescience in what Mac had just said. There was something in his remark that was more than flattery, something presumptuous in Mac's words and they raised questions in van Rijn's mind.

His skewed eyes bore in and continued to hold Mac for a full five seconds!

Then the artist attended to his etching plate and let the plate slide off his fingers to allow the mordant to continue its work. Mac thought he narrowly escaped a cross-examination and he wasn't sure he could talk his way out of the reasons he thought he knew all about van Rijn's life's accomplishments.

However, Rembrandt wasn't finished with Mac. He turned to him both serious and curious and said, "My life? Indeed, Meneer MacRitchie, what do you think you know about my life?"

Mac's mouth went dry under Rembrandts' study. He swallowed. Rembrandt waited. He said, "You don't know anything about my life. How could you?"

Finally Mac thought of something: "Well," Mac said with a shrug, "You are famous all over Europe, from your prints, and your paintings." This seemed safe for him to say, he thought, *Everybody knows that. Don't they?*

"You have seen my paintings? How? You've just arrived, Rabbi Aboab told me. *Only Sunday!*" The artist's pitched voice rose. "You can't have seen my paintings. You haven't had the time. As for my prints, the rabbi only owns *one*—that I know of—and not a very good one—a man playing cards." He took a breath and then added, "Don't tell the rabbi I said that."

Rembrandt continued to look intently at Mac, waiting for some confession he thought that Mac was keeping from him. "What do you know about me? What is it you have come here for? I sense that you are withholding something, and I won't have it, indeed, Meneer MacRitchie, not in my house!"

Mac looked down, ashamed. Things had been going so well up until now. He thought, *Should I tell?*

327

No. I could crush the man standing before me if I told him what I know—that Titus and Hendrickje would soon be dead, that Cornelia would be the only one in this little family to survive for long, that Rembrandt's remains would be buried in a pauper's grave, and that his remains' location would be forgotten forever. I couldn't bear to tell him.

Mac felt a heavy burden. This knowledge of Rembrandt's future weighed him down. He couldn't think what to say; and still Rembrandt's eyes held him as he waited for Mac's explanation.

Rembrandt lowered his voice and demanded icily, "What do you want?" Mac dreaded this confrontation. Whatever he said must not reach the other room and alarm Cornelia and Hendrickje.

Mac blurted, "I want to go out!"

Mac's words and the spontaneity of this answer completely baffled Rembrandt. He was speechless. He blinked at Mac and then he recovered with a changed expression—going suddenly from one of dark suspicion to glee; it was like someone had thrown an electric switch!

"OK!" said Rembrandt.

The American's suggestion to go out was inexplicable—like many of the things that came out of his mouth; but it so happened that—right now— *going out* sounded like a good idea to van Rijn!

Rembrandt repeated: "OK!" and he laughed with gusto at his cleverness for having remembered the Native American Indian word, *"Ok,"* which meant, *"Yes!"*

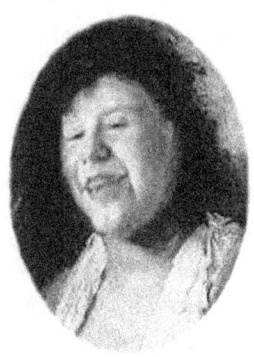

Chapter 40
In A Tavern

Seated at a small round table in a tavern with Rembrandt, Mac was blinking his eyes and straining to see through the smoke of candles, oil lamps, and tobacco. His eyes burned. It was a busy night and many men sat at the few tables or they stood around in small groups, and quite a few of them were puffing on extremely long-stemmed white pipes, adding to the smoky haze.

Cleverly fixed on a ship's wheel chandelier that hung on chains, fat candles gave a good light to the table where Rembrandt and Mac had been given places to sit opposite one another. Van Rijn took note that his American guest looked up above their table and studied the ship's wheel with interest. Mac tilted his head this way and that as he tried to figure out how the chandelier had been put together.

Rembrandt leaned across to be heard better and told Mac, "My friend made that. That's the man who greeted us when we came in—the one over there with the wooden leg. He comes from Leiden, as I do." Rembrandt gazed at the candles for a moment, and

329

then continued, "He lost his leg at sea in 'fifty-three in the *Battle of Gabbard Bank*. An English cannonball went right through the galley. He was a ship's cook then, and he still cooks today. He runs this tavern like a tight ship!"

Back at Rembrandt's house, only a half-hour ago, it had been a tense moment for him as Rembrandt had reproached Mac for his well-intentioned remarks because it had been taken by van Rijn that the American presumed to know too much about his life's work—more than Mac had any way of knowing.

Mac had artlessly changed the subject to defuse the situation and had said, he *wanted to go out*! Mac erupted with the words so spontaneously it blindsided Rembrandt. Thus Mac broke away from the issue without revealing anything of his history—knowledge he had that Mac dare not disclose.

It was a mad idea, but it worked! Rembrandt's unease over why Mac seemed to think that he knew so much about him had vanished and his suspicion of Mac' motives were forgotten. Van Rijn had agreed to go out; in fact, Rembrandt was glad—glad to be with somebody to whom he owed no money, and glad for a release from his home confinement.

With the rabbi's cash deposit in his pocket, plus the prospect of more money from van Leest the next day, now van Rijn had the means to treat the American and perhaps get back to the discussion of the *endorse* in exchange for the beautiful little etching press. Some wine and dinner might help to strike a deal, Rembrandt thought.

At the other side of the room a beefy woman waved over the heads of several drinkers and smiled at van Rijn. Rembrandt signaled back, raised his hand and waggled two fingers and made a sign to bring them dinners. Before long she brought two green glass roemers of red wine and set them on the table. She flashed a polite smile at Mac and turned her attention to van Rijn and began an amiable chat in Dutch.

"Your food will be coming soon, Rembrandt van Rijn, *honing*. I haven't seen you here for a long time! What have you been doing? Painting?"

"Oh, busy. Very busy, Mevrouw Hooters," Rembrandt replied, and then quickly he asked, "What are you serving? My guest and I are hungry!"

"*Konijnen stoofpot met eende vet!*"[92]

Rembrandt turned to Mac, who had gone back to his study of the ship's wheel, and he reached across and touched Mac's arm to get his attention. Van Rijn said, "We're in luck, Meneer MacRitchie! We're having rabbit stew with duck fat!"

The woman gave a parting smile to Mac as she turned and went back to check on their order. Mac looked unsettled when Rembrandt told him what was on the menu.

Van Rijn studied Mac. "I saw that face you made. Don't you like rabbit?"

Without thinking Mac said, "I don't eat any meat—red, white or fowl—or rabbit."

"Why? What's wrong with you? Are you sick?"

"No, not sick. But, in America, I eat only vegetables, fish, and shellfish. I'm a *pescaterian*." At this, Rembrandt looked blank, so Mac thought to elaborate: "Do you know the word, *vegetarian*?"

Van Rijn dissembled, "No, I never heard of it. So! You're not sick? Good! I will drink to your good health, Meneer MacRitchie," and, with a wink and a nod, van Rijn raised his roemer of wine. He didn't

---

[92] Rabbit stew with duck fat.

know what a "vegetarian" was, and he didn't really care to know.

Mac rallied and reached for the other wine glass and said, "And to you, Master Rembrandt, and to your health, too," and Mac also tried the wine. Over the rim of his glass, watching his host, Mac noticed that Rembrandt's eyes wandered off, his attention being drawn past Mac to watch someone behind him. Was it Vrouw Hooters, maybe?

Curious, Mac turned to see who—or what—was distracting van Rijn. He noticed there was a man in a hat standing on the edge a small group of drinkers, staring his way. Mac realized it was a man whose face he hoped he would never see again!

Mac swiveled back and he muttered, *"Oh no!"* and tried to shrink down in his seat, but he knew it was probably too late. When their eyes had met for just a split second, the man nodded and confirmed that, *Yes, he knew Mac!* It was the horse-dung boat skipper, there could be no doubt for he wore Mac's blue plume in his seaman's hat.

His dog was with him, alert with ears perked up and a glare for Mac. He took the lead as his master, frowning, weaved across the room toward Mac's table. Mac turned his face toward the chandelier again and braced himself with an indifferent air. Not Rembrandt, however; he stared openly and with interest at the approaching man and his dog.

Now the skipper stood at Mac's side and slurred in heavily-accented English, "Still in Amsterdam, *Engelsman?*" The boatman was drunk. Mac looked up at him as innocently as he could and kept his cool. He smiled but, choked with terror, he could say nothing. The man went on, "Oh, ja, I remember you, *Engelsman*. How come you here? You have money for drink? You go off with the procuress, so you must have money . . . but you save it for the whore! You stow away on my boat and not pay! You think you damn smart, but you don' fool me. You think you can fool me, *Engelsman,* eh?"

Rembrandt watched the encounter silently. Mac's mouth felt full of cotton and he still couldn't think of anything to say.

The man drew closer. "You pay me now! No foreign money, *Engels*! Good Dutch money!"

Mac took a deep breath. The dog was watching Mac with its head cocked sideways and it gave a low grumble; but it did not bark. *Not a good sign*, thought Mac, *because 'if a barking dog doesn't bite,' but this one doesn't bark, then that means . . ..*

The tavern had quieted down as others noticed something interesting was about to happen between the belligerent seaman and the foreigner sitting at the table. A few recognized Rembrandt, and they pointed and mumbled to one another.

Calmly, Rembrandt spoke up, in Dutch, saying, "Friend, this man is my guest. If he owes you, then allow me to pay for him."

Rembrandt's words pleased the man, and van Rijn said a few more things in Dutch to him as he reached into his coat, produced a purse, took out some coins and passed them across the table. Mac took them and—relieved for the moment—handed the coins up to the skipper. The dog stiffened and licked his chops as it followed Mac's exposed wrist, ready to leap into action.

The drunk took the coins and studied them. Mollified, he then focused on Rembrandt. In Dutch, and not as loudly as he had when he bullied Mac, the sailor asked, "*Wie ben jij, Meneer?*"[93] He wanted to

---

[93] Who are you, Sir?

know whom it was that he addressed.

"*Ik ben Rembrandt Hermanszoon van Rijn.*"[94]

The skipper put the coins in a pocket of his great coat and patted it fondly. He rubbed his stubbly chin and gave thought to the name. "Rembrandt," he repeated. He knew that name. "Hmm. *De fijnschilder?*[95]"

Rembrandt nodded pleasantly.

After a pause the seaman asked, "*Spreek je goed Engels, Mijneer van Rijn?*"[96]

"*Ja. Ik spreek goed Engels.*"[97]

"Tell this one I spit on the English! English kill my *broer* in *Scheveningen*,"[98] he instructed Rembrandt. All the while he talked to van Rijn he kept his eyes locked on Mac. The dog growled and quivered with anticipation that he should soon be able to show his stuff.

From out of nowhere, the tavern owner appeared and stood behind the skipper. He was now ready to take control of the situation and he put a firm hand on the seaman's shoulder as he crooned in Dutch, "Harkenszoon, my friend, you left your drink at the bar. Come back. Your friends are there. They say '*come back.*' Your pipe has gone out. Let me refill your bowl with good black tobacco."

Mac didn't understand a word, but he could tell by the tone of it that it was a most amiable and warm solicitation. The tavern owner had everything back under control. The skipper, willing to give it up as he had obtained some money, gave Mac one last black

---

[94] I am Rembrandt Hermanszoon van Rijn.

[95] The fine painter?

[96] Do you speak good English well, Mister van Rijn?

[97] Yes, I speak good English.

[98] [The] English killed my brother in [the battle of] Scheveningen.

look and turned away. The tavern owner—the picture of an experienced arbiter—led him back to the others, stumping ahead on his peg leg. The crowd noise level raised once more as people resumed what they had been doing before the confrontation had turned their heads.

Mac's heart was beating fast. A few seconds ago he had felt like dog meat, but now things were back to normal. Rembrandt looked at Mac, baffled.

"Do you *know* him? What was he talking about?" he asked Mac. "You, a *stowaway*?"

"It was how I made my way to the wharf at Binnen-Amstel Sunday morning," Mac explained. "There was a problem and it seemed the only way— the only solution." Mac hoped Rembrandt would not press him further. "I'm sorry to have put you out. I would say you saved my neck! I am most grateful, Meneer van Rijn."

To Mac, even if Rembrandt did want to find out more about his dung boat arrival, satisfying van Rijn's now-piqued curiosity didn't seem like such a challenge after what Mac had just been through.

If Rembrandt *did* want to know more, he would have to wait because, at the moment, Vrouw Hooters was setting out their plates and tableware. The well-peppered, thick rabbit stew came in a type of stubby-legged, black iron Dutch oven. A cook's helper followed her and brought biscuits, a bowl of cold quartered red beets and another of potatoes—plus the usual gob of butter. The helper ladled stew into ceramic bowls. The dull silver spoons, knives and forks had carved, red-hued wood handles, stained dark by long use.

Rembrandt regarded Mac as he considered the stew, with glistening puddles of clear, yellowish duck fat that floated on top. Mac's stomach growled so loud that it was audible to Rembrandt, even over the noise of the tavern!

"You are hungry!" van Rijn said, and feigned an offer: "I could ask if there's any fish, if you prefer."

Mac was quick to answer. "No, this is fine, I'm happy to have it. It's just that I am still shaky after that seaman and his dog came over. I appreciate your help, and also for this meal, Meneer van Rijn. I shouldn't have mentioned my fish-eating habit. Thank you for this food. I will have at it, and gladly."

Mac was sincere in his gratitude on all counts. He picked up a biscuit, split it and spread some butter on it. The first bite tasted of lard, so he swabbed on more butter to hide the flavor. He thought about Mevrouw Schwarzesherz' sweetened fig jam again, waiting back at Aboab's.

The encounter with the dung boat skipper had made him forget for few minutes how hungry he was; but now his appetite came roaring back with a vengeance. As Mac had gone without lunch, he was starving and beginning to feel the effects of the wine. Even the greasy rabbit stew looked good—duck fat and all. Swallowing his first bite of biscuit, he then drank some more wine to fortify himself and get ready to partake of the stew.

"The wine is delicious," Mac said after he had swallowed. "Where does it come from?"

Rembrandt said, "Oh . . . France I suppose, most likely," and he speared a chunk of grey rabbit flesh, picked a slim bone out of it, popped the meat into his mouth and chewed. After he swallowed, he took another drink of wine and launched into the important matters that were on his mind.

"Now," Rembrandt began as he set down his glass, "we should talk about the days ahead. I must tell you that Rabbi Aboab is preoccupied tomorrow, from dawn until dark, I am told, catching up with his synagogue duties. He has fallen behind in his obligations." Rembrandt was quiet as he suspended a biscuit in the duck fat, held it and watched while it soaked up the golden, glistening grease.

Mac interjected: "That's probably my fault, I'm afraid. I've taken up a lot of the rabbi's time. He's too considerate."

Rembrandt waved off Mac's remark. "Not so. Not so. He is taken with you. He said as much while sitting for me yesterday. Great man, the rabbi, but he's not often so generous to us gentiles. I am surprised, truth being told, at his feelings about you. Yes, he likes you, indeed."

"He was good to me. So was Dieners; and so have you been, Meneer van Rijn."

Rembrandt, satisfied that the biscuit he held in the fat was saturated, put it into his mouth and followed it with another piece of meat. He didn't finish swallowing; he talked eagerly—with food in his mouth—as he wanted to get their schedule settled.

"Friday afternoon, the day after tomorrow, is the beginning of the Sabbath, and so Rabbi Aboab will be gone to the synagogue all day tomorrow getting ready."

Rembrandt chewed and thought through more details. Mac speared a piece of red beet, put the whole thing in his mouth and followed it with another bite of his biscuit. It was a way to mask its saltiness and the lard.

Van Rijn said, "The point is, don't be surprised if you waken tomorrow in an empty house—and the same on the next day and Saturday, too. Then, on Sunday the rabbi told me that he leaves early for Tulpenburg to fetch his wife home."

Mac was impressed with how much and how fast

Rembrandt could speak and eat. Even having almost finished his meal, Rembrandt had continued to talk; he wasn't finished with their itinerary quite yet. Mac's own bowl was still full as he had filled up on biscuits, beets and butter. He was not yet ready to eat the rabbit.

Rembrandt told Mac his plan. "The rabbi and I discussed everything and agreed that you will come to my house straightaway each morning. You will find that I am an early riser. Tomorrow, we'll have a bite to eat—nothing fancy mind you—and get to printing. Bring supplies if you want, and the plate—the one that you had with you."

Mac would be glad to show van Rijn that old printing plate, but he hoped he wouldn't ask him to bring his printmaker chest, too, as it was bound to lead to a hullabaloo.

Mac took a big spoonful of the rabbit stew and gagged it down with another bite of well-buttered biscuit. He thought, *The cook could take a lesson from Faye*, and he yearned for her vegetarian stew and biscuits. *Will I ever eat her cooking again?*

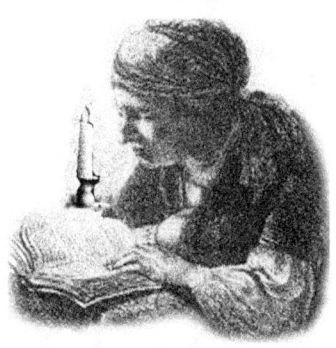

Chapter 41
A good day to die

Later that evening, after he and Rembrandt had left the tavern and said goodnight, Mac returned to Aboab's home. True to Rembrandt's forecast, Mac was met by Dieners alone, who said that the next day the rabbi would be entirely devoted to catching up on his work for the synagogue. It would be the same on Friday, until late at night as it would be the start of the Sabbath. Mac would not see the rabbi on either of these nights, but Dieners said that he should not worry because he would find the bed in the garret ready and waiting.

In the morning, Mahault would be coming as usual. Mac was to take breakfast at Rembrandt's as he wished, as everything had been arranged with Huisvrouw Hendrickje van Rijn.

Mac was tired and climbed the stairs to the garret, pulled himself up into the bunk and, not wanting to get cold, he did not bother to undress. Pulling the comforter over himself—up to his chin—he went into a deep sleep almost immediately.

Meanwhile, at her house a distance away, the

Black Widow slumped in a chair in the corner of her sitting room next to a little table. On it were a candle, a glass and a bottle of sweet wine. She had only the one candle for light—all that she needed—and she stared into the dark and sipped her wine.

The Scotsman vexed her, and she cursed him in the darkness. She was certain he was a sorcerer, and her nemesis. On her third glass of wine, she (like unwary Mac, who was now asleep at Aboab's) would doze off in her rocker. The wine would help her sleep long and hard this night.

Hours later, Mevrouw Schwarzesherz' girl, Mahault, rose in the early hours and tiptoed through the hall past the Black Widow's bedroom. The door was closed as usual. Mahault paused and listened; she could hear Vrouw Schwarzesherz' snores. The girl continued on to the next stairway that led down to the basement laboratory.

Carrying a small candle for light, Mahault entered the lab, closed the door and bolted it without the slightest sound. Although Mahault could not speak, her ears were as sharp as a bat's and she could hear if anyone approached. The workroom was off-limits when her mistress wasn't keeping an eye on her.

The girl knew, from having served her wine late last night that Vrouw Schwarzesherz had drunk a lot while cursing and boasting into her goblet, unaware that her plotting was overheard by Mahault. When the girl heard the woman's vitriol, her damning words had the effect of emboldening Mahault to step up to the challenge and somehow try to save Mac from the Black Widow's ways.

In the lab, the girl lit another, larger candle and an oil lamp; then she retrieved and opened the medicinal tome, turned the pages and found the place she had studied before. Mahault read the Latin text over again. This would become Mahault's recipe for *good* work. Thoughts of doing good deeds came to mind, and a feeling that she knew ways to do a kindness this breaking day, if needed. She smiled.

On Wednesday, when she passed through the rabbi's kitchen, she had checked to see that their larder still held the jar of fig preserves, and the basket of marinated apples that Pieter delivered was still there. That was a good thing, because there would be no time for extra baking before the Sabbath and therefore no using of them.

The foreigner was safe for today, as well as for the next few days because Dieners would be away most of the time. The van Rijns were taking care of their guest's meals, Dieners had told Mahault. The fig and apple concoctions would stay where they were—maybe forgotten, and the apples might rot.

Mahault took the foreign coin from her pocket—the American penny that Mac had given to her that awful morning when the Madam took him away. She held it close to the candlelight and examined the letters and images on the coin, but they made no sense. Even the Latin phrase that she found, *e pluribus unum*[99], or "*uit velen een*,"[100] puzzled her.

These words and images did not bode evil. Strange it was that Mevrouw Schwarzesherz was compelled to exorcize iniquity from the coin. On the other hand, her mistress feared everything the Meneer MacRitchie touched.

Mahault recalled that Pieter had told her he thought that Mevrouw Schwarzesherz' troubles began when the Scotsman said or showed something to her that terrified the old woman. What could it have been? Probably the innocent visitor possessed nothing

[99] Out of many, one.
[100] Out many, one.

at all to be afraid of, but the Black Widow saw the evil eye in all things that she didn't understand or esoteric fragments from her studies of black magic.

Whatever frightened the Black Widow, it was no wonder that she coveted the Scotsman's chest. That was clear in view of the things that Vrouw Schwarzesherz had said, drinking herself to sleep last night. Mahault had overheard her bragging that—in the end—she would have his *kist*.

Small wonder! Mahault would like to see inside the chest once more, and to taste again that strange dark substance in the bright red box with Rembrandt's name in gold, but her conscience said *no*. She had a new, more important mission now, and all the more vital since Mahault had personal experience with the secrets in his chest.

Having seen—and tasted—examples of the magic it contained, she felt fortunate. She thought, *Yes, I feel privileged; I feel I was chosen as his protector!* Fate had given her to see the important role that she could play.

In their special language, Mahault told her sister, and her sister agreed and advised her—should it be necessary—to shield the innocent man from the Black Widow's poison. Mahault found the recipe for the antitoxin against the substances with which Vrouw Schwarzesherz had laced the fig preserves and apples. This morning, in Mevrouw Schwarzesherz' own, private alchemy lab and while everyone in the house was still sleeping, Mahault set about preparing the remedy, selecting the powders first, which she would mix with a liquid.

A gray, puffball of a mouse scurried along a shelf just above Mahault's eye level and froze, taken aback at finding another living thing here. With her sharp ears Mahault's heard the mouse's tiny claws on the wood shelf and, when it stopped, she could sense its presence as it watched her. Without raising her bowed head, slowly Mahault turned her eyes up and met the black, beady eyes of the mouse.

She whispered softly and low, "*Goedemorgen muis*."[101] The mouse's ears twitched at the sound of her strained voice. Unafraid, it watched as the girl carefully funneled her liquid mixture into a tiny glass vial. She tightly inserted a cork and slipped the vial into her housemaid's livery pocket.

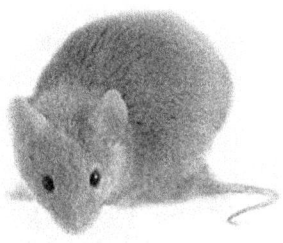

The garret was cold. What it could have been that awakened Mac may have been the sound of someone coming up the stairs to bring lighted candles. Or did he dream that someone spoke? Maybe it was a sound from the street below. Whatever, or whoever it was, Mac did not care; but he noticed that there was a candle burning on the desktop below the bunk; and the sconce oil lamp on the wall was lighted, too. While asleep he thought he had heard someone speak; but there was no one.

He wondered, *How can they live in these cold conditions, so many years before central heating?* He had noticed other rooms had fireplaces or corner heaters, but not in the garret. Wearing Rembrandt's heavy clothing for pajamas was a good idea but they

---

[101] Good morning, mouse.

still smelled of the tobacco smoke from his night at
the tavern.

Approaching day showed through the window,
and Mac heard a burst of startled seagulls' cries that
sounded like a glee club doing a round of, "Get up!
Get up!" He pushed the comforter down to his feet
and took himself down from the upper bunk, stretched
and looked around.

In what felt like private and quiet time, Mac
decided that he could write in his journal. There was
so much to tell; but Mac never allowed himself
pondering as to whom to tell his adventures, or
questioned how would it be possible that anyone in
his true time would read his journal.

He sat down at the desk, moved the candle to the
side, dropped the front panel of his printmaker chest,
and took out his journal and pen. The feel of the
ballpoint in his fingers was another reminder of the
distance of centuries over which countless inventions
had not yet been invented—inventions such as his
ballpoint pen and machines that made paper
aplenty—all that Mac took for granted.

He began to write: *Thursday, they're getting
ready for the Sabbath, and there will be no one here
but me for awhile . . ..* For an entire hour Mac
described events and his thoughts and logged the
events of the past few days.

Outside, as Mac wrote, things picked up in the
city. The carillon across the street began to ring.
Roosters crowed somewhere in the far distance. Mac
heard the sound of raindrops tapping on the octagonal
window as it started to rain. The sound of rain
drumming on the roof reminded him of Seattle, the
patter of rain outside their bedroom window sounded
just like it did here and now. Mac's heart ached with
homesickness, his eyes teared up and he couldn't

write any more.

His stomach growled. It seemed to him that he was always hungry. Mac figured that the carillon playing indicated it must be eight o'clock, the time that Rembrandt had said last night that he could go next door to his house for breakfast.

Mac could hear someone coming up the stairs and he assumed that it would be Mahault. He was correct. The girl appeared out of the near-darkness of the stairwell, carrying the basin, a pitcher of water, and a fresh washcloth. In the light of a candle she held, her face was angelic.

Mac nodded to her over his shoulder and she did not avoid eye contact as she had the other time they met. With the faintest trace of a smile, she nodded back. Their embarrassing first encounter was now forgiven and forgotten. When she had set down the toilet utensils on the wash stand, she approached Mac and offered him yet another note.

He took the folded paper and opened it to read: *"Sir, my sister informs me that Mevrouw Schwarzesherz has dark designs on you. My sister asks that I write to warn you that the woman is capable of evil. Take care, Sir, and again, thank you for your kindness toward my beloved sister."*

Mac turned to explain to Mahault how the Madam had taken a turn of heart, but Mahault had left. *She is mistaken*, Mac thought. *She doesn't know about the gifts Madam Schwarzesherz sent, and the apology she wrote.*

345

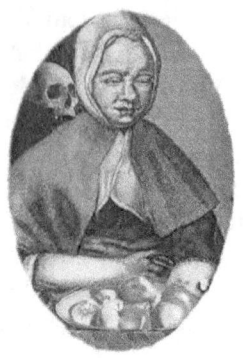

Chapter 42
Fig Newtons to die for

Hard rain was falling as Mac dashed over to Rembrandt's door and knocked hard. He was met by Hendrickje. She seemed to be in a happy mood. Clearly glad to see him, she held the door open wide.

"Welkom! Kom binnen! Het regent pijp stammen, is het niet?"[102] she said as she stepped back and invited Mac to come in. This was the most affable that Hendrickje had been toward Mac since the time of their first meeting. What she said in Dutch, Mac assumed, was about the rain; so he nodded, grinned and pretended to understand her. She led him into the middle room. Rembrandt was at the table and Cornelia was sitting beside him. She stared at Mac while she munched on a slice of bread. Hendrickje continued past Mac and went into the kitchen.

Rembrandt said, "What my wife just said to you, Meneer MacRitchie, was, '*It's raining pipestems.*' Stay awhile and I vow you will be speaking Dutch

---

[102] Welcome! Come in! It is raining pipestems is it not?

before long. I have been up since cock's crow. Is there anyone next door at Rabbi Aboab's house?"

"Everyone left before I wakened. I only saw the maid, Mahault."

"Ah! Mahault de Witte. A good girl. Yes. Helps Hendrickje sometimes. The girl comes from a good family. Poor as a church mouse. And Catholic. Pity her, indentured to that witch, the Black Widow." Rembrandt bit into a piece of bread and chewed, gazing up at the candles in the chandelier hanging overhead. He appeared to be lost in thought and Mac was forgotten. A few seconds passed and then van Rijn looked over at Mac standing behind a chair, expectantly.

"Oh Meneer MacRitchie, for God's sake—don't stand on ceremony! Sit down and eat," he commanded, and waved Mac to a place at the table. Hendrickje came in from the kitchen with tea and a plate with bread and cheese.

Mac nodded to her and he tried out a polite Dutch phrase that he had picked up: *"Dank u,"* he said to her back, as Hendrickje had already turned toward the kitchen.

Rembrandt directed his daughter, "Cornelia, *doe onze gast de groeten."*[103] He told her to try out an American greeting for Mac—a phrase in English that he helped her to memorize.

Cornelia ceased chewing, swallowed, and looked down at her plate. Her lips moved as she silently rehearsed what she had learned; then she looked up and said, "Goowould mornang Mithter MacReethie." She gave Mac a toothless, heart-melting smile and her cherubic cheeks glowed.

Mac complimented her: "Very good! You're

---

[103] Cornelia, do our guest greetings.

learning English!" Cornelia withdrew her smile. Mac corrected, "You're learning *American*!" That sounded better, and her smile came back.

She looked at her father for his approval. Rembrandt's eyes twinkled as he smiled and he prompted her to go on; there was more for Mac.

"Our Little Cake has something to show you," Rembrandt clarified, and he reminded her, "*Laat hem je souvenir zien.*"[104] Quickly, from under her chin, she held up a delicate silver chain to show Mac a pewter charm—the tiny windmill that David Lingelbach had given her at the amusement park. It dangled from her chubby fist and turned. Mac leaned forward to admire it from across the table.

He couldn't actually tell what the thing was from where he sat; regardless he said, "Very nice," and he asked Rembrandt, "How do you say, '*Very nice*' in Dutch?"

Van Rijn translated, "*Heel mooi.*"[105]

"*Heel mooey*," Mac repeated, and Cornelia broke out giggling at the way Mac pronounced the Dutch expression.

"Now eat, Meneer MacRitchie," Rembrandt said, "We've a long day ahead." Mac obeyed.

After awhile, his hunger somewhat satiated, Mac paused eating, leaned back in his chair and to van Rijn he said, "Sir, I have a favor to ask of Hendrickje. May I prevail upon her? Will you translate my wish to her? That is, of course, if *you* approve of my request."

"What is this 'favor'?"

"I have been given some apples—and also fig preserves, and I wonder if I might press upon your hospitality and ask if Hendrickje can make a pastry

---

[104] Let him see your souvenir.
[105] Very nice.

with them? I'd like to share these fruits with you."

Mac's strange suggestion was met with one of Rembrandt's "surprise faces," like one that Mac was certain he had seen among the artist's self-portrait etchings in history books.

"*Pastry*?" he questioned, and van Rijn began to chuckle as Mac nodded. He wondered, *Is the American joking? I never know what he's going to say next! Pastry?*

Mac clarified: "Yes. I miss American cooking. There is a fig pastry we call "Fig Newtons." Also, I miss apple-fig pie. I have the ingredients. They're over at Aboab's house. I hoped Dieners might make some, but he's so busy, and I'm wondering . . .."

Rembrandt cut Mac off before he could elaborate and shouted to Hendrickje, busy in the kitchen. His wife came and he spoke to her rapidly in Dutch, passing along Mac's extraordinary request for a "Dutch apple-fig pastry."

Hendrickje was surprised by Mac's appeal, but she was quick to understand, and she nodded to the affirmative: *Yes, she could do that*—although it seemed to Mac that she did so without enthusiasm.

"Thank you. *Dank u!* I'll get the things right now," Mac said, as he pushed back his chair, excused himself, and headed to the front door. Behind him he heard van Rijn and Hendrickje discussing something; he could have been mistaken, yet their words— foreign to him—sounded acerbic.

Outside, the rain had dwindled to a sprinkle as Mac hustled back and entered Aboab's house. He passed through the hallway toward the kitchen. It was still and quiet in the house, the tick-tock of the clock was the only sound he heard.

Mac went through to the kitchen. It was dim, as all the candles were snuffed out and no lamps burned.

The smell of candle smoke hung in the air, as though someone had just blown the candles out in the past few minutes. Soft, gray light filtered through the raindrop-festooned windowpane. On an impulse, Mac went to the window in time to see Mahault exit through the back gate. He heard the gate swing back with a thump as it shut behind her.

The basket of apples was still where it had been and in the larder he found the fig preserves. Mac put the jar in the basket with the apples. He stood for a moment and contemplated whether he should get some item from his printmaker's chest to share with Rembrandt—something appropriate that would not inspire questions. Van Rijn had been impressed by the ink tube. Mac's *kist* contained other wonders, but he decided that each thing—no matter how ordinary it might seem in Mac's time—could trigger queries that would put him at risk.

Rembrandt van Rijn was no dummy and was getting suspicious; Mac was running out of answers;. He surmised that Rembrandt would never recognize that his huge ego served as a defensive shield. If van Rijn were open-minded, interested and inquired about Mac's origins and the future world, van Rijn might have benefited from the American professor's insights.

Rembrandt was not as philosophical as Aboab had shown himself to be when Mac had revealed his origin. In this Aboab was remarkable; but Rembrandt would want know the future but he would be devastated if the truth of his future came out in a cross-examination of Mac, the time-traveler.

Mac visualized the artist's arrogance as being like a suit of armor and protected him against what Mac knew was to happen over Rembrandt's nine remaining years. So it was best that Mac would not show anything more except what he deemed to be harmless—such as the antique plate in his pocket—and that, also, would be for later and not sooner than needed. When he left and closed the front door, he noticed the rain had let up.

When Mac arrived back in Rembrandt's house, he saw that the dishes were already cleared from the table in the middle room and what was left of his breakfast was replaced with his press, along with a damp book of paper, the new etching plate and other printing supplies. As he had not actually finished eating, Mac was still hungry and he wished that they had left out the bread and cheese.

Mac carried the apple basket through to the kitchen. In passing he noticed that Cornelia was still at the table. Her chin rested on her folded arms. Dolefully, she meditated on the etching press. In the kitchen, Hendrickje was able to communicate to Mac that Rembrandt had stepped out momentarily to meet someone on business, and that Mac should wait in the other room with Cornelia.

When Mac came back into the middle room, Cornelia straightened up and smiled at him as Mac sat down opposite her, next to the press. Inspired to venture a demonstration for her, Mac thought he would teach the child something—something that could not possibly do any harm to the child and to which her mother would not object.

He addressed the girl in American: "Cornelia, I am glad you like my press," and he patted his press lovingly. Mac trusted that he would be understood by his gestures and his tone.

She blinked and lowered her head slightly but did not break eye contact. Cornelia was shy, yet she was also curious.

"There is a secret in it," Mac continued. He put

his hand under the press' woodwork and felt with his fingertips for a hidden, wind-up key to a spring-driven device he had built in the wood supports. With three practiced twists he wound it up and then he let it go.

A music box played, resonant in its wooden hiding place! The melody tinkling from under the press' rollers was the *"Canon in D,"* by Johann Pachelbel—a favorite of Mac's. It would be popularly-known as *The Wedding Song* in the 20th Century. Mac was ignorant of the fact that the real-life, boy Pachelbel was just a year older than the six-year old sitting opposite him.

Cornelia's expression was angelic; the music held her spellbound. Mac was moved to see her enraptured by the song. After three repetitions of the music, the notes slowed and stopped. It was only a short fragment of Pachelbel's *Canon*, played by a tiny music box movement. Mac was about to rewind it and play it again but, at that very moment, the carillonneur across the street began to play a hymn because it was now nine o'clock.

This was the kind of chance merging of sounds that always set off Mac's imagination. He felt as if he were hearing the soundtrack in a movie and that he was in the movie! His bliss was interrupted when he heard Cornelia's voice. Mac realized that she had been trying to get his attention and tell him something.

"Meneer?" she said—for the third time, *"Bedankt voor de muthiek."*[106] She had removed the pewter charm from her silver necklace. Solemn-faced, she held it out to Mac. *"Ik wil u di geven,"*[107] then she lisped, for the second time. *"Bedankt voor de*

---

[106] Thanks for the music.
[107] I want to give you this.

muthiek."

It was her offering to Mac, and in that way Cornelia thanked him for the music. He took it. Up close he could see that it was a tiny windmill.

Mac tapped his chest to make sure it was for him to keep. "For me?" he asked. Cornelia nodded. Mac couldn't see, behind his back, her mother stood for a moment in the doorway. She had been attracted by the music; Hendrickje saw Mac admire the charm momentarily before he pocketed it.

He gave a nod to Cornelia and said, *"Dank u."* Hendrickje backed away into the kitchen so as not to be noticed. She touched lightly at her eyes and went back to Mac's pie-making.

***

It was during the period of the musical and gift exchange between Mac and Cornelia that Rembrandt had gone across the street to talk business in a rendezvous with Jacques van Leest at the amusement park. Van Rijn brought the card publisher up-to-date on what had happened since they met the other day. With tact, van Rijn avoided telling the publisher about meeting up with Mac and trying out his small press. "Trade secret," was all he would tell van Leest when asked about his quest for a press.

Terms were agreed upon, and van Leest paid Rembrandt a cash deposit. However, they had a little disagreement over what the end-product should be called. Rembrandt wanted to call the cards, *Rembrandt's Artistieke Speelkaarten.* Van Leest said *No.* Without making a final decision, they parted because Rembrandt had much to do. His newly-etched plate waited for him at The Blue Crown. When he returned to his apartment at a little after nine to start printing, his mood was good despite the difference over the publisher's opinion of the name for Rembrandt's playing cards.

In the course of the next six hours, with Mac as printer's assistant, a great deal of work was accomplished. Mac took Arent's place because Arent helped at the mill on Thursdays. Time passed quickly, and the Halfwood Press served Rembrandt well.

Now it was three o'clock. For the sixth time, the carillonneur at the Nieuwe Doolhof played his hourly hymn; and—as if the chime was a signal to quit for the day—Rembrandt stopped printing. He passed his hand over the bronze charcoal brazier that he used for heating his printing plate and so soften the stiff black ink. The heater cover was cool; the embers in the brazier bowl had turned to whitish-grey ashes.

In his 21st Century studio, Mac was used to having an electric hotplate to warm his etching ink. Rembrandt's heater was a Chinese import, similar to the Japanese hibachi, on which Mac and Faye broiled veggie burgers or fish.

The aroma of baking pie from Hendrickje's kitchen oven had dissipated by now. In the time that it had taken Rembrandt to print forty impressions, the cooking smells of the apples, figs and spices were spoiled by the odors of warm etching ink, solvents and turpentine. Mac wondered if the unhygienic smells would taint the apple-fig pie that Hendrickje had set to cool in the kitchen.

It was a busy workday and Van Rijn didn't eat lunch. Apparently it was an unspoken understanding that nothing was more important than the work. No one—and certainly not Mac—had suggested that they stop and eat. Fasting made the work harder and by now Mac was famished.

During the session, Cornelia had watched for

awhile, but she got bored. At two o'clock Hendrickje
had bundled her up and, carrying a basket, she told
van Rijn they were off to the fish market. After they
left he said, "You are welcome to have dinner here
tonight, Meneer MacRitchie. My wife will be serving
fish. You know Rabbi Aboab will not likely return
tonight until very late—if at all, and," he reminded
Mac, "Dieners won't be cooking."

Mac was pleased to have the invitation. "Thank
you. I don't want to put Mevrouw van Rijn out,
though," Mac said. "Already she has made a pie for
me, and that's enough. I don't like to trouble her
more." To Mac, Hendrickje looked overworked and
stressed-out.

Hearing Mac's response and his tone, Rembrandt
gave him a queer look, as if annoyed at what he said
or how he said it. Mac grasped that the way in which
he had so obsequiously answered sounded too much
like English courtliness—feigned and fussy—and
peculiar to the chauvinistic Rembrandt's ears.

Mac backpedaled and added, "But, *yes*, I will be
grateful for a fish dinner, indeed—and that fresh pie
for dessert."

"Ah, yes, about that pie!" said Rembrandt, as he
remembered something that had to be announced and
could not wait. He cleared his throat. He had words
that might embarrass the American.

"I have an unusual request. You need to know
that my wife doesn't allow Cornelia to eat sweet
desserts. It's bad for her teeth and also our girl tends
toward chubbiness. This subject of desserts is a
sensitive issue in our family." He cleared his throat
again. "Therefore, I must ask you to take your pie to
the rabbi's to enjoy. Out of sight, out of mind, you
understand."

Mac was discomfited, although he need not have

felt so as he had no knowledge of the family's ways and concerns. Hendrickje was correct; Cornelia shouldn't be tempted with sweet Dutch apple-fig pie, all things considered.

"Say no more, Meneer van Rijn," he said, and Mac acted without further comment while Rembrandt turned to the business of cleaning up the printing area.

Mac went into the kitchen and collected the pie, which sat on the table with a linen cloth over it. In less than a minute he was back next door in Aboab's kitchen. He set the pie on the table. It looked good, with its top crust golden and extra-large slits in it oozing tears of thick sugary syrup. Mac thought, *Hendrickje and Faye could have a good chat on the subject of pie-making!*

As Mac hadn't eaten since breakfast, and since there was no telling when dinner would be served, he decided to have some pie in order to ward off the growling complaints of his stomach. He got a knife and cut out a wedge to taste. Thick cream oozed from where it had been drizzled through the slits. Mac bit off the pointed end of the first piece.

It was okay—but maybe a bit too much nutmeg to his taste, plus it had an odd, musky under-taste which Mac owed to sitting in the tainted air, so heavy with all the inks and oil smells from the printing session. He was afraid of that.

Hendrickje's pie was fair, nevertheless, quite edible, in fact and the rich cream was a good idea. He finished the sample and then cut another piece. He couldn't stop.

He cut another, and Mac ate his fill.

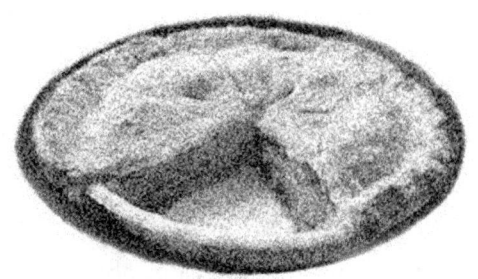

Chapter 43
Sweet Revenge

The pie was good going down and satisfied his hunger for now, but Mac experienced a bloated feeling and his legs felt as heavy as lead. *Why do I feel so sleepy?* He thought, *I should be excited to get back to Rembrandt's, but now. . . I just want to rest.* To lie down for awhile in the garret, he took the stairs. Going up, his head in a fog, he could barely make it to the top.

Shouldn't have eaten all that pie. Sugar on an empty stomach . . . that was a bad idea. Really sleepy. These were Mac's thoughts as he reached the top. He was in a sweat by the time he made the room. *I feel drunk. Got to lie down.*

Although groggy, he noticed that his journal lay on the desk. It struck him that while he rested in his bunk he could jot some notes about the printing session with Rembrandt—write while the master's methods were still fresh in his mind.

Writing might make this drowsiness pass. He picked up the journal; his pen was still tucked in between the pages. *More comfortable if I lie down. Better than sitting at the desk. So dizzy, probably fall off the chair. Apples must have been fermented or something. It tasted odd, that's for sure.*

Mac tossed his journal onto the bunk bed and with effort he pulled himself up the short ladder. Lying on the bed with his journal propped on his chest, he tried to think of what to write. His mind was in turmoil. He felt hot, which was strange for such a cold day. After a few seconds—his mind coming to a standstill—he knew he wouldn't be able to write. He put his pen in his shirt pocket. The book fell to the side.

Mac knew that he was bound to go to sleep, but he was aware enough to think to put his journal out of sight of anyone who might happen to come to waken him. He stuffed the book into a space between the mattress and the bunk-box side wall, and he thought, *Don't forget it. No one must know.* He mumbled, *mustn't know, huh Faye?*

In the silence of the empty house, Mac laid his head back and drifted off, boiling with fever.

***

The carillon chimed the hour—but Mac could not have heard it. He had been "dead to the world" for over an hour as the Black Witch's fruit and castoreum recipe worked toward its fatal purpose.

It was now five o'clock. As the carillon's final bell-notes died out, Mahault entered the back of van Rijn's house to help Hendrickje prepare the evening meal.

Like Mac, Rembrandt also slept—taking a long nap on the daybed in the middle room. His new prints were pinned on a twine line that he stretched from one bedstead post to another, the row of drying prints resembling little black-and-white celebratory flags— all of them with Rembrandt's grinning face on them.

Cornelia was in the front room, near the window overlooking the street. Wrapped in a thick Afghan to keep warm, she cradled a doll in her arms. She hummed a melody to it, a tune which she had heard in the morning. It was the *Canon in D*.

Hendrickje was feeling lonely in the kitchen, yet she didn't say much to Mahault as the maid was not conversant except by using sign-language and miming. Rembrandt's wife was too tired and worried to make the effort beyond saying anything that was necessary. She was even more fatigued than usual because of the frenetic activities that had taken place over the past two days. The new developments only added more worries to the uncertainty about their rent money.

Hendrickje was worried about Cornelia's future, too. How would van Rijn ever build their daughter's dowry at the rate things were going? What remained of Saskia's money and valuables belonged to Titus, according to Saskia's will and the binding of the law that governed her estate.

Hendrickje was reminded now of Titus, and she wondered, *What is taking him so long to get back from Leiden? What will he say when he finds out about all the dealings van Rijn has started without talking to him about it first—and buying that press?*

Hendrickje opened and rolled away grey paper that wrapped a sizable fish. Its mouth was open and its death-glazed unseeing eyes stared up at her. Mahault came to her side to look at the fish and, as she touched Hendrickje's arm, smiled and gestured toward the fish and signed that she had a question: Mahault meant, *"A special dinner?"*

What Mahault wanted to know was clear enough to Hendrickje; she was well-accustomed to Mahault's sign language. Hendrickje said, "Yes, Mahault, a fish dinner, as we have a guest tonight—the foreigner, Meneer MacRitchie. He's staying at Rabbi Aboab's. You know him, don't you?"

A private thought made Mahault smile as she nodded and thought, '*Know him?' I've slept with him!*

Hendrickje noted Mahault's sunny grin at her mention of Meneer MacRitchie—and she interpreted Mahault's reaction to mean, "*Yes, he's nice.*"

Hendrickje nodded, and said, "Yes, he *is* nice. And my husband seems to like him. They've been printing half the day, and now van Rijn is napping. The American is at Aboab's house." She turned to look at the mantle clock that sat on a shelf on the other wall.

She added, "I thought he would be back by now. I made a pie for him. That strange man wanted me to make a pastry with some apples and fig preserves that had been given to him. So I did. He took the pie next door."

Mahault's smile vanished, and Hendrickje noticed the change in her expression—one second she looked happy—now sudden concern and questioning evident on the girl's face. Hendrickje asked, "What? Don't you understand, *pie*? Apple fig pie?"

Mahault nodded slowly as she understood what Hendrickje had said sunk in. Then, Mahault shook her head *No! No!* This confused Hendrickje, and so she corrected as she thought that Mahault meant, *No pie! No sweets!* Mahault knew about the house rule about *no sweet desserts*.

"Ah, but of course, you remembered Cornelia is not to have sweets, yes it's true—how smart of you to remember! Bad for the teeth, and not good for us, either! So, van Rijn told Meneer MacRitchie to take his pie to Rabbi Aboab's house." With this clarified, Hendrickje reached for a knife and remarked, "Out of sight, out of mind, you know," and she began to slice off the head of the fish.

Once again, Mahault touched her arm and Hendrickje stopped cutting to see what she wanted. With a gesture and more signs, Mahault pointed at the clock and made out what she wanted to know: *How long ago did Meneer MacRitchie go?*

Hendrickje frowned at this query and she wondered, *Well, this is odd! Why is Mahault so interested?*

"Are you asking '*How long ago did he go to Rabbi Aboab's house?*' Is that what you mean?"

Mahault nodded briskly, *Yes.*

"Oh, I guess it must have been about an hour or two, perhaps three o'clock." Mahault eyes widened. As she backed toward the door she signed that she would be back soon, turned and was gone! Hendrickje was astonished. She shrugged and returned to the task of beheading the fish.

Five minutes later, Mahault came back. She was out of breath and animated, with gestures to indicate Hendrickje had to come with her to Aboab's house—and *now!* Hendrickje stood open-mouthed, stock-still and unbelieving so Mahault came over to her and boldly took Hendrickje's arm and tried to pull her toward the back door.

Shocked at Mahault's strange behavior, Hendrickje jerked her arm back. She objected, "*No!* You stop that, girl, I can't go with you!"

With more sign language, more expressive face-making, Mahault repeatedly mimed someone asleep, her head leaned on praying hands, eyes closed, so as to explain to Hendrickje, *Meneer MacRitchie is asleep!*

Hendrickje understood the charade and explained, "Well, he's probably tired!" She stepped back from

Mahault, her hands on her hips—irritated and amazed at Mahault's audacity over such a trifling thing—the American napping. Hendrickje's explanation did not satisfy; it only made Mahault start to bawl and make unpleasant throaty sounds.

Suddenly, awakened by the sounds of Hendrickje's scolding and with Mahault carrying on, Rembrandt appeared in the doorway to the middle room. "What's going on here?" he shouted. "What's the matter with Mahault? Why is she so upset? Lord! She sounds like she's having a cow!"

"She saw that MacRitchie is asleep over at Aboab Fonseca's house."

"Asleep? So what? He's probably tired," said Rembrandt. This only made Mahault's howls worse and then she did the unthinkable: she went to van Rijn, grabbed Rembrandt by his arm and tried to pull him toward the back door!

He jerked away and said, "Unhand me! What in Hades possesses you, girl! Are you mad?"

"*Hij is stervende!*"[108] Mahault proclaimed, mouthing her words between sobs in a labored baritone, with her never-used, hoarse voice she loudly added a demand, "*Je moet mee komen!*"[109]

Mahault moaned and rolled her eyes, her little body trembling with fear. Her words, '*The man is dying,*' and '*you must come up with me,*' were the first words that she had spoken to anyone in almost ten years.

The van Rijns froze and stood with their mouths open, stared and stunned. Mahault looked hopefully at one face and the other, back and forth. She decided they would be of no help and she ran out the back door. She didn't bother to look back to see if either of

---

[108] He is dying!
[109] You must come up with me!

them followed her.

She was soon again in the garret. Mac seemed to have wakened but he was delirious, sweating, and twitching. Finally, after a few minutes, Rembrandt did come up the stairs to the garret, and he found Mahault standing on the chair so that she could be at Mac's level. Rembrandt took one step up the bunk ladder to look at Mac, who lay sweating with his eyes closed, forehead shining wet, head lying on his matted wig, unkempt like something dead.

"Oh my God! It's the fever!" Rembrandt whispered. "Good thing Hendrickje didn't come. I'll go warn her," and he went down the stairs and left Mahault alone with Mac. Mahault anticipated that van Rijn would not be coming back any time soon.

Mahault knew it had to happen. She knew the score, and now she knew that she had to use the vial of antitoxin she had in her pocket. Mahault was certain that this was not typhoid fever in Mac, neither was it the plague, nor cholera. It was the Black Widow's concoction of arsenic and castoreum. Although Mahault was not positive that the antidote would work, it was her only hope. She had to try.

"*Quod potest occidere curationis, ita dicit Paracelsus*,"[110] Mahault whispered to Mac, whose mouth hung open like Hendrickje's dead fish's. Even if Mac could have heard her, he would not have understood the Latin that came from Mahault's mouth: "*What can kill, can cure, so sayeth Paracelsus.*"

Mac was oblivious and knocking on heaven's door. Muttering a quick, silent prayer in Latin, she emptied the liquid in the vial into his mouth and with her hand on his chin she forced his mouth to stay shut

---

[110] What can kill can also cure, sayeth Perecelsius.

while Mac involuntarily swallowed it.

Mac's periodic convulsions were a long time in slowing. As she waited and watched to see the results of her administration of the antidote, Mahault wished that Rembrandt would come back so she could somehow allay his fears. There were also Dieners and the Rabbi Aboab to think about. As she wondered what to do, as if on cue, she heard the front door shut—someone had come—an answer to her wish! Ten seconds later, she heard Dieners' unmistakable voice call up the stairs from below, "Hallo!" in English.

Mahault hurried to the stairs and was halfway down when she met Dieners hobbling on his way up. He was surprised to see her at this time of day.

"Mahault! It's you. What are you doing here? Where's Meneer MacRitchie? I saw . . .."

She stopped him and mimed the sleepy-head pose, waggled her head and gestured up toward the garret. It was effective.

"Meneer MacRitchie's asleep." Dieners understood. "He is asleep? Hah! We've overworked him I guess. Can't take it, can he! Ha ha," he said, turning to go back downstairs.

Mahault followed him to the kitchen and Dieners pointed at the partly eaten pie. "What's this? Where did this pie come from? Who ate . . .?" began Dieners; but he guessed the story almost instantly. His suspicions regarding the gifts from Vrouw Schwarzesherz came back to him in a rush.

"Drek!" He looked at Mahault for confirmation to confirm what he himself had deduced. She nodded her head vigorously and pointed toward van Rijn's house.

"Hendrickje made the . . .!" Dieners said. "It's almost half gone! Did the foreigner eat all that?"

Mahault confirmed, *Yes, he did.*

Dieners scratched his head briskly. "That's bad. *Very bad!* That witch Vrouw Schwarzesherz had it in for him. She probably poisoned those things she sent. I suspected it. *If he ate all that . . ..*" There was instant agreement from Mahault.

"I must get a doctor," and Dieners turned and trotted toward the door, but Mahault ran after him and grabbed his shoulder and stopped him in his tracks. Unused to being caught that way, Dieners whirled back and saw her take something from a pocket to show him. It was an empty glass vial.

As he realized what she had, Dieners relaxed and then he chuckled. Dieners had long-suspected Mahault was more than she appeared to be. He knew Mahault's family, that they were good people. She was not merely the Black Widow's indentured handmaiden, a chambermaid and cook's helper! She was Vrouw Schwarzesherz' shadow; and—as it was now revealed, Mahault was Vrouw Schwarzesherz' nemesis.

As much as the Black Widow practiced black magic, Mahault, at times, reversed the ill effects with white magic. He thought, *Mahault knew how to make a remedy for Vrouw Schwarzesherz' poison!* The pieces fit—the empty vial she showed him told the whole story. Dieners took the vial, looked up at Mahault and nodded. She smiled. It would be their secret.

No one would ever guess.

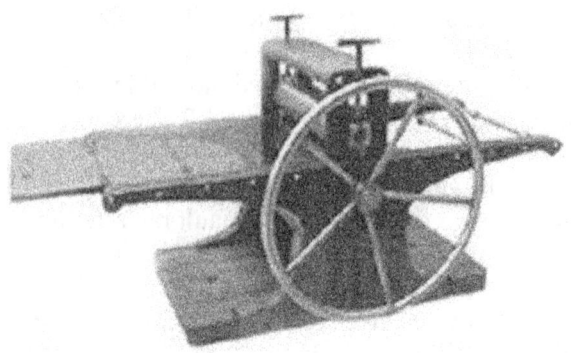

Chapter 44
Awakening

Mahault and Dieners went together to the Rembrandts where they found Hendrickje in a panic and wailing, expecting the worse for their family. Rembrandt was helplessly trying to console his wife. She had broken down when van Rijn told her it looked like MacRitchie had the fever. She expected the worst, fearing more for Cornelia than anyone else—her first and only child. Cornelia was huddled in the Afghan, her eyes wide and on the verge of tears at seeing her mother in such a state.

They were surprised and their fears rekindled to see Mahault come back with Dieners, but Dieners was bold in his telling of what was actually the matter with MacRitchie. Dieners assured them that it was not contagion. Neither Rembrandt nor Hendrickje knew the whole story about the foreigner and his brush with Mevrouw Schwarzesherz, nor did they know that she was the one who sent the fig paste and apples. It was impossible for them to follow Dieners' explanation; he didn't try hard to make it clear—wisely enough.

Awakening

At best it was a kind of mixed up story. Dieners couldn't tell them everything there was to know about Meneer MacRitchie. Actually, in spite that his telling was a fragmented and confused story, all the van Rijns cared about was that the sickened visitor was not carrying one of the dread diseases that they had seen sweep through Amsterdam. With that made clear, they were convinced that they did not have to worry. But they also knew that Mac would not be joining them for dinner.

Dieners had little time and left to rejoin Aboab and assist the rabbi in his work at the synagogue. The Rembrandt's dinner was delayed, of course, but within a few hours, life at the Rembrandt home had returned to a semblance of normalcy.

Mahault returned to the garret to check up on Mac—who was in a deep sleep, and finally it was time that she had to go back to the chores that awaited her at the house of Vrouw Schwarzesherz. Mahault was reluctant to leave, but she believed Mac would probably sleep while the antitoxin did its job.

When Mahault returned the next morning, Friday, Mac was still asleep. His breathing was shallow. One might have thought that he was comatose, but when she put her fingers on his brow, his temperature felt about normal.

***

Whenever Mahault came back to the Schwarzesherz house from Aboab da Fonseca's, the Black Widow always asked her about, "the Scotsman." However, her probing questions to Mahault got her no satisfaction; Mahault seemed not to understand her questions at all. It was annoying to Vrouw Schwarzesherz. Mahault was not worried that she would be caught in her ploy by Mevrouw Schwarzesherz.

Whenever she got a chance, Mahault spent more time in the laboratory—more time than usual; and Mevrouw Schwarzesherz spent more time with her wine because she was worried. Something was going on at the Aboab house. The Black Widow could feel it in the air, and she summoned various spirits as she sought to know what it could be. There was nothing for her to do but wonder when the Scotsman would eat the treats that she had gone to so much trouble to prepare for him.

As Vrouw Schwarzesherz passed the time drinking, she used her imagination to picture the most likely outcomes of her clever plot. She amazed herself with her own cunning. Her plan was that when MacRitchie died (and she was sure that he would as her signature potion always worked) she could then come forward as the one who had first discovered him in his hour of need, and thus prove her good intentions by also having sent gifts to the Scotsman. She could claim possession of his koffer as repayment for expenditures that she had made on his behalf.

He owed her!

***

Finally, a little after noon on Saturday, Mac raised himself up on his elbows and looked around. He had trouble focusing. There was something on the wall he couldn't understand. He scrunched his eyes tightly until they watered, and looked again. It was a dark, shapeless object. Then he realized that it was his great Flemish hat. He hadn't seen it for days. Then he saw his costume hanging on a peg right below it. It was then that he realized he was dressed only is his shirt and shorts. Someone had undressed him! Then he lay back down and tried to think. *What day is it?* His head throbbed and his eyes ached and soon Mac was back asleep.

At six that evening, Dieners came to him, climbed up on the chair, shook Mac's shoulder and asked him if he would like to come down for a bite to eat.

"Not now. I'm not hungry." Mac mumbled.

"You should drink some water," Dieners said. "It is pure, we have safe, pure water from the Tulpenburg springs," he said. "I will leave it in a decanter on the desk for you." Then Dieners returned to his work with Rabbi Aboab as now it was the Sabbath—the end of a week that had been unusually busy for the rabbi after so many unexpected events.

Very early Sunday morning Mac woke up. He still had a headache, but it seemed to have subsided. It was still dark, and he thought he could hear high-pitched ringing bells, but then he realized he had an extreme case of tinnitus.

He lifted himself up on his elbows and looked up to the octagonal window. There was a clear sky and a full moon, casting blue moonlight in the room. With heavy-lidded eyes and unsteady footing, he carefully made his way down the ladder. He remembered that Dieners' had told him there was water, and that it was safe to drink. For some reason the cold didn't bother him.

In the wan light Mac found the chair in its usual place by the desk and sat down heavily. The glint of moonlight on the decanter caught his eye and he took it, removed the stopper, and drank. He was thirsty, but he restrained himself in case too much too soon would not set well on his empty stomach. Mac's senses started to come back.

The clothes Rembrandt had loaned him were

gone, but his Flemish costume pants and waistcoat were hanging on the peg under the hat. With great effort he got up and dressed. The exertion made him thirsty; he sat down and took another drink of water. He put the decanter out of the way so he could put down his head. He went to sleep on the desk that way—with his head on his folded arms.

Mac slept for an hour, and wakened as someone tapped him on his shoulder. He opened one eye and saw that the room was lighter, and he could hear a rooster crowing, and the carillon rang. He didn't count how many. He raised his head and saw Mahault. Mac nodded to her, put his head down and closed his eyes again.

Mahault lighted the oil lamp on the wall, set a candle on top of the chest out of the way, and she tapped Mac's shoulder again. He thought he dreamed it, but he raised his head again and looked, blinked dully. It really was Mahault he saw, and not a dream; now she smiled.

She moved the decanter a little to suggest he drink some water. His mouth was dry and tasted like copper with a bitter under-taste. Mahault had brought him a pan, warm water and a cloth. She left him and went downstairs. She felt confident that Mac would be all right, and glad that she had helped. She had done a good thing.

Dieners waited for Mac in the kitchen as he thought by now that Mac would be coming out of his lethargy and that he should be hungry when he came down. Rabbi Fonseca was not at home, as he had already left in a carriage to go to Tulpenburg to get his wife and bring her home. Dieners had a lot to do to get ready for Huisvrouw da Fonseca's return.

Mac came down the stairs at last. He felt none too steady but at least he was vertical again. He thought

Dieners was especially congenial toward his him this morning. He even asked Mac what he would like for breakfast, and Mac asked for a soft-cooked egg, bread and cheese. Mac was dispirited and said little. He had a dull headache, no appetite, and he was grateful that there was no herring.

"How do you feel?" Dieners asked him.

"I feel heavy as lead. I ate too much pie, did you see it?" Mac noticed that the uneaten pie was gone.

"Oh, the pie, yes; unfortunately I had to throw it out. A rat had made a mess of it," Dieners said with a chuckle.

The humor of Dieners' statement was lost on Mac. "Hendrickje made it for me yesterday," Mac explained. "It wasn't very good. Don't tell her I said that. I was so hungry that I ate too much of it. It made me groggy, and now I have a headache. Please don't tell Hendrickje, Meneer Dieners. She did her best. She works so hard."

"I won't tell her," Dieners promised. "By the way, Rabbi Aboab won't be coming back until late. He has gone to get his wife and also to see his daughter. He asked me to extend to you his apologies. He is looking forward to introducing you to Mevrouw da Fonseca."

Mac half-listened, but something didn't register when Dieners had given his accounting. With a puckered brow he said, "I thought he was going on Sunday. To get his wife . . .."

"It *is* Sunday," said Dieners. "You slept for two days! You were sick, Meneer MacRitchie, but now you are well, thanks to Mahault. She got you through the worst of it. By the way, Mahault laundered Rembrandt's clothes you were wearing and she returned them to van Rijn. I see you are back in your own attire."

371

Mac studied Dieners for a long time; you couldn't say he looked surprised. "Sick?" he asked.

"Yes. I think the pie caused it," said Dieners, but as he would not explain more; he rambled on with cheer. "Now you'll be fine. The rabbi was very worried, but now everything is all right. You can stay in bed until you feel well enough to rejoin Meneer van Rijn. He was worried, too. I must say, Rembrandt seemed quite concerned—which is unlike him, if I may say so."

Mac felt confused with his head full of cobwebs and he wasn't sure of anything, but he said, "I see. I understand. I think I should go back to Rembrandt's house and see what his plans are, find out if he has need of me. But, as this is Sunday, won't he be at church?"

Dieners nodded and then wobbled his head 'no.' "Yes, it's Sunday, but no, van Rijn isn't a churchgoer. I talked with him earlier this morning while you were still sleeping. He said if you are feeling all right, to please come to him after you've had something to eat."

When Mac went next door things were much as Dieners had said they would be, yet, in some ways, different. In the same way that Dieners had been especially accommodating to Mac, Rembrandt and Hendrickje were effusive toward him, welcoming him as though they had not seen him for a long time and, repeatedly, they asked how he felt, and was he all right.

Mac thought the van Rijns' behavior to be a bit smarmy, but he enjoyed their welcome and their attention. They even served him a luxury—coffee—something he hadn't had in a week. They seldom had coffee in the van Rijn house and Mac had assumed coffee didn't exist as yet in Amsterdam—but he assumed wrong. The coffee they served wasn't good; of course Mac did not say so. He asked for cream and a little sugar.

Sipping the coffee, Mac looked around and it was only then that he noticed that his press was nowhere to be seen. It crossed Mac's mind that something must have happened to it, and that's why the Rembrandts were being especially nice; yet there was no mention of his press to Mac.

Van Rijn had plans and laid them out for Mac right away. He explained that there was to be a meeting with van Leest this very day, and within the hour. His playing card-publisher was going to stop in on his way to church in order to see a sample of the prints—even though the ink on them was not yet dry.

"What I'm going to ask you to do now may sound strange to your ears, Meneer MacRitchie, and please do not take offense: Will you take away your press? You see, I don't want van Leest to know the details about your new machine. Not yet."

Rembrandt was anxious about Mac's press. This did, indeed, sound odd to Mac's ears. He was surprised but he said nothing as Rembrandt went to a tall armoire and opened it. He had put the press out of sight in an alcove inside—next to the stack of prints. As van Rijn brought Mac the press, he went on with his explanation.

"I only want van Leest to see that I did, in fact, get my etching printed. You see, I had said 'no' to his proposal at first because I had no press. Then, when he asked me why I had changed my mind about making artist's cards, I didn't tell him about your visit and how you brought your wonderful little press."

Mac nodded, but he considered that van Rijn's game was manipulative, much more so than necessary. He wondered, *But why hide the press?*

Mac's face must have betrayed his thoughts, as Rembrandt was quick to explain further: "I don't know how you do business in New Amsterdam, but, here in the Mother country, if you want to maximize your profits, you don't tell anything to anyone about your methods. My—access to—your press is proprietary knowledge." Rembrandt concluded, "I can see by your face that you don't understand, but, at least for now, take back your press and wait at Rabbi Aboab's house. Please."

Mac nodded, but he felt disappointed. "Okay," he said.

Rembrandt laughed. "Ha! *Okay*! Yes!" Rembrandt had more: "There's one more thing before you go. I've been thinking about your press. When I first saw it, I confess that I thought—from the size of it, that it was a child's toy and could not be a true printing press. Then it came to me that it is astute to have a small press for small prints. Also, a small press won't take up space like the press I used to own."

This was a familiar refrain to Mac—the press's economy of means had been his favorite selling point. The words of the renowned Rembrandt made him smile and Mac ventured, "Sir, I would like it if you would write that down—and sign it for me."

"Write it down? What for?"

"It would be an endorsement," Mac said.

Van Rijn broke out laughing. "Ha! You joke with me again! No, no, I prefer not to. I'll tell you what I've decided: I know a wood crafter who makes furnishings for ships. He can make a small press, like yours, but designed like the one that I used to have. Oh, I know he will laugh at the idea of such a wee press! Ha ha. But I'll show him. I'll show everyone. I could even keep my wee wooden press a secret if I wanted to—keep it in a cupboard and hidden if necessary!" Rembrandt laughed at the image of a press fitted in his armoire.

"That works," agreed Mac. "That's what I . . .."

Rembrandt cut him off: "Wait! I almost forgot! There was a plate you had with you. Aboab told me. You wanted to print it. May I look at it?" Mac took the plate out of his pocket. Van Rijn was surprised when he saw it. "What? But this is still coated? Why is that?"

"I couldn't get that stuff off."

Rembrandt tilted the plate this way and that to catch the light. "Where did you get this?"

Mac improvised: "An immigrant. From New Amsterdam." He thought, *Not so far-fetched because it's from Maine, not far from New York—New Amsterdam.*

Rembrandt's mouth puckered as he thought. He said, "Hmm. Well . . .," and nothing more and gave the plate back to Mac. Van Rijn went into the kitchen and, momentarily, came back with a small, tightly-stoppered brown bottle and a few sheets of paper. "Take this and clean it over at Aboab's home, and take this paper, too—we don't want the spirits to hurt the rabbi's furniture." He gestured to the press and said, "Van Leest will be here soon, so, please, if you will indulge me."

It didn't take Mac long to clear out his press and get back to Aboab's house. As he approached the front steps, he met Dieners coming out the door.

"I'm going to the market," Dieners said. "I see that you have your machine. What's the matter? Was Rembrandt unimpressed?"

"No, he liked it well enough, but he needed some open space," Mac said. "The press was in the way, and he asked me to keep it here awhile."

"Then, as soon as I get back, will you show me

printing? I didn't see you finish, you may remember."

"I do remember, yes, and now I have a plate and some paper. I will print for you to pay for my dinner!" Dieners nodded and smiled at the prospect of a demonstration. He turned and went off to the market, a basket swinging at his side.

Mac went up the steps and in the door. Aboab's house was beginning to feel like a second home even though it was no place like home.

By this time, Mahault was finished with her duties, gone for the day and Mac found that he was alone. Cleaning supplies stood about, evidence that Dieners' had been getting ready for Huisvrouw da Fonseca's homecoming sometime later that day.

With his press cradled in his arms, Mac side-stepped up the staircase crab-like to navigate the narrow staircase. In the garret Mac found that Mahault had cleared the decanter and the candle away, but the top of the desk was still too crowded to be able set the press down and still have enough room to finish cleaning the plate.

To make room, Mac opened the front of the chest, slid the press into its place and closed up the chest's door. He put a piece of paper down to protect the desktop and set the plate on it, then unstopped the bottle that Rembrandt had sent with him. With a few drops of the solvent dribbled onto the plate, Mac began to rub it vigorously with a rag. His rubbing jiggled the desk, and as he rubbed harder and harder, the chest's drop-down door fell open from all the shaking. Mac shut the door up again and locked it so as to keep it shut.

He put more drops on the plate and rubbed again. Now the little etched, coppery face was clearing as the black coating softened a little and rubbed away. He saw that the face was upside down, so Mac rotated the plate and rubbed some more. He thought, *This stuff is stubborn. It's like epoxy paint!*

Mac wished he had some lacquer thinner. At home he had everything in his studio; but not in this place. To himself he muttered, *There's no place like my studio*, and he rubbed harder.

From somewhere overhead, it seemed that Mac heard a woman's voice cry out a word, but he couldn't make out what she said. He thought, *Could that be the Missus already? Missus Da Fonseca? Back so soon? Oh my . . ..* He started rubbing again.

The woman cried out again, and this time it was more distinct: *"Mac!"*—his nickname. Faye cried out a third time, right in Mac's ear: *"Mac!"*

Faye?

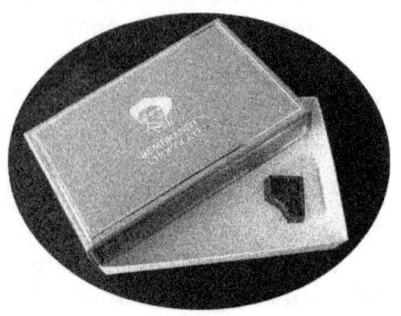

Chapter 45
Party Time

"*Mac, wake up!*

Faye was near tears. Mac's head was resting in the crook of her arm. Her voice broke as she shouted louder, "*Mac! W-w-wake up*! Don't scare me like this!" Mac's head lolled to the side. He jerked it back and his eyes popped open.

Faye had found Mac lying on the floor of his shop, and she immediately sat on the floor and cradled his head in her lap, almost burying him in the fluffy crinoline of her costume gown.

"Mac! Don't you ever *do* that! You hear? You scared me to death. What *were* you doing, anyway?"

Faye's Marie Antoinette wig slipped a little on her head and so with her other hand she put it right and wiped her cheek with her palm. The ballpoint beauty spot was smeared. She heaved a sigh of relief to see Mac coming around and said, "Did you pass out?"

Mac stared at her in disbelief. "I passed out? Is that what?"

"Yes, I guess so," said Faye. "I waited for you

378

awhile, then I came in and found you! You looked like you were dead, Hon! What happened?"

"I don't know. I was . . . it was the lacquer thinner . . . maybe," Mac answered, but he was confused. "How long was I out?"

"Um, about five minutes. I beeped the horn for you to come. Then I started to worry because I couldn't see you through the window so I came in and you there you were, lying on the floor. At first I thought you were being funny!"

Mac thought this over for a second, and then he rolled off Faye's lap and raised himself to his feet, saying nothing; and to Faye, he seemed oddly indifferent to her accounting of what happened—not remotely interested.

Faye got up, too. Hesitantly, she asked, "How do you feel?"

"I feel fine," Mac said. He gave her a quizzical look. "Really, I do."

"You're sure?"

"Yes. Faye, I'm sorry about what happened. It was nothing. Don't ever worry about me. I'll be more careful." He looked around the shop in wonderment, as if he was uncertain of exactly what he was promising to be more careful about; his eyes settled momentarily on the lacquer thinner can that sat by itself on the counter. He looked at the clock and said, "We'd better go!"

Faye said, "Okay, but don't forget what you came in here for—the chocolate for the party," and she went to the shop door and opened it.

Mac watched her. He looked confused.

Standing by the door, Faye reminded him, "Remember, in the chest? *Chocolates.* Rembrandt's?"

Mac furrowed his brow, then said, "Oh, right," and he went to the printmaker chest. It was locked.

He reached into his pocket for the key. He found it mixed with other things—some change, his USB flash drive, some lint, and a little oddly-shaped metal object which he didn't recognize. He returned the other things to his pocket and used the key to open the drop-down door of the chest.

The front of the chest came open and he took the box of chocolates out. From the doorway Faye eyed it and said, "Mac, that box has been opened, I think, look—the string is hanging. I think some little rat got into it, looks like," she accused good naturedly.

Mac looked. It did look odd. "No, Honey, it's just twisted I think." As he began to re-tie the gold string he stopped and his face brightened. "I remember now! I thought, why not take that camera we got? It's right here, and we could test it at the party if the batteries are okay."

Faye turned, "Sure, but let's get going. We're already late."

Mac took out the camera and clutched it together with the box of chocolates, turned off the lights and off they went to the party.

***

At Dennis' house a woman in a period livery of an old-timey European housemaid opened the door, and a rushing hubbub of chatter and babble from the crowd met them. It was party time! She smiled as she saw the Queen and the Netherlander—she knew them in spite of their disguises.

"Hey hey *hey*, it's the MacRitchies!" She exclaimed, loud enough to be heard over the noisy crowd indoors so as to announce their arrival to the party-goers. A few people heard the greeter and noticed, and they went back to what they were doing before Nora got their attention.

Mac thought he recognized the woman's voice, but not her face because it was smudged with soot, and her hair was covered with a scullery maid's white hat with long ties hanging down. Her clothes were plain and gray. She held a feather duster and gave Mac's costumed chest a quick once over. Mac chuckled at the feather duster treatment, and after thinking for a second he knew who she was.

"Nora!"

"Not *Nora. Cinderella*! I'm Cinderella. I clean fireplaces! Also dusty old masters!" and she gave his great hat a swipe with the duster, while Mac tried to fend her off. Nora was one of Mac's best friends.

As they stood in the door she said haltingly, for effect: "You. Look. Great. Mac! Right out of a Vermeer painting. I see that you brought a queen with you! Come in, come in." She asked, "And who is she?" then aside, Nora added slyly, "As if I didn't know."

Faye stepped forward and showed that she was not above speaking to the help. "*Je suis la reine Marie-Antoinette,*"[111] she said, affecting her best accent for Nora's benefit. She handed Nora the bright red, gold-stamped box of Rembrandt's Chocolates.

"Ooohh—a box of chocolates. Thank you," said Nora as she took the box. "I'll put these on the table for everyone."

As she turned away a voice called from behind her, "Hey, you two! Welcome!" A tall, black man approached, with a patch over one eye and dressed in a long black coat, winking lights all over it and glossy, studded leather tights. The crowd parted and gave him wide berth as he strode to meet Mac and

---

[111] I am the Queen Marie Antoinette.

Faye with long steps, *thunking* as he loftily walked forward on stilts.

Mac was aghast. *Dennis on stilts!* Their host normally stood under four-feet tall; but on stilts he towered over Mac.

"Ho! Dennis. Damn! That. Is. Way. Cool, man!" said Mac, admiring the transformation of the dwarf to giant-height.

"Not Dennis! My name is *Ilosovic Stayne!*" he declared with a little snarl. Dennis swayed a little as he tried his best to keep his balance.

Nora came back and said, "He's the villain, the Red Queen's strong-man from the movie, 'Alice in Wonderland.'"

Dennis, role-playing the evil Stayne, shot a look down at Nora, "Off with her head!" he shouted, scowling, and then flashed her one of his killer smiles.

At this Mac remembered the camera and whipped it out from under his Flemish waistcoat and said, "Wait, hold still a sec, Stayne, I want to take your picture."

Mac pressed the shiny silver power button on the camera and the lens turret extended, making ready to shoot; but when Mac looked at the viewfinder screen to focus, he did a double-take. What he saw on the bright little viewing screen wasn't the tall Dennis. Instead, it showed a white washbasin and a chamber pot next to it. Mac realized that the camera was in playback mode.

"Oops!" he said, and explained to no one in particular, "We just got this camera on *craigslist*, and the seller didn't erase his photos. Hold it one more sec, Den . . . Stayne!" Mac selected the reformat command from the menu to erase all the previous owners' snapshots.

"Hurry up," said Dennis, as he swayed on his stilts, "I can't stand in one place for very long on these things."

Finished reformatting the camera's memory, Mac took his shot. "Got it!"

Dennis was pulled away by another guest wearing a Big Bird costume, and Faye was still talking to Nora. Mac turned to see a woman dressed in black, generously bejeweled and gliding toward him. He tried to guess what character she played. When she spoke he knew that she was Sherry disguised as—*what*? Her hair was wrapped in a black scarf and she wore a fringed shawl.

"You look beautiful . . . Sherry . . . I think. Let me guess what you are," and after a second Mac said, "I know! You're a gypsy fortune teller!"

"Wrong, Mac, I'm a procuress from a famous Dutch painting, as you should know, if you are—as you appear to be—Maestro Vermeer!" She leaned in close to Mac flirtatiously and examined his Netherlander's outfit from his hat and wig down to his boots.

Sherry continued: "I have in mind someone you should meet, Mac," and she touched Faye on her arm and intoned, "Oh Faye, if you don't mind, I want to have a private word with your man, here," and she took Mac's arm to lead him away.

Everyone laughed at Sherry's role-playing as a procuress. Her nature was far from that of a madam and the absurdity was hilarious to everyone in her circle.

"What's going on here," a deep voice resounded. "Did this woman proposition you Mac?" The voice was Carl's. He wore a dark robe and a fluffy white Santa Claus beard. If Carl had worn a kippeh instead of a Joker's Hat, he would have passed for an old

Jewish rabbi.

"Watch out for her, Faye," Carl warned. "She'll have him in bed with a young thing before you know it!"

Mac responded with, "None of your beeswax, Carl! Leave us alone."

It was a happy moment, like a reunion. Mac and Faye had more fun like this as the party progressed. It felt good to Mac to laugh and joke around, and he experienced a deep sense of relief, a kind of release that surprised him. Where did this feeling come from? Why did he feel so elated? He decided it was his habit of working alone in his studio all the time and too long away from his old friends—that must be it; he had been more lonely than he had realized. Now he felt good, so *at home*.

Mac took pictures until the camera's batteries ran down and then he pocketed the camera. He and Faye found a space to sit together on a couch. In front of them was a low, wide coffee table displaying a platter of lox, cream cheese, crackers and also several bottles of wine plus one champagne bottle in an ice bucket. There were Halloween treats and tiny, chilled cream puffs.

The red box that the Rembrandt Chocolates came in was on the table, also. It was empty except for one piece. The other pieces had been snatched up within minutes after Nora opened the box. Mac wondered why that one piece hadn't been taken. Then he noticed that a corner of it was bitten off; he thought, *No one wants to take a piece that someone else has already tried.*

The MacRitchie's remained seated on the couch for most of the evening, sipping champagne, snacking and talking with others. At one point Mac leaned over to Faye and muttered, "Nature calls."

"Well go then. I don't want hear about it!" she whispered, and waved him away.

In the bathroom, Mac washed his hands and, as he finished drying, he noticed in the mirror that his great Flemish hat was missing its plume. He dismissed the loss and thought it probably fell out in the studio incident. He stared at the mirror. Another thing was odd. His face seemed changed. Was it the rock-musician's wig? Of course. Yet the face was not his own, somehow.

I know I've seen a face like that before, Mac thought, *Maybe in a movie, or a book*.

Mac pulled a face in the mirror and mimicked Rembrandt's etchings that popped into his mind. He put on a surprised look, scowled, and opened his eyes wide and exaggerated a look of surprise—his mouth forming a perfect "O". His forehead wrinkled in a washboard of furrows, then went smooth again. Mac's cheeks sucked in and puffed out. *Wow. I may even look like Rembrandt. Better not drink any more champagne.*

He turned away to rejoin Faye and the others. The face in the mirror, however, remained until Mac switched off the bathroom light and he closed the door.

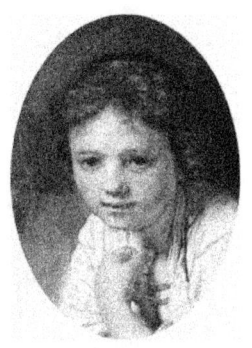

Chapter 46
To etch like Rembrandt

Mac hunkered over his laptop in his workshop on an improvised desk. He heard the familiar squeak of the door to his workshop open and shut. He knew without looking around that this would be Faye bringing him his two-o'clock coffee.

"Coffee," she called, and then, "What are you doing?" when she saw him sitting in the backmost corner, staring at his computer. "I thought you'd be working on your printmaker chest today."

"Hi. Not yet. I'm writing something. It started as a short essay, and—well, it kind of grew into several pages—sort of. I didn't want to tell you until I was further along."

"What's it about?"

"Time travel or a parallel universe. It's about a guy who goes back to the 17th Century. He's a printmaker."

"Do you think that will sell? Maybe instead of an artist, make him a bank robber, or a serial killer. Artists don't sell in the mass markets today."

"But I think a person has to write what they know

about, Faye. I've never robbed a bank or any of those things, good grief! This is *art*, you know."

"Hmm. Well, that's interesting. What's happening in the story now?"

"Well, this guy—my protagonist, meets up with Rembrandt, and he also meets Rembrandt's family. I researched the artist's life, and I learned that they had a little girl. I also learned that Rembrandt sometimes used his family as models for some of his paintings. He painted his wives. I wanted to find one of his paintings of a little girl, because I figure Rembrandt would use her as a model."

"What was her name?" Now Faye was by Mac's desktop and set down his coffee. She glanced at the computer screen, which showed dozens of images of paintings—mostly children.

Mac answered her question: "Cornelia."

"Are all those Cornelia, you think?" she asked, watching the screen as Mac scrolled down it with the wheel thing on the mouse.

"They're 17th Century paintings of children, some by Rembrandt and other artists of the period, like Vermeer, Bols, Leyster . . .." Mac paused as he homed in on one image and clicked on it to enlarge it.

"Well, I've got to go. I'll see you at dinner, Hon."

"Okay. Bye, Faye. And thanks for the coffee,"

In the image of the painting of the little girl that caught his eye, she girl smiled coyly out at the viewer and fingered something at her neckline with her finger and thumb—as if to play with it. Mac read the title: "*Young Girl at a window by Rembrandt van Rijn.*"

Mac zoomed in closer, and he wondered, *What's she got in her fingers?* The resolution of the image low, so that the more Mac enlarged it, the more pixilated the image became. He zoomed back out.

It was impossible for Mac to tell what the thing was that the girl held in her fingers. It wasn't a crucifix—as one might expect, but a fuzzy, grayish blob of pixilated paint. Despite its being hard to define, to Mac there was something familiar about the shape of it. As he stared at the portrait, his left hand fumbled its way into his pocket as though it had a mind of its own.

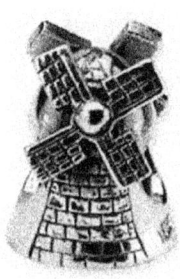

Inspired, Mac jerked his hand out of his pocket and looked around for his journal for something to write on. *Funny,* he thought, *I haven't seen my journal for awhile.* Instead, he took a legal pad and began to write, trying to do it in his best hand:

How to etch like Rembrandt.

Inspired, he was off instantly, but Mac thought of some problems if he was going to explain how to etch like Rembrandt. For one, no one was sure how Rembrandt etched. Van Rijn didn't leave notes; or, if he did, the notes were lost. What he used may not be obtained.

Problems with old-time etching with asphaltum etching grounds and the chemicals, such as hydrochloric acid—those mixtures known as *etchants* or *mordants*—would be hard to handle. To go with his Halfwood Press Project, Mac did, however, have a fairly safe method which he might describe to help others.

A review of Rembrandt's etchings on the Web gave Mac a boost. He got basic information to describe how Rembrandt made his 1660 etching, *Self portrait with a surprised look.*

Mac adapted his technique he called *laser toner etching* for the beginning etcher who wants to *Etch like Rembrandt.* By the time Faye called him for dinner that day, Mac had written over twelve pages on his article:

The chemical technique of etching was developed in the middle ages by Arabic armor makers, artillery, knife and gunsmiths as a means of applying decoration to weapons. It became a plate making technique when papermaking and printing developed. The word etching is derived from the Dutch word for eat, eten, and etching is spelled in Dutch, etsen. You get the idea an acid "eats" metal.

In the printmaking world, there are two steps to making prints. First is the plate making, and second is print making from the plate. Etching is a plate making technique based on the chemical effect of etchants on metal sheets, also called plates. Copper, zinc, magnesium and steel are most common, with

390

zinc being the most popular among beginners because it is cheaper and acid etches it fast. To etch like Rembrandt, copper is the preferred metal. As far as it is known, he used only copper for his etchings. He made some 290 etchings that are fine art; that is, his were not copies of other work which would mean prints as reproductions.

All etching techniques use chemicals. One is a relatively safe chemical—ferric chloride—which is a mineral salt. The hydrochloric acid in Dutch mordant was favored in Rembrandt's time but is not recommended for beginners.

Not only did he use etching, Rembrandt also used a direct drawing-on-metal method, called "drypoint," because no liquid acid is involved in making the plate. Its only drawback is that it produces a plate that wears out sooner than an etched or engraved plate.

For Rembrandt, etching was a creative process like drawing and painting, but with several advantages. One is the skill required, and every skilled artist knows the importance of practicing and improving artistic skills. To practice painting a great deal, the costs of painting imposes limits, not to mention costs of storing paintings waiting for owners to buy them.

Therefore there is another value of printmaking, which is economic. It costs less to make a print than it does to make a painting; and if you make a number of prints and are able to distribute and sell them, they reduce the cost of materials, supplies and labor needed for them.

A third reason creative artists use printmaking is because it is a process art that is divided into two processes: Plate making and print making, which means the artist can limit his or her work to the making of printing plates, and another person can do the printing. This might be merely a practical arrangement; but often times it becomes more a collaborative arrangement for teamwork.

You find collaboration in other art forms when two people, each with different strengths or talent, come up with better results than either one could have done alone. The sum of their effort together is greater than the sum of each one's parts.

A fourth value of printmaking is that a plate can be printed differently each time it is printed. This makes it like a musical score, as when a musician chooses to alter the tempo, key, or other aspect of a performance of a given composition. Dancers, too, may perform a dance routine differently. In this sense, printmaking is more like a performance art than strictly limited to its visual effects alone.

A fifth reason printmaking has survived over the centuries despite technological changes is because it is a kind of social art due to the collaborative nature of it, mentioned above, and it requires people of different skill sets. A machinist must make a press or the instruments; an ink maker must make the inks, a papermaker the paper, and so on.

Producers or publishers come in when the management of a project is too much for the artist, which brings business people into the picture. When people share equipment, such as a printing press, they create a kind of cottage industry. Not only equipment, but knowledge of all kinds is shared, too.

Considering what has been written here so far, the reader should bear in mind that two steps are involved in the art of printmaking—plate making and print making. This is, in my opinion, forgotten when teachers teach it. It should be emphasized that if someone makes a printing plate, it is not required that they also print the plate. It can bring in the division of labor, so called because printing is laborious and sometimes not part of the creative process that is seen in the plate making step.

Printing is laborious if it is paid labor only; but if printing is taken up by a person in close association and collusion with the maker of the plate—the artist in most instances—it contributes to the value of the fine art print.

An artist—a painter for example—who does not make a plate but only paints on a sheet of metal or plastic and runs it through a press is demonstrating how a monotype—as this is called—doesn't involve plate making at all! Likewise, finding a piece of flattened material (metal, plastic, paper, etc.) and applying ink to it and running it through a press with paper is proof that plate making can be automatic.

With these considerations to define the print in terms that Rembrandt appears to have used the art and craft, one can now proceed to adapt van Rijn's etching process to our times—the 21st Century. Historians tell us that he made many variations in his prints, using different papers, inking and preparing the plates differently, and reworking etched plates with drypoint and engraving, i.e., mixed media.

Etchers still cover their metal plates with a thin coat of acid-resistant mixture known as the etching ground or acid resist and these resists are often mixtures of asphalt, resin, wax or grease and they are sold today in liquid, paste or ball form. A ball form can be melted on a plate and rolled out to a smooth coat. Printmakers may make their own grounds.

Rembrandt, like most etchers, drew the image with a sharp point, a scribe, or a needle, so that where the point penetrated the etching ground the copper is exposed to the etchant, which comes next. It is said that he used a fairly soft, pasty etching ground of his own devising. For van Rijn, it meant he could draw in a free, loose manner—such as curly hair and lively facial features. Rembrandt almost always drew directly on the plate, perhaps with preliminary studies on paper with chalk as a guideline. Rarely, if ever, would he transfer a drawing onto the etching ground.

Drawing for making an etching is always a process with a little surprise to it because the final print will be a reversal of the original image. What was on the left side will be on the right. Lettering and numbers in the art will be backward. Artists sometimes use a mirror to correct for this, but this is difficult.

Rembrandt put the plate in a dish of hydrochloric acid diluted with water, and perhaps potassium chloride and acetic acid. No one is sure precisely what formula he used, but there is a popular etchant called Dutch Mordant (mordant is another word for etching solution and etchant). The exposed parts are etched away, producing lines and textures in the surface of the metal. The longer the plate is left in, the deeper these get. How long to leave it is a matter of practice, trial-and-error, or lookup tables.

The etching ground—the resist—is removed before the print making step. The clean plate is inked with a suitable ink, usually oil-based and sticky. The surface is wiped clean by hand so that it is clear of ink except for the ink caught in the lines and textures.

You soften a suitable paper; usually a thick type of rag paper, by dampening it and then it is suitable to make the print. With a press designed for the purpose—such as a Halfwood Press with its two steel rollers that pass a flat bed between them—you set up with felt blankets to cushion the plate and paper. You lay the inked plate on the bed; the damp paper over it and follow with the felt blankets on top. These go through the press by turning the wheel.

The pressure between the top roller and the plate is so extreme that the paper is forced into the lines and textures where the ink is and produces an image. It is a reversed impression of the image on the plate. The lines that have been bitten deeply may be darker than the more shallow or delicate ones.

Textures that are deep will hold and release more ink than delicate tones.

This printing method is called "intaglio printing" with the ink coming from lines and textures that were made in the original surface of the plate and the way the ink was rubbed into the lines and the surface wiped clean.

Intaglio printing refers _only_ to the printing. The etched plate might print by another process — such as by relief printing. That etching made the plate doesn't mean it has to be printed intaglio. Also, intaglio and relief are sometimes combined, as when one color of ink might be below the surface, and another color might be on the top surface. Two colors are printed at one time through the press.

Printmaking as an art form is complicated, and writing about it is difficult because although there are many rules to observe, in fact the only "rules" are those of chemistry and physics. Rules apply, for example, as in cold, still etchant it takes longer to etch a plate than in warm, turbulent etchant. Heavy pressure in printing gives different results compared to light pressure as a rule.

Plate making for intaglio and relief printing often does not involve chemicals, but instruments, to make the plate. Already mentioned was drypoint. Engraving is a process that uses an instrument called a burin, or graver. It has a V-shaped point which cuts a sharp-edged line which typically starts and ends in a point. Sometimes artists invent their own instruments to make their images more true to their liking or to save time. Electric engravers, for example, are popular among plate-making artists.

Rembrandt's first plates were pure etchings, without drypoint. He initially used drypoint only for small additions or corrections. From about 1640 he became increasingly interested in the painterly effects of the velvety drypoint line, and seemed unconcerned with the fact the plates wore out quickly. He combined drypoint with the burin drawn straight onto the copper.

Another instrument is the burnisher, a hardened, polished steel shaft with a rubbing point that can erase fine lines or burnish away unwanted scratches. A scraper, like the burnisher, is another instrument which can be used for corrections or as a drawing instrument. Over time, these instruments were joined by dozens of others as the commercial pressure for finer detail was great. Mezzotint, aquatint and—finally—halftone photographic screens became the norm.

Deliberate variation by inking the plate differently is possible, either by the artist who makes the plate and prints it, or by the printer charged with printing the job. More or less ink can be left in the impression, so the mood of an impression can change. This variable is called 'surface tone,' a result of the kind of ink used and the manner in which the plate is wiped.

When the lines and tones are re-worked, it is called making a 'state-change.' In modern times, these notations are often indicated on the print as a technical aid. Art collectors sometimes want to have rare and unusual "state prints" instead of the published edition.

Almost all Rembrandt's etchings exist in more than one state, sometimes as many as ten or more. Often the changes are slight, amounting to little more than minor additions or corrections. Sometimes they are so drastic that the result is a new composition. The changes are documented the moment the print is made, which gave rise to the "moment number" as a new way of fixing this time factor.

A variation in printmaking is when a fresh print, while still damp, is run back through the press with another sheet of paper on it. It produces a print-of-a-print (a counterproof) which naturally, being reversed twice, looks like the original composition as made on the plate. It is so the artist wishing to make minor adjustments to the plate can find the spots easier. Another kind of print is the maculature, a print pulled to get more ink out of the plate which results in a very light image.

Finally, there is the monoprint, where only one such impression is made, but more could be made if it was desirable. This is not the same as a monotype, which is a transfer painting and, since it cannot be printed exactly the same again, it is not a print.

A limited number of impressions can be made from a metal or wood printing plate, depending on the metal. Steel last longer than copper and zinc, for example. A drypoint plate might be worn out in ten or fifteen impressions.

Prints of the same state may vary considerably as the plate and the burr become worn. While this is a nightmare for publishers, most creative artists take it in stride; some even view the process of wear and tear with more interest than if everything were made permanent.

The different origins of paper (e.g. European, Japanese and 'Chinese') give the printmaker an unlimited range of color and surface structures, all of which can be exploited artistically. A plate printed on different papers produces different effects. Many of Rembrandt's prints are on Japanese paper.

Many printmakers use the same methods Rembrandt did. They have good reasons to, as they will tell you. Some say the results are better; most will say it suits them to follow the ways of the old masters. A few might explain that they feel they are in touch with the old masters and the smells and feelings of the processes are important to their creative process!

What follows is a new way to explore etching that is in between the ways of the old masters, with their asphaltum-based etching grounds, their hydrochloric and nitric acid

404

solutions and materials which may be difficult to find and buy plus some etchants are hazardous to your health and your home plumbing!

By the end of the 20th Century, printmaking studios nationwide were beset with numerous warnings from doctors and the Occupational Safety Health Administration (OSHA), and schools that taught printmaking had to change their methods or stop teaching printmaking. These factors brought about a non-toxic printmaking movement so that students do not have to risk their health to practice printmaking.

Today there is a division between the toxic and non-toxic advocates. You may hear muttering in a printmaking demonstration when a teacher uses mineral spirits to clean a printing plate; a substitute for mineral spirits is vegetable oil or a solvent based on soybean oil. To suggest using lacquer thinner to clean a plate will raise great protests if it is not carried out in a ventilated space. There are inks based on oil and inks based on water-soluble mixtures that may contain oil but do not require oil solvents to clean. Where there is a will, there is a way, so I have included chocolate as an ink.

Thus far there are few perfect, easy-to-make replacements for the pasty etching ground said to have been the secret of Rembrandt's free-style of drawing on a copper plate.

There are few ways to etch a copper plate without an acid or mineral salt solution. As it seems there is no way to have our copper plate and completely non-toxic method, the following method is offered. I must say, however, that you proceed at your own risk and use all materials and supplies according to safety precautions.

Here is how I do my "laser transfer etchings." First, I eliminated the asphaltum-based etching ground. Instead I use a black-and-white laser printer and laminator to get my etching ground on to the copper plate., as used by Rembrandt. Copper is a beautiful metal and thin copper fits most budgets. Costly engraver's copper and thicker copper plates are sold by art suppliers. Copper circuit board (PCB, a copper-clad plastic) will work.

With software graphics program, make a solid, filled rectangle a little larger than your printing plate. Rembrandt did not make big prints, so choose small for your etching— under five-by-seven inches.

Call up your printing program and position your rectangle on the page where it will make efficient use of paper. Letter-sized paper, for example, has room for two rectangles if you wish to make a five-by-seven print. A page layout program, such as Adobe InDesign or Microsoft Publisher, lets you position your rectangles.

Load your black-and-white laser printer paper carrier with silicon-coated paper. You don't buy this in a store; it comes with peel-off label stock. Like the throwaway backing from Contact paper, such papers have a shiny, slick coating of silicon on it that gives the release-effect.

These papers are the carrier to transfer laser toner to a metal plate. A laser printer has a heating element in it that fuses the toner to these papers on the shiny, coated side; the same toner will melt and stick to a metal (or wood) surface if you iron it on. You should set your printer for maximum blacks if it provides a switch or this option in its software controls. The laser toner in the toner cartridge is a powdered form of plastic. I like Hewlett-Packard (HP) toners best.

The black rectangle on your silicon-coated paper is like a thin etching resist because and, when toner is melted as a coating on the metal, the metal will not be eaten away by an etchant.

A printed design, drawing, or photographic image instead of a solid black lets etchers have lettering, numbers and other difficult images in their etching plates. Any image you can print in a laser toner you can etch into metal for printmaking and metal design projects, i.e., jewelry, badges, etc.

With your black rectangle of laser toner, now turn on your iron or your personal laminator. A personal laminator is like the ones used in convenience shops like FedEx Kinko's. A nine-inch model is recommended as the most versatile, but a smaller model will suffice. A hand iron, on high, will do the job, but it's trickier.

Prepare your copper plate by first checking that the edges are not sharp or burred. A sharp edge will damage the laminator, if you use one. Anyway, you will need to bevel and soften the edges of the plate to print it later on; do it now.

Remove all traces of oils and greases, fingerprints and dirt from the copper surface with vinegar and whiting or cleaners such as Comet or Bon Ami. If you use a scrubbing pad, it leaves a tone on the plate; "tooth" on the plate, even if it is just a haze, may help toner that is going to be fused to the plate to stick. Rub the plate with #000 steel wool enhances the toner's adhesion. Also clean the back of the plate.

You have a silicon-coated paper with a fragile black rectangle on it. Although the toner will not stick to the silicon very well (nothing will stick to silicon). Thus, if you scratch the toner, it will leave a line in the black.

You are ready to prepare to draw to etch like Rembrandt would draw on a pasty etching ground but you will be drawing through laser toner on silicon-coated paper instead of asphaltum-coated copper. You fuse the toner to the metal in the next step, which will result in a reversed composition.

The finished print from the plate will turn it around. You may want to write words on the print; your writing will come out the same way at the end of the printing.

With the laminator warmed up or hand iron hot, pre-warm the plate by putting through your laminator once. Alternatively, with a sheet of paper to prevent scratching, run a hot iron over it. This speeds up fusing. Place the black rectangle (on which you drew your lines) on the copper and feed into the laminator.

If the metal is thin, such as 22 gauge, it will probably stick slightly the first time through, but not if not hot enough. The plate is too hot to touch so use pliers to pick up the plate by its edge. Pass it through again, or continue ironing until you can lift a corner and see that the toner is transferred to the plate.

Peel off the silicon-coated paper. You may see a few spots that did not stick, a result of dust on the plate. They will have to be touched up with a spot of some kind of resist such as a magic markers or nail polish.

Before beginning the etching, as the toner is not fused well enough to be strong against the corrosive effect of the etchant, it needs to heated on a hotplate or electric coil range so high that it melts. Hold the plate with pliers and heat the plate until the black toner changes from dull to satin, indicating that it is hot enough. It may even smoke—a good indication.

When cool, coat the back of the plate because the back is exposed to the etchant and your solution will become weak. The easiest way is with strips of plastic shipping tape.

The best type of etchant is ferric chloride. This mineral salt causes a precipitation effect, so the plate should be upside down or on its edge so the precipitate will fall away from the surface and not clog it and thus stop the process.

If you use a plastic photographer's tray, glass cake or casserole pan, then you can suspend the plate face-down with a long strip of shipping tape that reaches all the way across the pan and sticks to two opposing edges.

Attach the plate by its backside in the middle of this long strip of tape, and you can

412

lift it and suspend it, face down, in the pan slightly off the tray bottom. Stick the two ends of the tape to the top edge of the tray's opposite edges so the plate hangs suspended. When you pour the ferric chloride in to cover the plate, the precipitate will fall out of the etching happening on the underside of the suspended plate.

To be sure there are no air bubbles trapped on the plate, rock it back and forth so the liquid will sweep away any bubbles.

The time that you should etch depends on how deep you want your lines, and to a beginner this is a mystery. Generally the depth depends on temperature. Also, if the solution is fresh it will work faster than if it is old and weak. If you agitate, sweep or bubble the solution with a fish tank air pump, the etchant works faster.

All things considered, five to fifteen minutes will get results. If you etch for 20 to 40 minutes, it will be deep; if your composition has closely-set lines, they may even erode sideways, causing an "erasing" effect called crevé. Rinse the plate with water, dry it, and look closely with a magnifier, such as a photographer's lupe, to see depth.

When you have cleaned off the plate, there is no going back. You cannot replace the toner when it's gone.

To clean the plate use #000 steel wool and rub. If the toner is fused well, this is hard work but safe. Lacquer thinner, which is a highly toxic chemical, dissolves the toner instantly but you must use it carefully, with ample ventilation or go outdoors. You should never be able to smell the solvent while you are using it. Use a window fan by an open window to pull the fumes away from you.

Use gloves, such as rubber gloves or nitrile exam gloves for protection. Lacquer thinner will go right through your skin as it is a mixture of tuluol, alcohol and other toxic solvents and can lead to brain damage and mental illness. For more information, read

414

resources on the Web or in books like, *Artist Beware*, by Dr. McCann.

If you are printing the plate by the intaglio method, as Rembrandt did, use etching ink. Water-based etching inks are available.

Work the ink into the etched areas and lines with a credit card or rubber scraper, a rag or gloved finger. Wipe off the surface ink and print it intaglio in an etching press. Use printmaking paper softened by soaking and blotting off the excess water.

The idea of using a chocolate bar for inking an etched copper plate is for making a miniature etching presses kids can use and works around the problem of cleaning up regular printing inks.

A chocolate bar is like an oil stick which painters use. Rub the bar across the plate and chocolate will stick in the lines and textures. When you have chocolate in the lines and textures, make the press and paper ready. Warm the plate and print. Warming a metal *plate makes the chocolate soft to print.*

This paper has not addressed other areas of interest, such as galvanic etching, or etching with safe solutions and electricity. Another area is plastic plates printed by 3-D printing.

Still another is not etching but engraving using a CNC router-computer controlled engraving for wood and plastic plate-making.

The end

Mac had written nonstop for over two hours and he thought he had covered everything. As he concentrated he unconsciously puckered up his lips and stared at his writing, deep in thought After a few seconds, he added a postscript:

These are far and away from etching like Rembrandt. However, if they had been available to him in the 1600's, I think he would have made art with them.

This is how the story ended, and Mac leaned way back in his chair and thought *wouldn't it cool if Rembrandt came up in time to this, the 21st Century?*

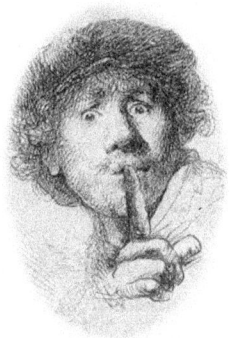

Denouement

This Denouement is in six parts:

In Part 1: Part one starts below, where you may read a rundown of the events that happened after that November Sunday in 1660 when Mac—along with his printmaker chest and its contents, vanished from the garret of Rabbi Aboab's house. He had been in Amsterdam one week.

Part 2: To call this book "historical fiction" would be partly accurate because some characters named in this story were alive in 1660, and part two provides brief descriptions of the real, historical figures in the story besides Rembrandt van Rijn.

Part 3: Part three describes the fictional characters—such as Macia Schwarzesherz, Mahault, etc.

Part 4: Part four is a mock interview of the author, Bill Ritchie.

Part 5: Part five gives you recipes for the baking mentioned in the novel. These were made by Lynda Ritchie; all are real so you may try them at home.

Part 6: Part six, "About the Author," is a brief biography of the author.

Part 1 of the Denouement – The aftermath

Mac's disappearance triggered events that created quite a buzz in the Rozengracht neighborhood of Amsterdam in November, 1660. When Dieners van Catarina returned from the market, he was first to discover that the mysterious American Colonial, William Handyside MacRitchie, and his koffer were missing. The Rembrandt family was next to learn about Mac's disappearance; and third, Mahault. Of course, word spread to reach everyone who had met MacRitchie during his week there.

Both Rabbi Aboab and Rembrandt reported Meneer MacRitchie's (and his printmaker chest) disappearance to the authorities, and an investigation was launched.

Vrouw Macia Schwarzesherz was arrested on suspicion of murder and theft. But, since Mac's body was never found and there was no trace of the chest, she couldn't be convicted for those crimes. However, when the authorities searched her house pursuant to their investigation, they found her alchemical trove. They suspected her of poison-making which implicated her in a number of unsolved poisoning deaths, so she went to trial.

During Macia Schwarzesherz' trial, Mahault was cross-examined as an accomplice to the crime, but she was never really suspected of complicity. She had said not a word, of course, and many people testified as to her good character.

Pieter, too, was called on the stand and his testimony was taken in due course, but yielded little. The documented poisonings (most of which were instances of wives getting rid of their husbands) plus the rumor that Schwarzesherz had eaten her own husband years before were enough to sentence her to the Gouda *Spinhuis* (a women's house of correction) where she spent the rest of her life.

Rembrandt—well-pleased with the Mini Halfwood Press that Mac had introduced to him, used the money (from van Leest and Rabbi Aboab's portrait fee) to hire a craftsman to build a one-fourth scale model of his old etching press; it was made all of wood and was to be put into service for the card project. However, van Leest decided that the intaglio printing method was too slow and too labor-intensive for making playing cards. As a result, Rembrandt made only a few cards. They showed five self portraits of Rembrandt, drawn by the artist from the memory of his earlier self-portraits.

Arent de Gelder (usually spelled *Aert*) stayed with Rembrandt to the end, and made good on his commitment to be van Rijn's protégé. He was Rembrandt's last student; he is rumored to have completed some of Rembrandt's unfinished paintings after van Rijn' death. Arent de Gelder's work can be seen today in major museum collections.

Whether Arent was related to the actual van Gelder Zonen Paper Company—which dates back to the 1660s, is the author's speculation. Arent's use of copper-point drawing is fiction, although this technique does work; the author used copper-point and silver-point in his own drawings in the 1960s.

The blackened, partly cleaned plate (which Dieners found on the desktop where Meneer MacRitchie left it) ended up with Rembrandt. It was one of the few clues that remained left behind that indicated his visitor had actually existed. Van Rijn never finished cleaning off the black coating on the plate; if he had, he would have recognized it to be an etching of his own from years before. One can't help but wonder what would happen if Rembrandt tried to clean the black coating off that plate.

The second and third clues remained with Mahault—the penny and MacRitchie's journal, which Mahault found when she was changing the bunk bedclothes. She showed the book to her sister who was able to read some of it despite the sloppy handwriting. The two had no idea what Mac was writing about as most of it was nonsense to them. They never showed it to anyone. As the pages were thin paper compared to paper made in the 17th Century, they were torn out and used for toilet paper.

There was a fourth clue—the one-dollar bill with which Mac paid his room and board, but this, as well as the blue, fake Ostrich plume, was never seen again.

Part 2 of the Denouement - Real people and places

Disclaimer: The following has not been reviewed for accuracy and last names are listed alphabetically. – BR

Daniel Berillos was Rabbi Aboab's son-in-law, married to Judith, daughter of Aboab and Ester. In the story he appeared in the company of Daniel de Pinto, who visited Aboab on behalf of Geerincx seeking storage space while a floor was to be repaired.

Rabbi Isaac Aboab da Fonseca, who was fifty-five years old at the time-setting of this story, lived another thirty-three years and made significant contributions to Amsterdam's Portuguese-Sephardic community. The Portuguese synagogue in Amsterdam (the *Esnoga*) was inaugurated fifteen years later. There is no known portrait of Aboab "by Rembrandt" and there appear to be only two images of the famous rabbi known to exist. Aboab did not live next door to Rembrandt, and he probably did not live on the Rozengracht. He had a wife, Ester, and a married daughter, Julia.

Samuel Geerincx is one of the two men acting together who bought Rembrandt's house at auction. He was a silk merchant; the other man was a shoemaker. The story's incident of the floor-tile is fabricated. [As a note of interest: The author plans to make a board game based on this novel and the tiles may figure as a game mechanic.]

Arent (also spelled **Aert**) **de Gelder** was one of Rembrandt's last pupils while in Amsterdam, studying in the Rozengracht studio from 1661 to 1663 and—according to some accounts, he continued to assist until van Rijn's death. I played with his age since he was about 15 when he was a student, and put him to work for the van Rijns at a younger age to fit my timeline. The fact that his family name is the same as the famous Van Gelder Zonen paper company is a coincidence and not verified but a good fit for this story.

Jacques van Leest was a well-known playing card publisher; and Rembrandt did, in fact, rent the apartment, **The Blue Crown** from van Leest. Van Rijn lived there with his wife and their daughter, Cornelia. Also Titus lived there until he married. Hendrickje died in this house, and, in 1669, Rembrandt died there, too. Rembrandt never made artist's cards for van Leest. There is only one etching by Rembrandt remotely connected to playing cards, the "Man Playing Cards," shown below, dated about 1641.

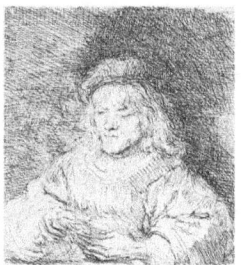

Jan Lievens shared a studio with Rembrandt when—in their twenties, they were just starting their careers. Some historians believe that the two engaged in friendly competition and high-spirited art collaborations. It is true that they saw little of each other in their old age and true also that Lievens lived near the Rozengracht where Rembrandt lived.

David Linglebach, formerly a tavern keeper from Frankfurt who moved to Amsterdam, called himself *Kunstmeester* (Master Artist) and was a specialist in fountains and fireworks. He leased property on Rozengracht for the "Nieuwe Doolhof" across from the apartment (The Blue Crown) where Rembrandt spent his last years. The amusement park featured automata, displays and a carillon.

Abraham and Isaac Pereira arrived in Amsterdam about 1644 and became main figures in the flourishing trading enterprises in Amsterdam. Jewish merchants such as these men were important as persons with in-demand skills during the Dutch Golden Age. They labored assiduously in the causes of the Dutch people and contributed materially to the prosperity of the Dutch Republic. They would not likely have been a threat to a visitor like Mac as the author portrayed them; it is more likely that they would have been welcoming because the protagonist's situation was similar their own, that is to say, as Jews they were outsiders in the Republic.

Daniel Pinto lived next door to Rembrandt's former home on the Breestraat and therefore was to be the neighbor of Geerincx after the artist's house was auctioned to Geerincx and his associate. Pinto's relationship with Rembrandt was soured by a financial disagreement prior to van Rijn's loss. Specifically, Rembrandt refused to pay his share of the repairs to the foundation under the common wall of their adjoined houses.

The DePinto family, wealthy Jews in Amsterdam, had a villa called *Tulpenburg*, near Ouderkerk where—in the story, there is mention of Rabbi Aboab's wife and daughter were away on holiday the week Mac stayed at Aboab's house. The holiday by Aboab's wife and daughter is fiction, but the Tulpenburg is real and today is part of the city of Utrecht.

Rembrandt Hermanszoon van Rijn was about

423

54 years old in this story, with nine years remaining to him; and they were to be unhappy ones. He had few commissions in these times and many setbacks. Added to his sorrows were the deaths of Hendrickje and his son Titus. Rembrandt's days of making etchings were apparently over by 1660 as he had lost everything in his bankruptcy. His last etchings may have been the ones that he made to illustrate a book for Menasseh Ben Israel, another leader and a publisher in the Jewish community. The reader is invited to read Simon Schama's book, "Rembrandt's Eyes" for more general knowledge of Rembrandt and his times.

Cornelia van Rijn was the last survivor of Rembrandt's immediate household to grow into adulthood. She was born in 1654 (a year after the mentioned German-born Johann Pachelbel, composer of the "Canon in D"). She inherited what remained of the van Rijn money which actually had come to her from Saskia's dowry. She married a minor artist, and the couple migrated to a Dutch colony in the East Indies to live.

Titus van Rijn, Rembrandt's only son (from his first marriage to Saskia) was referred to but never "met" in this story. Titus and Hendrickje took out a business license in December, 1660 (the month following the time-setting of this story) in order to salvage and protect Rembrandt's legacy. Titus married a few years later, and the couple had a child. Titus died of plague in 1668, predeceasing Rembrandt by a year. His wife and child also died of diseases, which meant that Cornelia was the only surviving member of van Rijn's family to grow into adulthood.

Rembrandt's House at 4 Jodenbreestraat, Amsterdam (the house he bought when his career was at its peak) is today *Het Museum Rembrandtshuis*, a branch of the *Rijksmuseum*. The Website shows restored rooms in the house and how they may have looked in the artist's day. The view of the printing room and press is included. Also, it is shown on the *Park West Gallery Tour* Website (http://www.tinyurl.com/6vfxhh8), where one can see a video of a printer using the press to print a replica of a Rembrandt etching.

The "loose tiles" in what used to be Rembrandt's printing studio is fiction but the author got the idea for the problem when he looked at pictures of the printing room, which has, in fact, a tiled floor. [A dollhouse based on Rembrandt's house, also on the Web, shows the printing room being located in the attic, which is confusing. Who knows?]

Baruch Spinoza, the lens crafter's name that Mac noticed on the magnifying glass, was famously excommunicated by a council on which Rabbi Aboab served a few years prior to 1660. Reference to his name is of minor importance to the story, but the author included a passing reference to suggest a personal conflict between Aboab's duty to his community and his personal, liberal philosophy.

Hendrickje Stoffels, who was Rembrandt's second wife and the mother of Cornelia, died in 1663, worn out, tired and susceptible to the maladies of those dark times. She may have died of typhoid fever, cholera or tuberculosis—any one of which was a common cause of death in those days.

Part 3 of the Denouement - Fictional characters

William Handyside MacRitchie is an autobiographical character, the name derivative from the author's given name, William Harley Ritchie. The Ritchie clan is a sub-clan of the MacIntosh. The author's wife, Lynda **Faye** Fisher Ritchie, allowed the use of her name, and is regarded as *Koningin van de Queen Anne* pie *and bread-maker* besides being first to read and make corrections and suggestions in this book's manuscript. She also made and tested the recipes, excluding the castoreum.

Macia Schwarzesherz, a fictional character, fled Poland with her husband after stealing a rare alchemical book. They came to Amsterdam where they opened a perfume manufacturing business. Their marriage was acrimonious, and her husband disappeared. Neighbors suspected that she murdered him; but as there was no body, she was never arrested. There was a rumor that she had eaten him to get rid of the evidence. She was interested in practical kabbalism, sometimes considered to be a kind of black magic. She claimed that she could heal people or remove (or impose) curses. She had abundant apothecary and alchemical supplies necessary for her perfumes. She knew how to make poisons, too, and was probably paid in gold for her services. Her nickname, *Black Widow*, came from the rumor of cannibalism.

Mahault de Witte and **Pieter de Wit** – After the "Black Widow" was sent to the *Gouda Spinhuis,* a correctional facility for women, the young couples' families and friends pooled their resources, formed a corporation and purchased the Schwarzesherz house

426

as it was put up for auction. Mahault and Pieter were thereafter made the permanent staff by the corporation. The couple was eventually married and they used their savings to take deed of the property. Mahault's trauma-related mutism faded and her voice returned. When they had their first child, Pieter remodeled a room to become a nursery, and he found the cache of gold that had been hidden by the Black Widow. With this windfall, Pieter decided to give up his plan to sign on a merchant ship and he stayed home instead.

Dieners van Catarina lived on in the house of Rabbi Isaac Aboab da Fonseca as his loyal adopted son, manservant and manager of the household.

De Gelder the Elder, the father of Arent, is fictionally portrayed as the inventor of the Hollander Beater that became the industry standard pulp-making machine for papermaking. The actual van Gelder Zonen Paper Company began sometime before 1690 and lasted until 1980. [The author, as a printmaker, used some of this company's fine papers in the 1970s.]

Nora, Dennis, Sherry and **Carl**—the names given to the party-goers in Chapter 18—are owing to the names of the author's oldest Seattle friends in the arts. They had been graduate students at the University of Washington School Of Art. Bill Ritchie expresses his advance apologies to them for the made-up physical and character portrayals. These individuals are in no way like the characters in the story except for their friendliness and good-natured personalities. Nora (Norie) and her husband Ralph are notable for their annual winter season parties that served the author in writing his description of the atmosphere in the closing paragraphs.

Part 4 of the Denouement - Mock Interview with the Author

Q: What made you decide to write this book?

I made a wooden toy etching press, a working scale model of the one in the Rembrandtshuis Museum in Amsterdam. I saw the real one in 1969. Now, etching presses are made of steel. I want to invent a printmaking teaching method that uses toys and games with the press in parts that you put together like LEGO. I needed a method-of-play and I thought if I wrote a novel, the novel would inform me as to what the game-play would be. The novel would be an idea book, you might say.

Q: Does this novel reflect your own experience?

I'm an old-world printmaker, and I design presses. My ancestral clan name is MacRitchie, a sub-clan of the MacIntosh. I drew my character on my life although I never passed out sniffing lacquer thinner, nor have I had any out-of-body experiences. I write what I know about, my philosophy and my techniques. My wife's middle name is Faye; so, the story leans toward autobiography.

Q: You were an art professor?

Yes, I was a professor of printmaking for 19 years at the University Of Washington School Of Art in Seattle. I left it in 1985 to be an artist and free-lance teacher.

Q: Was that when you became a writer?

No. I only wrote journals and essays while I was in college in the 'sixties. After college I wrote self-help books and on-demand books, videos and such.

Q: What attracted you to Rembrandt?

Rembrandt is among the most interesting artists in the history of printmaking. Salvador Dali is another one. I got the idea of producing collectible etching presses with books about artists' lives—historical fiction based on famous printmakers. For my toy press idea, I started with Rembrandt. I'd also like to do Munch, Picasso, Dali and others . . ..

Q: What were some influences on your book?

When I was a child I read books by Louise Andrews Kent, in which the hero kid goes along on great expeditions. She applied the plot to Marco Polo, Magellan, Columbus, Vasco da Gama, and others, the titles of which all started with, "He Went With . . .." They were all about The Quest.

In the old days of TV, Walter Cronkite introduced the series titled, "You Are There." Those episodes were unforgettable! Another influence was Peter Watkins' mockumentary film, "Edvard Munch," and Munch was another important printmaker I'd like to write about.

Q: Was there a movie on Rembrandt?

Yes, I know of several. In 1936, "Rembrandt," in which he was played by Charles Laughton. In 1942 a German language film came out, and in 2007 there was a Rembrandt movie—the English title of which is, "Night Watchers." Also there was a short animated children's film made a few years ago about Rembrandt and his art.

Q: How accurate is your story, historically?

I relied on several books about the artist and the period and about Jews in Amsterdam, and also paper manufacturing. I printed on van Gelder Zonen paper in the 1970s, and, by coincidence, Arent Gelder was Rembrandt's last student. Rabbi Aboab is real and his

429

work in Brazil is documented. He was a humanist and interested in mysticism. That he would adopt an African infant is a stretch. The homes of Rembrandt are known, especially the one that is the Rembrandt Museum. His landlord on the Rozengracht was in fact a playing-card publisher. Rembrandt's relationship with his neighbor is known to have been discordant. So there are a few true facts in my story.

Q: What's with the playing cards?

Three things: My printmaking teaching method uses cards that are similar to playing cards. They are known as collectible or trading cards. Artists make what are called Artist Trading Cards. Secondly, van Leest, Rembrandt's landlord, published playing cards. It was lucky that van Leest was in the card business. Third, Rembrandt made many small etchings, some of which would be the size of playing cards. My ideas for games to teach printmaking use all of these.

End of Mock Interview

Part 5 of the Denouement - Recipes

Suikerbrood (Sugar Loaf)

Yeast Dough:
1/4 cup warm water
1 pkg. active dry yeast
3/4 cup scalded lukewarm milk
1/4 cup sugar
1 tsp. salt
1 egg
1/4 cup soft shortening
3 1/2 to 3 3/4 cups sifted flour

Dissolve yeast in warm water. Add milk, sugar, salt, egg, shortening and half of flour. Mix until smooth. Add enough flour to handle easily. Turn onto floured surface; knead until smooth. Round up in greased bowl. Cover with damp cloth. Let rise in warm place (85 degrees) until double, about 1 1/2 hr. Punch down; let rise again until almost double, about 30 minutes. Roll dough into oblong 16 x 8". Sprinkle with mixture of 3 tbsp. sugar and 2 tsp. cinnamon. Roll up tightly, starting with narrow end. Seal edge. Place sealed edge down in greased loaf pan, 9 x 5 x 3". Let rise until double, about 50 min. Heat oven to 375 degrees. Bake about 35 min. or until nicely browned.

It was the fragrance of freshly-baked sugar loaves that brought van Leest to Dieners' kitchen. Hendrickje had some in a basket, a gift to another woman who sometimes took care of their daughter, Cornelia. The sugar loaf is the same as our cinnamon bread, but, in the 17th Century, the sugar was from Brazil and is shown in some online recipes as other kinds of sugar that are coarser and form gooey bubbles in the bread. Ginger syrup is also closer to the real thing in the novel. The bread is mentioned again when Arent buys a loaf for his mother. It is traditionally a gift to expectant mothers.

Gefuldekuiken (Almond Sugar Cookies)

1 cup butter
1 cup sugar
1 egg yolk
1/2 tsp. vanilla flavoring
1/2 tsp. almond flavoring
2 Cups sifted flour
1/2 tsp. salt
1/4 tsp. baking soda

Cream butter and sugar. Add egg yolk and flavorings. Add flour, salt and soda. Roll into walnut sized balls. Press down with palm of hand. Refrigerate for 5 minutes, then press with sugared glass. Bake at 350 degrees for 7 - 8 min. Turn pan after 5 min.

This is a kind of cookie, or biscuit, which Arent gave to Mac on their walk between Geerincx' house (the floor project) and Arent's paper-mill home. Rembrandt's student wanted to buy a sugar loaf for his parents, and he also bought two gefuldekuiken *as treats for himself and Mac, who, at the time, was pretending to be the mute helpmate to Arent.*

Fig Bars

Ingredients for crust:
1 cup shortening

1 cup sugar or brown sugar
2 cups flour
1 tsp. baking soda
2 cups oats
1 tsp. nutmeg
1 tsp. cinnamon
1 cup chopped pecans
Pinch of salt

Ingredients for fig filling:
2 cups fresh, ripe chopped figs
3/4 cup sugar
3/4 cup water

To prepare fig filling, combine the chopped figs, 3/4 cup of sugar and 3/4 cup of water in a medium sized saucepan over medium high heat. Cook the mixture, stirring constantly, until mixture thickens to a jam-like consistency. Once the mixture has thickened, set aside and let it cool completely.

Preheat oven to 400 degrees. While the fig filling is cooling, prepare the cookie crust.

Combine 1 cup of shortening, 1 cup of sugar, 2 cups of flour, 1 tsp. of baking soda, pinch of salt, 1 tsp. nutmeg, and 1 tsp. cinnamon in large mixing bowl. Use your hands to mix the ingredients into a crumb mixture. Stir in 2 cups of oats and 1 cup of chopped pecans until thoroughly combined.

In a rectangular shaped baking pan, add half of the mixture, and press down lightly with your hands to flatten the mixture so that it covers the entire bottom of the baking pan. Spread the completely cooled fig filling over the dough mixture in the baking pan. Cover the top with dollops of remaining dough and pat lightly, then sprinkle top with more cinnamon. Bake for 35-40 min. or until crust is golden. Check at 25-30 minutes. Cut into squares or bars when still warm.

The title of Chapter 16, Fig Newtons to Die For, *came before I realized that finding a Fig Newton recipe was difficult, and it was unlikely Hendrickje would know how to make them. However, the title was cute and I left it, even though it would be apple fig pie that was the actual desert Hendrickje baked. Lynda (Faye), my wife, actually makes an apple fig pie. She has never added castoreum or arsenic to it.*

Apple Fig Pie

Filling:
3/4 cups sugar
1 tsp. cinnamon
3 tbsp. flour
1 cup chopped fresh figs
6 cups sliced pared apples
1 1/2 tbsp. butter

Prepare the filling (except the butter) and mix ingredients well. Let it sit while preparing the crust. Preheat oven to 425 degrees.

Pastry for double-crust 9 inch pie:
2 cups sifted flour
1 tsp. salt
2/3 cup plus 2 tbsp. cold shortening
1/4 cup water

Sift flour with salt. Blend shortening with flour and salt; toss water lightly around in bowl and mix with a fork. Ball up the dough and divide in two portions - one slightly larger for the bottom crust.

Roll out and place larger crust in 9-inch pie pan. Pour the filling into the pastry-lined pie pan. Dot with the butter. Seal and flute the crust. Bake 50 to 60 min., or until crust is nicely browned and apples are cooked through.

This is a killer pie! However, you have to possess the skill of a Lynda Faye to bring it off well. Do not try making apple fig pie with castoreum and arsenic at home.

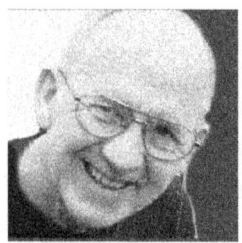

Bill Ritchie, about 2004

Part 6 of the Denouement - About the Author

Bill Ritchie lives in Seattle with his wife, Lynda. Educated in state colleges in Washington State and California in the 1960s, he taught printmaking at the University of Washington from 1966 to 1985. A year after his last sabbatical Ritchie left the university inventing a new printmaking teaching method for blended distance learning. Using video and computers, he has strived to restore the unique, personal aspects of art professors' offerings which he thought were being devalued and lost. His lifework became an "asset management and legacy transfer scheme," a game-like practice that he code-named *Emeralda: Games for the Gifts of Life*.

Ritchie teaches that printmaking is greater than the sum of handcraft and techniques or the manners of drawing and painting. His own printmaking has been a seamless blend of video, film, and computer graphics. "Everything in art is printmaking in one form or another," he tells his students. "When I opened my eyes to art, I was looking at a print."

Creative writing, especially historic fiction, is another way to teach. Story-telling, video games and distance learning call for a balance of creativity and invention in which any experience—including printmaking, can be shared. Toward this end the books that Ritchie publishes are exercises that advance him in a teacher's role.

In 2004 Ritchie designed his first Halfwood Etching press with a 24-inch wide bed. A professional steel Wright, named Tom Kughler, produced a one-fourth scale model of it, and Ritchie named this one, "Mini Halfwood Press," and later he designed the Printmaker Chest (both of which he included in this story). Most recently, he designed the "WeeWoodie Rembrandt" press pictured in this book. His Website for the Halfwood Presses is www.printmakingworld.com and his personal, artist/teacher's Website is www.ritchie-art.com.

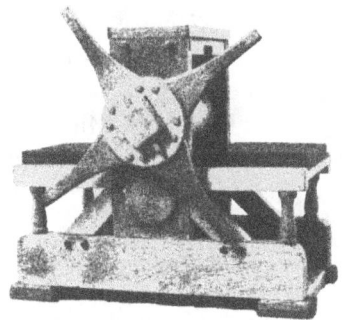

Prototype of the WeeWoodie Rembrandt Press

Acknowledgements

I want to thank Lynda Ritchie, my wife, and Nellie Sunderland, our younger daughter, for reading through the first drafts, making corrections and offering extensive suggestions. A special thanks goes to Ernest Horvers, Chocolatier of Rembrandt's Chocolate Company, and his family for donating the Rembrandt's Chocolates and also for jumping in at the last minute to correct my Dutch language usages, plus young Corey who offered ideas for a video game using the WeeWoodie Rembrandt press. Larry Jellin, my neighbor, helped me with early-morning conversations centering on the early stages of my writing. Also Doctor Simon Schama, (although I don't know him) whose books, *Rembrandt's Eyes* and *The Embarrassment of Riches* were like a time-traveler's guidebooks for me. The book, *Rembrandt's Jews*, by Steven Nadler, was also beneficial. Also Tom and Margie Kughler, Rick Miller, Ron Myhre and Warren Ralls for their work in the making of the Halfwood Press, a dream coming true, of which this novel is a related element.

"I would not have come to this privileged point in the art of writing were it not for the hundred-plus people who purchased Halfwood Presses and several Printmaker Chests that I designed and built. Without these printmakers' feedback (not to mention

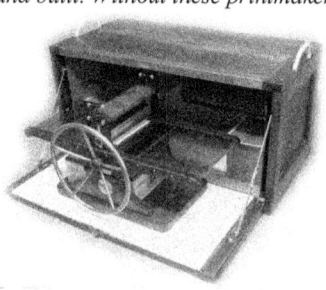

augmenting our family's livelihood by their purchases) this book would never have been conceived and published." ***BR***

At left: The author's Halfwood Press and Printmaker Chest, "Everything you need to be a printmaker; just add creative juice."

Bill Ritchie's PressGhost Series

Books and publications by Bill Ritchie, many of which he offers in the "PressGhost," a USB flash memory drive built into Halfwood Etching Presses. His publications are available from amazon.com, createspace.com, lulu.com and, soon, Barnes & Noble. Some are ebook (Kindle, Nook) versions.

Halfwood Press – The Story
Swipe: A screenplay
Art of Selling Prints: Between Production and Livelihood
Printmaking Camp – A Graphic Novel
Cascades: Ten years of great notions
Video Dig Reloaded: Soul of a new art show
Travel Tapes: A professor's Big Gamble
Emeralda Inventor Interviews: 31 days in fantasy videos
Artsport 'Zines: Ritchie Mined (Kindle only)
E'Studios 'Zines: Ritchie Mined (Kindle only)
MacRitchie's 'Zines: Ritchie Mined (Kindle only)
O'Studios 'Zines: Ritchie Mined (Kindle only)
Perfect Press 'Zines: Ritchie Mined (Kindle only)
Perfect Studios 'Zines: Ritchie Mined (Kindle only)
RIISMA 'Zines: Ritchie Mined (Kindle only)
SPEACON 'Zines: Ritchie Mined (Kindle only)
Video 'Zines: Ritchie Mined (Kindle only)
Video 'N Print 'Zines: Ritchie Mined (Kindle only)
(An Unusual Childhood, Editor, Memoir of H. J. Reeves,
also available as an AudioBook at Audible.com and iTunes)

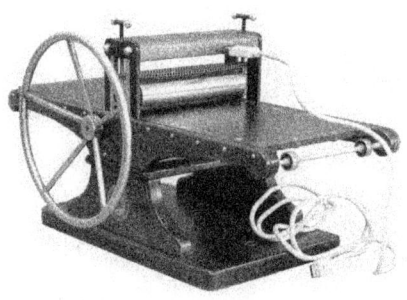

The author's design of a small etching press with the "PressGhost" plug-in feature. The photo shows the cable for connecting to a USB port on a digital device for downloading the printmaking information stored on the flash drive.

Rembrandt's Ghost in the New Machine

Printed in USA by CreateSpace.com,
an amazon.com company

www.ingramcontent.com/pod-product-compliance
Lightning Source LLC
Chambersburg PA
CBHW051437170526
45166CB00001B/20